Healthful Herbs

Feverfew—often used before aspirin became popular, feverfew builds resistance to migraine attacks.

Garlic—one of the most useful plants in the herbal pharmacopoeia, acts as an antibiotic and potent spice.

Sarsparilla—contains testosterone and influences male sexual potency.

Chamomile—has anti-spasmodic and anti-inflammatory qualities which are excellent for relief—and eventual cure—of ulcers.

With an emphasis on sound, proven principles of use, *Herbs for All Seasons* offers effective, all-natural suggestions for your "kitchen pharmacy" as well as information on cultivating and cooking herbs for flavor and beauty. Find out why modern pharmaceutical companies are using herbs in the preparation of sophisticated drugs and why herbal knowledge is being sought by the U.N.'s Food and Health Organization. This fascinating guide will tell you all you need to know about the history and variety of uses of . . .

Herbs for All Seasons

Other books by Sally Freeman

Drugs and Civilization

The Kitchen Almanac

The Green World

Herbs for All Seasons

Growing and Gathering Herbs
for
Flavor, Health, and Beauty

Sally Freeman

Illustrations by Gretchen K. Halpert
Additional Illustrations by Burt Levitsky

A PLUME BOOK

To my parents, Helen and Arthur Wilcox

PLUME
Published by the Penguin Group
Penguin Books USA Inc., 375 Hudson Street, New York, New York 10014, U.S.A.
Penguin Books Ltd, 27 Wrights Lane, London W8 5TZ, England
Penguin Books Australia Ltd, Ringwood, Victoria, Australia
Penguin Books Canada Ltd, 2801 John Street, Markham, Ontario, Canada L3R 1B4
Penguin Books (N.Z.) Ltd, 182–190 Wairau Road, Auckland 10, New Zealand

Penguin Books Ltd, Registered Offices: Harmondsworth, Middlesex, England

First published by Plume, an imprint of New American Library,
a division of Penguin Books USA Inc.

First Printing, March, 1991
10 9 8 7 6 5 4 3 2

Grateful acknowledgment to the Library of the New York Botanical Garden, Bronx, New York, for permission to reprint the drawing of the European Mandrake on page 33.

REGISTERED TRADEMARK—MARCA REGISTRADA

LIBRARY OF CONGRESS CATALOGING IN PUBLICATION DATA
Freeman, Sally.
    Herbs for all seasons : growing and gathering herbs for flavor,
health, and beauty / by Sally Freeman ; illustrations by Gretchen K. Halpert ; additional
    illustrations by Burt Levitsky.
        Includes bibliographical references and index.
        ISBN 0-452-26584-3
        1. Herbs.   2. Herb gardening.   3. Herbs—Therapeutic use.   4. Cookery (Herbs)
    5. Herbal cosmetics.   6. Herbals.   I. Title.
SB351. H5F74 1991   90-46570
635'.7—dc20   CIP

Printed in the United States of America
Set in Berkley
Designed by Patrice Fodero

Note to the Reader: The ideas, procedures, and suggestions contained in this book are not intended as a substitute for consulting with your physician. All matters regarding your health require medical supervision.

BOOKS ARE AVAILABLE AT QUANTITY DISCOUNTS WHEN USED TO PROMOTE PRODUCTS OR SERVICES. FOR INFORMATION PLEASE WRITE TO PREMIUM MARKETING DIVISION, PENGUIN BOOKS USA INC., 375 HUDSON STREET, NEW YORK, NEW YORK 10014.

Contents

Acknowledgments

In researching and writing this book I am grateful for the efforts and support of my family and friends, with special thanks to my editor Alexia Dorszynski for her insight, creativity and sensitivity in vetting this manuscript; my agent, Wendy Lipkind; Theodore Strongin and Judy Rosenburg for the computer; Pat Repert for gardening advice; and the New York Botanical Garden Library, especially Lothian Lynas for her research suggestions; the Brooklyn Botanic Garden Library, especially Marie Giasi; the New York Public Library, particularly the Rare Books staff, Olga Melbardis, and Loretta Nieminski for research material and suggestions; and Kathy Hamel Peifer, who suggested this book. And to Willa Speiser for a first-rate copy edit.

Herbs for sipping
Herbs for seasoning
Herbs for casting spells
Herbs to keep you well

Introduction

For a time during the early 1970s, I lived in the mountains of northern New Mexico near a tiny settlement that qualified as a town because it had its own post office and general store. I seldom patronized the general store; its hours were erratic and mysterious and its offerings limited to a few dusty tins of sardines, a box or two of saltine crackers, and a loaf or two of squishy white bread. Like most of my close neighbors, I shopped for coffee, flour, and other staples in the nearest town of any real size, a forty-five-minute drive from where I lived. Most of our food was homegrown: goat's milk and goat cheeses curdled with the "cheese plant" gathered from the mountainside; vegetables seasoned with wild or homegrown herbs; eggs, beef, goat, and rabbit, also raised at home; occasionally venison. Once, when a stray rattlesnake took up residence beneath one of our adobe houses, we ate that, too.

The valley in which we lived was 7,500 feet above sea level, an altitude that made for a short growing season. The soil, composed of generous amounts of rock, sand, and adobe, was only marginally fertile, and the weather was capricious. Spring winds ripped through the valley for several weeks each March with a force that could tear the tin roof from a house or knock over an outhouse. Snowstorms in late spring sometimes killed the fruit blossoms, which meant there would be no harvest of wild apples that year. The first frost often came in August, and before that, there was drought.

During the first summer I spent in the valley the drought lasted throughout the growing season, and the only vegetation that thrived in the gardens were weeds. Fortunately, the weeds were edible ones, so I developed quite a culinary repertoire around the lamb's-quarters that carpeted the site of an abandoned pigpen, the purslane that sprawled over the sun-baked mud of the garden, and the watercress that grew by the spring. The rabbits were grateful for the Russian thistle—about all that thrived in the fields—and we, in turn, were grateful for the rabbit that enlivened our weedy meals.

It seemed that those edible weeds were nature's way of compensating for such a stingy harvest of conventional crops that summer. The land was, at best, a challenge to the gardener even in good seasons. But poor soil, so inhospitable to most cultivated plants, is also the soil most favorable to those wild greens, often more nutritious than domestic ones, and the wild herbs that restored health after a long, vitamin-deprived winter.

Mexicans who had settled in the valley long before the Anglos arrived made full use of the hidden riches the land had to offer and had developed an extensive herbal pharmacopoeia. Mama Torres, who lived a few miles away, was generous in sharing her extensive herbal knowledge with those who came to visit, admire her herb garden, and chat over a cup of tea.

Her herbal knowledge was vitally important to those of us who lived three miles from the nearest telephone and without immediate access to doctors. As it happened, there were no serious illnesses or injuries during the time I lived in the valley. The rigorous lifestyle, which entailed a good deal of physical work outdoors and a minimum of chemicals in the air, food, and water, was no doubt responsible for the prevailing hardiness and lack of stress-related ailments. Should the need arise, there were, of course, hospitals and doctors and wonder drugs available, if not within the immediate vicinity, then at least within an hour's drive. But for the most part, the everyday aches and pains, sniffles, and blahs, which in more populated areas might be treated by a doctor, were here treated at home with many of the same remedies that had been used by the early Mexican settlers, and the American Indians who preceded them, and before that, over two thousand years ago, by the early Greek founders of Western medicine.

It puts you in touch with history, living that way, and, more important, it puts you in touch with yourself. Not only did I feel proud of my self-sufficiency in basic matters of survival, I reveled in the sensuality of it all.

Swallowing a pill for colic or indigestion, for example, does not compare to the experience of taking down a jar of peppermint leaves gathered on a sunny summer afternoon and brewing a cup of wonderfully fragrant and warming tea. This experience not only dispels the stomachache but, as the medieval herbalists used to say, "comforteth the heart." A gardener serving up in January a pesto made in August from homegrown basil, or an amateur winemaker sipping dandelion wine made with blossoms gathered the spring before, knows this feeling well.

My experiment with living off the land in New Mexico took place some fifteen years ago, when such ventures were quite popular among a small, disgruntled minority. I enjoyed it because it was a culmination of other, briefer experiences in natural living and reading and writing about the subject.

Now I spend part of my year in New York City, and note with some amusement that much of what was once dismissed as the concerns of fanatics, little old ladies in tennis shoes, and social rebels is now served up as "New Age" to people who carry tennis shoes along with their briefcases. You can find herb teas in most supermarkets these days, along with name-brand cosmetics made with herbs, and name-brand cereals, soups, and sauces that cost more because of all the nasty stuff they *don't* put into them.

In the past twenty years or so, most people have become increasingly aware that the blessings of chemistry are mixed. Chemicals used in agriculture poison our water supply, industrial chemicals pollute the air—and some of us are getting sick. Highly publicized pharmaceutical disasters such as the birth defects in children born to women who took thalidomide, the rare form of vaginal cancer found in some women whose mothers took diethylstilbestrol, and the drug dependencies resulting from prolonged use of certain tranquilizers and sleeping pills have taught us that some synthetic drugs may not be as safe as we had once supposed.

It is no secret by now that the average doctor, with little time or energy to spare, relies mostly on advertising supplied by drug companies for his or her pharmaceutical knowledge. In addition, it is not uncommon for a patient to be taking more than one drug, and the synergistic effect of some drug combinations is still unknown. Recent studies show that overmedication and adverse reactions to drugs are not only prevalent but are particularly dangerous for people over sixty-five, who by and large take up to twice the quantity of prescribed drugs that younger people do, and, because of the effects of aging, may have a more acute reaction to combinations of drugs.

Meanwhile, in many parts of the world, most notably in Asia and Africa as well as in areas of the Americas, herbal medicine is still practiced. The practical advantages of these natural healing methods are manifold. The ingredients are relatively inexpensive—often even free—and easy to come by, unwanted side effects are, for the most part, avoided, and, most important, they work.

In recent years, these ancient healing methods have attracted the attention of the Western medical world. Botanicals used by the Chinese, by Native Americans, and by Africans have been studied for their contributions to state-of-the-art medicine. Increasingly, the major pharmaceutical houses are sending researchers into the jungles and mountains to seek cures in the plant world rather than in the laboratory.

Currently, the World Health Organization is launching a global campaign to make greater use of traditional medicines, which in many areas offer a low-cost form of health care that is readily accepted by residents who are wary of modern medicine. In Africa, for example, shamans and herbalists are sharing their knowledge with university-trained researchers who conduct laboratory analyses in an attempt to identify the active ingredients of the leaves, roots, and tree bark used in folk medicine. Similar cooperative ventures have been undertaken with native healers on American Indian reservations. The results of such research are being published in contemporary medical journals as well as in the increasing number of publications devoted to alternative medicine.

There was a time, not long ago, when herbs were part of everyone's daily life. The housewife at work in her kitchen knew which herb to give her baby for colic; her husband, at work in the fields, knew which plant to apply if he injured himself. Herbal tisanes were served at afternoon tea and for aperitifs, and a wide range of herbs, some now out of fashion, were used for flavoring food—often a necessity in the days before refrigeration, when meats were not always as fresh as they might be.

In many parts of America, home remedies are still used for a variety of ailments. Although we associate herbal healing with rural areas where the plants can be gathered and grown, the variety and range of folk medicine is most strikingly evident in metropolitan areas. In New York City, for example, you can readily find a botanica that sells herbs used in the Caribbean and Latin America. Some of these herbs originally came from Africa and have been used for many generations by Afro-Americans. You can also find shops that sell African botanicals, Chinese pharmacies filled with mysterious roots and leaves used in Chinese medicine for thousands of years, and shops that are aromatic with the herbs and spices of India and the Middle East. In addition to this cosmopolitan array, there are homeopathic pharmacies, health food stores, shops that specialize in a wide range of herbs from many countries, and New Age centers all over the city that teach people how to use them.

In the following pages, I will tell you about some of my adventures in herbalism, and what scientists are learning about this fascinating field. Many of the herbs I discuss will be well known to you. You may already have them sitting on your kitchen spice shelf or growing in your vegetable garden, your front lawn, by the roadside, or even between the cracks in pavements.

Even if you never go so far as to set up an herbal pharmacy in your kitchen, discovering the virtues of the humble plants you meet on your daily walks puts you in touch with a very old tradition, and with a marvelous cast of characters, from physicians, gardeners, and monks to shamans and witches, who have created that tradition through the centuries.

Introduction

Part One

An Herbal Chronicle

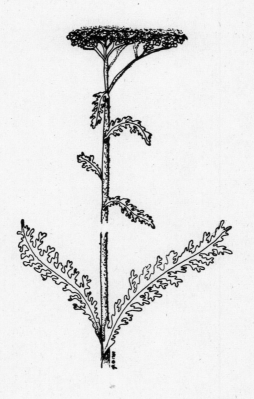

Chapter 1

Simples, Stills, and Barnacle Geese

An old huntress of everything the forest produces—bluebells, wild strawberries, hazelnuts, foxgloves, blackberries—would set off "to the lilies" before dawn, pass by the Dutch Ponds and their overtrodden environs, taking care that no one followed her. She would head homeward at the hour when the green forest turns blue. Her long stride, the stride of a robust, aging woman, would set swinging all around her the bunches of lily of the valley hanging head down, twenty, thirty, fifty bunches.

From For an Herbarium *by Colette*

Four hundred years ago, when being the lady of the manor was a profession requiring the utmost versatility and skill, the most active place in the home, besides the kitchen, was a workroom lined with shelves that glittered with rainbow hues of cordials, creams, and conserves. Dominating this room was the apparatus that inspired its name: the stillroom.

Inspired by the Austrian *Buch Zu Distilleren* [Distillery Book]

(1513), the first detailed work to initiate its readers into the mysteries of distilling, stillrooms were the rage in sixteenth-century Europe, and there was scarcely a manor house without one. Here the mistress distilled the heart-warming cordials that took the curse off winter evenings spent in drafty parlors, and the "waters" that whitened and softened her skin. Here also, hung to dry from rafters or sealed in bottles and jars, were the herbs and edible flowers that seasoned the manor's casseroles and stews and supplied the working materials for the most significant of milady's manifold roles.

In those days, when such medical services as existed were not readily available, the housewife was not only the family housekeeper, chef, and gardener, or the supervisor of such tasks, but also the apothecary and physician. Her main resources were her herb garden filled with a variety of plants—many no longer grown today except by specialists; some, like the onion, now classified as vegetables—and her stillroom book.

Basically a collection of recipes, the book was often a family heirloom passed down from mother to daughter, annotated and expanded by each new generation. In its handwritten pages one might find instructions for making such delicacies as Marigold Cream, a golden milk pudding tinted and seasoned with fresh marigold petals, as well as wines, cordials, and syrups to comfort the heart, soothe a sore throat, or sweeten a sour stomach. Stillroom books—treasured works, classics of domestic literature—survived for countless generations. By the nineteenth century, the stillroom book had become the "receipt book." No longer in manuscript form, receipt books were printed and widely distributed, in time evolving into one of the most lucrative areas of modern publishing: cookbooks.

Although they kept no stillrooms and usually did not have the reading and writing skills for keeping a stillroom book, the lady of the manor's less wealthy colleagues in the homemaking trade also tended herb gardens in the tiny plots surrounding their cottages, using the herbs for home remedies they had learned from their mothers and grandmothers.

As the mistress of the sixteenth-century manor was leafing through her stillroom book and the cottage housewife was in the fields gathering "simples," or medicinal herbs, learned men all over Europe, most of them amateur botanists and professional physicians, were writing herbals. These new herbals were partly based on classic works written by Greek and Latin authors of antiquity, but they also included observations and discoveries about plants native to England, Germany, and other countries where the books were written. Not for centuries had there been such widespread and intense writing activity in the field of botanical medicine. Spanning only two centuries, this period, which ended about 1670, is known as the golden age of herbalism.

In those days the village never lacked for women who gathered simples. "Just so many death risks!" Sido would say. But I would sneak away and follow them into the woods anyway. They spoke little and smelled good. The aroma of sinful wormwood and mint from the marshes dogged their steps.

Colette

The use of herbs in healing is thought to have originated in Egypt, Sumeria, and China. The ancient peoples believed these humble but powerful plants were created from the flesh of the gods. The most complete herbal that has survived from antiquity is the *Papyrus Ebers*, copied around 1550 B.C., but written perhaps five to twenty centuries earlier. Also surviving are a Sumerian tablet dating back to 3000 B.C. and a Chinese herbal, Emperor Shen Nung's *Pent' Sao Ching*, written in 2700 B.C.

In the West, most of what was known about plants in general and herbs in particular was based on the writings of three classical authors: Theophrastus, Pliny, and Dioscorides. Theophrastus had been Aristotle's pupil, and in 322 B.C. became the philosopher's successor in governing the school of Athens. Like his teacher, Theophrastus was a student of natural history. *Historia Plantarum*, Theophrastus' ten-volume natural history of plants, laid the foundation for what was later to become the science of botany.

Somewhat later, during the first century A.D., Pliny the Elder, a Roman naturalist, undertook the staggering task of compiling what was known at the time about the nature of the physical universe. His thirty-seven-volume *Historia Naturalis* [Natural History] dealt with geography, anthropology, mineralogy, and botany; sixteen volumes were devoted to plants and their medical uses. Himself a natural wonder, Pliny worked from dawn until one or two o'clock in the morning at a variety of careers that included law and the military (he served as captain in the army, commander of naval fleets, and governor of Spain) as well as writing and scholarly pursuits. Pliny's writing is now regarded more as folklore than science, and thus offers little of academic interest to contemporary scientists, but his chatty accounts are still enjoyed for their stylistic charm.

Formidable as the accomplishments of Theophrastus and Pliny were, it was the latter's Greek contemporary Dioscorides who made the most significant contribution to medicine. Little is known of the man himself, save that he was a soldier and may have served as physician to Nero's army. His *De Materia Medica* [Materials of Medicine], the first Western herbal, was a systematic study of the medicinal uses of herbs and is regarded as the foundation of pharmacology. Dioscorides was to be the final authority on pharmacology for the next fifteen hundred years.

After the conquest of Byzantium, Greek scholars brought the writings of Dioscorides to the East, where his work became a vital influence on the medical practices of the Moslem world. In the West, his *Materials of Medicine* (translated into Latin as *De Materia Medica)* was copied and preserved in monasteries through the Middle Ages.

These monasteries not only preserved classical culture but also were centers of medical knowledge and experimental horticulture. The study of medicine and horticulture was enriched and expanded by traveling monks who returned from their journeys bringing new species of flowers, fruits, vegetables, and herbs, and by visitors from other monastic communities, who brought with them prize specimens from their gardens and orchards and shared what they had learned of how to grow and use them.

The typical monastery featured both a doctor's house and an adjoining infirmary. Nearby was the "physic" (medicinal) garden, where grew the herbs used in treating not only the monastic community but also the residents of the surrounding countryside who came to the monastery for medical treatment. The care offered at the monastery was far superior to most in an age when ignorance and superstition were the norm. (In fact, during the Middle Ages, the monk's only real competitor in the medical trade was the "white witch," whom you will meet in the next chapter.) Monks also served as distillers, using herbs to flavor the superb liqueurs that rounded out the otherwise austere monastery meals.

Free from the worldly distractions of family and career, a good number of the men and women who retired to monasteries and convents at that time contributed much to our culture, copying and preserving classical manuscripts and writing original works. *Physica* [Natural Medicine], the first German natural history and the first herbal written by a woman, was conceived within the walls of a convent. A compilation of folk remedies that had been developed and used in the convent, *Physica* was written by Hildegard of Bingen, an abbess and mystic noted for her learning and her influence on medieval religious thought.

The invention of printing in the mid-fifteenth century made possible a wider distribution of books. Herbals were early candidates for the press because they were interesting both to the wealthy physicians who practiced herbal medicine and to merchants engaged in the highly profitable herb and spice trade. The herbals were beautifully crafted and lavishly illustrated, showcasing the artists and engravers who illustrated them and assuring them a prominent place in the history of illustration.

One of the most beautiful of these herbals was written and illustrated by Leonhart Fuchs, one of the fathers of German botany. Published in 1542, the herbal is exemplary not only for Fuchs's knowledge of plants but also for his illustrative woodcuts. Remarkably lifelike, these wood engravings pictured the plant, including the root system, in detail, thus making field identification possible. Some of the illustrations were the first European representations of certain North American plants such as the pumpkin gourd. Smaller, pirated editions of Fuchs's woodcuts were used to illustrate herbals by other writers—not an uncommon practice in an age when the works of artists and writers were not protected by copyright.

Theophrastus's *Historia Plantarum* and Dioscorides' *De Materia Medica* were among the first books to be printed. The publication of Dioscorides' work was important for two reasons, the more obvious one being that the medical knowledge of the founders of Western medicine was now accessible to the international healing community. The other is that it inspired botanists to make field identifications of those plants native to their local surroundings. These native plants were classified according to their botanical characteristics rather than their medical uses, formerly the traditional method of classifying flora. The new system was a major development in the history of science; as a result, botany evolved as a separate science, independent of medicine.

The publication of Dioscorides' *De Materia Medica* was followed by the publication of botanical works from all over the European continent and Britain, where there was intense interest in herbalism. The works of many classical and contemporary authors were translated into English, the first being the anonymous *Grete Herbal,* a compilation of Anglo Saxon herbal remedies written in 1526. The most notorious of these translations was made by Nicholas Culpeper, a London physician, gardener, and herbalist who outraged the medical establishment by publishing, in 1649, an English translation of the London College of Physician's pharmacopoeia, which was originally written in Latin and was intended only for physicians. Not only did Culpeper make available information that hitherto had been available only to those who read Latin, he further thumbed his nose at certain members of the establishment by adding his own not altogether flattering observations about their formulas, describing the august gentlemen who used them as "a company of proud, insulting, domineering doctors, whose wits were born about 500 years before themselves."

Culpeper's disdain for his fellow physicians had been voiced earlier by Leonhart Fuchs, who, in his own herbal, complained that hardly one doctor in a hundred had knowledge of so much as a handful of plants, depending instead on mostly illiterate apothecaries. These local apothecaries in turn relied on the peasants who gathered their herbs for them—somewhat, we might suppose, as many modern physicians rely on the advertising brochures supplied by the pharmaceutical house to provide them with information about the preparations they dispense.

During the Renaissance, the science of botany progressed rapidly. The printing press helped greatly in promoting the exchange of botanical information; so did the universities, which now included, botany in their curricula. Travel was another important factor. Renaissance botanists gathered new knowledge and shared what they had learned during their travels, which were sometimes made necessary by persecution from the Catholic church, the dominant faith in Europe at that time.

Spanish botanists who traveled to India incorporated Asian spices into their herbals along with the writings of the Persian philosopher-physician Avicenna. Those who embarked on voyages to the New World returned with the medical lore of the Aztecs, who named plants according to their habitats and medicinal properties rather than their botanical characteristics. The most important of the New World studies was written by Francesco Hernandez, physician to King Philip II. In 1570 Hernandez embarked on a royal expedition to New Spain, as Mexico was then called, to inventory the plants of the region. Hernandez's *Treasury of the Medicinal Things of New Spain,* the first natural history of the New World, was the result of his seven years of travel through Mexico. Unfortunately, the work was never published in its entirety because King Philip, after having it bound in silver- and gold-tooled leather, had it buried in the royal library, where it languished until a friar-apothecary translated extracts from Latin to Spanish. These translated extracts, Agnes Arber in *Herbals, Their Origins and Evolution* tells us, were finally published in 1615 in Mexico, years after the author and the translator had died.

Meanwhile, in England, two more pioneering works had been published. William Turner, a physician, theologian, herbalist, and botanist published the first original English herbal in 1568. A Protestant whose religious beliefs conflicted with the dogma of the Church of England, Turner traveled extensively on the Continent after graduating from Cambridge, studying medicine and botany during his expatriate years. Upon returning to England he made extensive studies of the herbs that grew in his surrounding countryside. Eventually, Turner recorded what he had learned from his travels and his studies of local flora in English, the language that would be understood by his fellow countrymen, including the many surgeons and apothecaries who could not read Latin.

Nearly thirty years later, Turner's work was followed by an endeavor that was far less original, yet immensely popular at the time and still in print to this day—Gerard's *Herbal*. Actually, the substance of the work was not Gerard's, but that of the Dutch botanist Rembert Dodoens. Dodoens's work had been translated into English by a Dr. Priest, who died before the translation was published. Gerard managed to obtain Priest's translation and claimed Dodoens's work as his own.

Although Dodoens provided the bulk of the scholarship, the spirit of the herbal is Gerard's. Written in a warm, conversational style, the herbal brings the English countryside to life and infuses Dodoens's rather dry factual presentation with charm and immediacy. In writing of Solomon seal, for example, Gerard remarks, "The root of Solomons seale stamped while it is fresh and greene, and applied, taketh away in one night, or two at the most, any bruise, blacke or blew spots gotten by fals or womens wilfulnesse, in stumbling upon their hasty husbands fists, or such like."

Besides being a practicing physician, Gerard was famous among his fellow Londoners for his gardening skills. In addition to being supervisor of gardens for both Lord Burleigh and the London College of Physicians, he grew as many as a thousand plants in his own garden. "It groweth in my garden," is a boast that is repeated throughout the book. He is also specific about where a plant might be found growing in the wild. For example, in writing about the various species of *Orchis* (a member of the orchid family), he directs the reader who seeks the variety "resembling the white Butter-fly" to look for it "upon the declining of the hill at the end of Hampsted Heath, neere to a small cottage there in the way side, as yee goe from London to Henden [,] a village near by."

Although historians of herbals are quick to point out Gerard's indebtedness to Dodoens, the modern reader, browsing through his pages, doesn't usually care whence the botanical research came. It is Gerard's observations and literary style that have made the book a classic, and passages such as those concerning the Barnacle Goose that make the book such a delight to read. The last "plant" Gerard describes is the "Barnacle tree." This peculiar species, according to its popular legend, produces, instead of a fruit, a certain shell "of a white color tending to russet . . . which falling into the water do become fowles, which we call Barnacles; in the North of England, brant geese; and in Lancashire, tree geese." Gerard asserts that he has actually gathered some of these shells, which resemble mussels, and in some that "neerer came to ripeness I found living things that were very naked, in shape like a Bird; in others, the Birds covered with softe downe, the shell halfe open, and the Bird ready to fall out, which no doubt were the Fowles called Barnacles." Some commentators regard the Barnacle entry as a lapse in Gerard's usually skeptical approach to folklore (see "Mandrake" in the next chapter). I think it is more likely that his "eyewitness account" was written with tongue in cheek and all his wits about him, perhaps to remind the critical reader that while much of the research was Dodoens's, the playful spirit was very much his own.

The third of the triumvirate of great English herbalists was John Parkinson, also a physician and gardener, and best known for his *Paradisi in Sole Paradisis Terrestris* [A Garden of Pleasant Flowers], published in 1629. Still in print, the work is regarded as one of the greatest of all gardening books. *Paradisi* is by no means limited to gardening, however, but also describes medicinal uses of the plants discussed. In 1640, when Parkinson was seventy-three, he published *Theatrum Botanicum,* an herbal. Largely a compilation from earlier sources, *Theatrum Botanicum* is outstanding for its scope. Thirty-eight hundred plants are discussed, many of them collected during the author's travels, others brought to him by visitors from abroad. Parkinson's garden, which provided the herbs for his medical practice, included plants from the Orient, Russia, and America as well as several native plants, such as the Welsh poppy, which were his own discoveries.

Although the works of Turner, Parkinson, and Gerard were the most extensive of the English herbals published during that time, two smaller works were also widely read. The authors, Nicholas Culpeper and William Coles, each embraced one of two conflicting theories of herbalism: the astrological approach and the doctrine of signatures.

According to astrological theory, which had been popular for centuries and still has its followers today, each part of the human body, as well as the herbs used for treating it, is governed by a different planet. Hence, a medicinal herb should be gathered when the ruling planet is rising and administered for those diseases caused by the "sympathy" or "antipathy" of a particular planet. Thus: "Dandelion is ruled by Jupiter, and therefore will be good for the blood, acting as an aperient [gentle laxative], resolvent [reducer of inflammation or swelling], and diuretic [releaser of water from body tissues], or on the urine." To a modern follower of astrology or a reader of farmers' almanacs, the reasoning here will be familiar. A student of herbals would also recognize the applications, for the dandilion has been used for just such purposes for thousands of years.

This passage about the dandelion is quoted from a sprightly discourse entitled *The English Physician or an Astrological Discourse of the Vulgar Herbs of This Nation being a Compleat Method of Phys-*

The Bishop of Worcesters Admirably Curing Powder
Take black tips of crabs claws when the Sun enters into Cancer, which is every year on the eleventh day of June, pick and wash them clean, and beat them into a fine powder, which finely searse, then take musk and civet, of each three grains, ambergreece twelve grains, rub them in the bottom of the Mortor, and then beat them and the powder of the claws together; then with a pound of this powder mix one ounce of the Magistery of Pearl. Then take ten skins of adders or Snakes or Slow Worms, cut them in pieces,

ick *Whereby a man may preserve his Body in health, or cure himself being sick, for three cents Charge, with such things as one-by grow in England, they being fit for most English Bodies.* A curious blend of folklore, astrology, and solid medical experience, the herbal was written by a young physician who devoted most of his practice to healing the poor using only native English herbs that he grew in his garden. He was the same Nicholas Culpeper who had affronted the College of Physicians by publishing an unauthorized translation of their pharmacopoeia. As we might expect, the College did not welcome this latest work by the sharp-tongued upstart—but that didn't affect its sales; the Culpeper herbal became so popular that pirated editions of it appeared into the nineteenth century.

The doctrine of signatures was based on the assumption that all plants were put on earth by God to cure the ills of man and animals. By studying the physical characteristics of a plant, so the reasoning goes, one could figure out what ailment it would cure. Thus, the dandelion, which has been used since ancient times to cure liver as well as kidney disorders, signaled its use by its golden color—yellow, like jaundice, a symptom of liver disease. Similarly, the walnut, which resembles the shape of the human brain, should be used to treat that organ, and the iris should be used as a poultice for bruises, which are purple. And what about plants that have no obvious signatures? William Coles, author of *The Art of Simpling,* which was published in 1656, asserted that God had created some plants without a distinguishing signature because "the rarity of it [i.e., the signature], which is the delight, would be taken away by too much harping on one string."

and put them into a Pipkin to a pinte and a half of spring water, cover it close and set it on a gentle fire to simper only, not to boyle, for ten or twelve hours, in which time it will be turned into a jelly, and therewith make the said powder into balls. If such skins are not to be gooten, then take six ounces of shaved harts horn, and boyl it to a jelly, and therewith make the solid powder into balls, the horn must be of a red deer, killed in August, when the moon is in Leo, for that is best. The dose is seven or eight grains in Beer or Wine.

From The Queen's Closet Opened, *probably written by Henrietta Maria, wife of Charles I*

Despite the ingenuity of Culpeper's and Coles's explanations, it would seem that both the astrological and doctrine of signatures theories were thought up to confirm what the herbalist already knew and served mainly to jog the memory. The two herbalists were contemporaries and acquaintances who ridiculed one another's dogmas while clinging tenaciously to their own. On one point, however, they adamantly agreed: only native plants should be used in healing. This theory had some wisdom at a time when travel by land or sea was slow and a patient might well perish before a foreign herb reached his shores. Also, many of the common herbs that are used to treat common disorders are universals (that is, they grow all over the world), and there is a marked similarity in the ways these herbs have been used by various cultures and nations. Also, since a number of different herbs can be used to treat a single disorder, the remedies for more ordinary complaints are likely to be found growing in our dooryards or down the road a piece.

Dubious medical theories such as the astrology of plants and the doctrine of signatures, coupled with the generous admixture of superstition and magic that accompany folk medicine, eventually led to the decline of herbalism as an acceptable form of medicine. As Culpeper and Coles were writing, the Golden Age of herbalists was drawing to a close. Drugs composed of minerals or man-made chemicals were introduced in the seventeenth century and soon became the official treatments for disease. The use of herbs in folk medicine, however, continued to flourish into the twentieth century, and at no time has the use of chemical drugs gone unchallenged.

In the nineteenth century, Samuel Hahnemann founded the system of homeopathic medicine, based on the principle that "like cures like." The theoretical basis for homeopathy had been espoused by Hippocrates and was based on the premise that the body's natural defenses could be marshalled against disease. Therefore, instead of eliminating the symptoms with synthetic chemicals, Hahnemann gave patients tiny doses of the herbs that would produce the same symptoms in a healthy person, thus stimulating the body's immune system to work to eliminate the disease. Naturopathy, another natural healing system, can be traced back to the Aesculapians Galen and Hippocrates. It consists of a common-sense regimen of good diet, fresh air, sunshine, and fasting to allow the body to heal naturally. Elements of both these approaches are incorporated in an eclectic system of mind/body healing known as holistic medicine. Holistic healing recognizes that the main responsibility for maintaining health lies with the patient; it includes such alternative disciplines as acupuncture, biofeedback, faith healing, folk medicine, megavitamins, meditation, and Yoga. Many of these therapies are now being incorporated into conventional medical practice.

Meanwhile, in the African bush, in Central America, North America, and other parts of the world, native healers and tribal shamans have long been making discoveries about botanical cures, quite independent of East or West. Whatever the orientation, the ancient art of healing is based on the very beginnings of science and religion, which, as you will see in the next chapter, are rooted in myth, magic, and patient attention to the natural world.

Chapter 2

Herbs, Myth, and Magic

Ages and people which sever the earth from the poetic spirit, or do not care, or stop their ears with knowledge with dust, find their veins grown hollow and their hearts an emptiness echoing to questioning. For the earth is ever more than the earth, more than the upper and the lower field, the tree and the hill. Here is mystery banded about the forehead with green, here are gods ascending, here is benignancy and the corn in the sun, here terror and night, here life, here death, here fire, here the wave coursing in the sea. It is this earth which is the true inheritance of man, his link with his human past, the source of his religion, ritual and song, the kingdom without whose splendour he lapses from his mysterious estate of man to a baser world which is without the other virtue and the other integrity of the animal.

From *Herbs and the Earth*
by Henry Beston

The link between religion, magic, and healing has existed since prehistoric times. This relationship remains vital in shamanism, thought to be the world's oldest religion and still very much alive in tribal communities in parts of Africa, South America, and Siberia. The shamans, who are priests and priestesses of this tribal religion, are also highly skilled botanical physicians. Their knowledge, closely guarded and specific, has been handed down through the centuries to successive generations of shamans who have experimented, sometimes at risk to health or life, to improve and expand upon the ancient body of empirical knowledge. Native healers such as these are the very people whom representatives of the World Health Organization, the World Wildlife Federation, and pharmaceutical companies are literally beating through the bush to find and interview in hopes of finding cures to diseases that have so far been unresponsive to Western medicine.

The bond between spiritual and medical power, real or supposed, exists not only in primitive religions, but also in the origins of Western medicine. In ancient Greece the best doctors were physician–priests, devotees of the mythical healer Aesculapius. The most famous of the Aesculapians were Hippocrates, the father of Western medicine, and Galen, the father of surgery. Thanks to medieval monks, the writings of these early Greek physicians were copied and preserved, to be rediscovered by healers down through the ages.

The Aesculapians had a wide knowledge of botanical remedies. They also recognized the interdependency between physical health and the unconscious. Our word *psychosomatic,* which refers to a symptom or disease caused by a psychological disturbance, comes from the Greek words for "body" and "soul," a reminder that our most sophisticated medical thinking takes account of the interconnection between spiritual and physical health—a concept that can be traced back to these early Greek practitioners.

That prayer has been as important as physic in healing has been a continuing theme in Christianity since the founding of the Catholic church. The New Testament has many stories of miraculous cures; medieval monks no doubt relied on prayer as often as they did upon herbal draughts to heal their patients. A similar connection exists in folk medicine throughout the world. In his account of European folk medicine, P. Kemp remarks, "There is no reference that can be read in the sense of medical doctor as distinct from the priest and magician earlier than A.D. 804." No doubt since prehistoric times, ceremonies that included prayers, chants, and rituals have been used in treating illnesses. Some medical researchers are now beginning to acknowledge that a patient's belief in the efficacy of ritual is not mere superstition, but may actually help the healing process. The positive mental attitude engendered by faith can stimulate hormonal activity that strengthens the immune system. It has been observed that comforting rituals can lead to a direct rise in the white blood count, the body's main defense against disease. As a result of these new findings, even orthodox Western physicians are experimenting with New Age techniques such as creative visualization to develop and enlist the patient's imaginative powers in the healing process.

For centuries, indigenous peoples have relied not only on healing rituals, but on the miraculous or magical properties of the medicines they have used. Some "remedies," such as ingesting urine or excrement, would seem more likely to hasten the invalid's passage into the next world rather than help him in this one; others were indeed panaceas at the time they were first used, and they are still used in medicine today. For example, the legendary healer Aescupalius, to whom the temples of the Aesculapians are dedicated, was said to have restored the stricken hero Hippolytus to life with a "magical simple." Archeological clues suggest that the simple Aesculapius used was the opium poppy. When patients first arrived at the Aesculapian temple, they were given opium, which, among other effects, causes vivid dreams. After the effects of the drug wore off, the dreams were reported to the physician, who then based his diagnosis and prescription on the content of the dream. Hippocrates, Galen, and other Aesculapians prescribed opium for a wide variety of ailments. Certain conditions, such as acute diarrhea, coughs, and intense pain, are still treated by paregoric, codeine, morphine, and other opium derivatives.

The belief in the magical efficacy of herbs goes back to the time before recorded history when primitive peoples believed that gods and spirits dwelled in trees and plants. Some of these gods and spirits were benign and offered protection; others were malevolent, and their vegetable residences were shunned by all except those who would invoke the evil spirits or use the plants associated with them for black magic and other sinister purposes.

Such animistic beliefs were later incorporated into the great mythologies of the world. In Greek mythology, for example, the old plant gods and tree spirits took on several identities: Dionysius, god of the grapevine; Iris, messenger of Zeus and Hera, whose path between heaven and earth was the rainbow; and Narcissus, who fell in love with his own reflected image and eventually changed into the flower that bears his name. And so on. The myths of all cultures are full of such stories, and so are the great religions, from the sacred lotus of Buddhism to the rose of Christianity, which symbolizes the Virgin Mary. The corn goddess, symbol of life's renewal and abundance, appears again and again in mythologies of the Old World and the New, from Demeter, who was the goddess of corn and barley in Greek mythology, to her counterparts in the Indian legends of North and South America.

So compelling were these vegetation myths that they persisted into the Christian era. The fathers of the Catholic church, tacitly acknowledging that they could not compete with the power of myth, transformed the heathen gods and goddesses into Christian saints. For example, Isis of Egyptian and Venus of Roman mythology became the Virgin Mary. Many flowers were dedicated to her, especially the lily and the white rose, symbols of her purity. The red rose, which in Greek mythology acquired its color from the blood of Aphrodite, goddess of love, was also beloved by the Turks, who claimed that the blood of Mohammed had stained the petals, and

Today the defunct Varenne has not lost all her powers. Her simples have merely narrowed their sphere of influence. The devil with purges, abortion colics, sleep troublers, and love-vanquishing herbs! But, as you can see, I still call on them for the stuff of dreams.

Colette

later by the Christians, who believed that it was the blood of Christian martyrs that had dyed the petals red.

Saint John ran a close second to the Virgin Mary in the number of plants associated with his name. His birthday, celebrated on the eve of the summer solstice, is one of the two most important festivals of the pagan year; the other was the winter solstice, when Christians celebrate the birth of Christ. Even today in some areas of the world it is customary to light bonfires on Midsummer Eve to drive off evil spirits and so protect animals and crops to insure a bountiful harvest. St. John's-wort was one of the herbs burned in these midsummer fires. Others were mugwort, yarrow, vervain, elder, figwort, fennel, chamomile, plantain, hawthorn, lavender, and male fern. Most of these plants were reputed to have sacred or demonic powers and were used for such purposes by priests, peasants, and witches.

Fern seed, for example, which is actually a spore and too tiny to be seen by the naked eye, supposedly puts forth golden blossoms on St. John's Day, or Midsummer Eve. A person who is lucky enough to find one of these minute "seeds" acquires the very useful skill of becoming invisible, as well as the even more valuable ability to find gold or buried treasure.

Mistletoe was also thought to bestow treasure-finding powers. Indeed, if any plant can be said to have played a starring role at both winter and summer solstice, it would be this parasitic evergreen, which attaches itself to trees, most notably the oak, home of the gods in many mythologies. The mistletoe was sacred to early Teutonic and Celtic tribes of northern Europe. Norse mythology held that the beloved god Balder had been killed by an arrow made of mistletoe. In Roman mythology, the mistletoe may have been the Golden Bough, key to the entrance of the Underworld. Druid priests of the ancient Celts used mistletoe in their fertility rites and as medicine for such a wide variety of ailments that it was known as "heal-all." According to ancient custom, mistletoe could only be gathered on Midsummer Eve by a Druid priest, clothed in white, who cut down the sacred plant with a golden sickle and gathered it in a white mantle, never allowing the plant to touch the earth. Our cus-

HERBS FOR ALL SEASONS
FREEMAN   GI PLUM Q $10.00
11/10/92   IBCOE D98596EL   1
Z88813   0-452-26584-3
                 PO NUMBER 11092FW

B

****

tom of hanging a sprig of mistletoe in the house at Christmas originated with the Druids, who used it to drive away evil spirits. For centuries the mistletoe was considered powerful protection against witchcraft. Although its effectiveness as a witch repellent may be questionable, the medicinal value of mistletoe is quite real. It was formerly used in domestic medicine for treating heart, circulatory, and digestive problems. Because mistletoe is toxic, other remedies are now used for such disorders, but even today children's leukemia is treated with extracts of mistletoe.

Of the herbs burned in the midsummer fires, yarrow is perhaps the most venerable. It was sacred to the ancient Chinese, and to this day the manipulation of fifty dried yarrow stalks is considered the most accurate method of consulting the *I Ching,* an ancient Chinese book of divination. *Achillea millefolium,* the botanical name for yarrow, was inspired by the Greek legend that the plant was used to treat the wounds of Achilles and his soldiers during the Trojan war. Also known as "soldier's woundwort" because of its ability to stop external and internal bleeding, yarrow is used as a tonic and blood builder as well as a styptic.

detail of flower

Yarrow-Achillea millefolium

Mugwort is also laden with mythic associations. According to legend, Saint John the Baptist wore a girdle of mugwort to sustain him in the wilderness. The name *mugwort* supposedly came from *muggiwurti,* an old Germanic word for "fly" or "gnat plant" (*wort* or *wurt* was the Anglo-Saxon word for "plant"), and refers to its use as an insect repellent since the time of Dioscorides. It is also possible that the name derives from mugwort's use in flavoring ale before hops were used for that purpose. The Japanese, noting the shape of the leaves, call the plant wild chrysanthemum and use it for flavoring soups. In addition to such mundane services, the versatile mugwort was also considered powerful protection against witches, the devil, and that vague but dreaded affliction known as "the evil eye." A sprig hung above the doorway protected the home from unwanted visitors of every sort, including the plague, lightning, carbuncles, and the quartan ague. A few leaves tucked inside the shoe would keep a traveler from becoming weary.

Not all of the herbs cast into the midsummer bonfire had attained the clear status of witch and devil chasers, however. Vervain, for example, had an ambiguous reputation. Gerard tells us that in Latin vervain is *Sacra herba,* a name assigned to any plant gathered to embellish the altar or other holy place; in the next breath, Gerard informs us that "the Divill did reveale it as a secret and divine medicine." Apparently, vervain at certain times and in certain places has been used variously by both witches and those who wish to protect themselves from them.

Two ingredients of the Saint John's Day fires would seem at first to be unlikely candidates for burning along with the guardians of hearth and home: the elder and the hawthorn. Both were loved by witches and approached warily or not at all by God-fearing folk. The word *hag,* often applied to witches, derives from the same word as *hedge*—and hedges were often composed of hawthorn. It was considered unlucky to bring a branch of hawthorn into the house, especially on May Day, for on Walpurgis Night, the last night of April, and one of the major holidays on the witch's calendar, a witch was most likely to turn herself into a hawthorn. The elder was thought to be a favorite resting place for sorcerers, and no self-respecting witch would be without such a bush or tree in her garden. Not only was she likely to clamber into its branches for a quiet moment of contemplation, but she might actually choose to live in the branches of an elder bush or tree. Accordingly, the elder in any form was banished from the domestic hearth. The wood was never used for furniture or cradles, nor would any cottager choose to live in any place where an elder grew in the vicinity. Clearing away the elders from one's neighborhood, moreover, was not to be undertaken lightly. First one had to apologize to the elder and the witch who might be living inside it. If the woodcutter neglected this formality, dire consequences might follow: he might lose a finger or even a limb or be stricken with some crippling illness.

In view of the superstitions regarding the hawthorn and the elder, one might wonder why they were burned on Midsummer Eve. The most reasonable explanation is that while other herbs were burned to drive away witches, burning elders and hawthorns might destroy the witches themselves.

Which brings us to the subject of the witch as medical practitioner.

As we noted in the last chapter, during the Middle Ages the monk's chief competitor in the art of healing was the white witch, or wise woman, who often was also the village midwife. How many of these women actually indulged in the down-and-dirty sorcery intended to blast crops and blight babies is a matter of some debate, particularly now, when feminist scholars are revising our earlier views of history. Branding her as a witch might have been a convenient way of disposing of any woman who might pose an economic or intellectual threat, or who was considered too independent or sexually alluring, or who offered stiff competition to the male-dominated medical trade because of her superior knowledge of botanical medicine.

This is not to say that witches who practiced magic did not exist. They had existed since ancient times and they did join together in covens during the Middle Ages and later, but the purpose of their weekly or seasonal meetings was usually not to worship the devil or devour young children. The object of a witches' sabbath was more likely to worship a goddess or the spirits of the woods and fields, and the rituals they practiced were often for the purpose of influencing events in the natural world, particularly the weather, upon which the lives and livelihoods of most rural people depend.

Some witches, it is true, did pose a threat to the religious, moral, or economic order by summoning demons, bewitching lovers, or causing milk to sour, cattle to sicken, and crops to fail. These were the black witches, however—certainly not the main practitioners of the craft. The majority of witches were of the gray or white variety, whom Dorothy Jacobs dubs "the GP's of their profession." The white witch used her power and knowledge to help people, and her services were often rendered free of charge. The gray witch was an equivocal figure, and it was to her that one applied for the more unsavory tasks: abortions, hexes, even perhaps putting a troublesome person out of the way permanently, as well as the cures, love philters, healings, and unhexings that constituted the white witch's ordinary workday.

But black, white, or gray, the one thing each of these witches had in common was her garden. In it she tended the herbs that she used in recipes that had been handed down through gener-

The implication that both well and ill-disposed spirits cause sickness, and also are masters of healing, is universal. . . . Judges, in the Middle Ages, ordered the accused witches to remove curses laid on other people, since only the witch himself knew how it could be done. . . . Only those who cause illness can remove it and are in a sense the patrons also of healing.
From Healing Rituals
by P. Kemp

ations of witches. The centerpiece of the witch's garden was the elder, and when she did not feel inclined to scoot up into its branches for a quiet think or appropriate it for her private apartment, it was likely that she used its products for more mundane purposes, such as making an elder flower ointment for softening the skin and soothing abrasions, or a tea for treating coughs, colds, kidney and urinary complaints, constipation, or rheumatism. If the witch were of the less benign sort, she might exploit the toxic qualities of the plant: the root and bark of the young plant, when taken in sufficient quantity, are powerful purgatives, as are the berries, which when eaten raw cause vomiting. Seeds of the red elderberry are poisonous.

The fearsome hawthorn might be brewed into a tea for use when a client complained of heart or nervous problems; the flowers and fruit strengthen the heart, normalize the blood pressure, and are helpful in nervous conditions, especially insomnia.

Another shrub or bush that one was likely to see in the witch's garden was the witch hazel, which she used for divining. Even those who had no commerce with witches and their craft acknowledged the magical powers of the witch hazel. According to legend, Saint Patrick used a branch of it to drive the snakes from Ireland. In bloom, a witch hazel bush bears a froth of tiny yellow flowers resembling forsythia. Anyone coming upon a flowering witch hazel might be easily persuaded that the bush does have magical properties, for it blooms in winter.

Hawthorn-Crataegus oxyacantha

One blustery winter day at the end of January, as I was walking through the Brooklyn Botanic Garden, muffled to the nose against the cutting winds, my attention was captured by a flash of sunny yellow that stood out in warm relief against the gray stone walls and the dry husks of the previous summer. I turned and, sure enough, there stood a witch hazel covered with yellow flowers, unexpected and cheering as a goddess of spring.

The word *witch* means "yielding," and refers to the suppleness of the branches, a quality that makes the witch hazel a likely candidate for use as a divining rod, which supposedly bends toward whatever it is meant to be finding. For this reason witch hazel was used for centuries to locate underground water and is still used for that purpose in rural areas all over the world. Even today, some professional well-drilling companies who are stymied in the search for water will call in a "dowser," or diviner. The dowser, who is believed to have psychic powers that assist in the work, arrives at the well-drilling scene bearing the tool of the trade: a forked branch of witch hazel. Holding one end of the fork in each hand with the apex of the triangle pointing straight ahead, the dowser will walk slowly over the property. When the witch hazel divines water, the apex of the forked branch will suddenly dip toward the earth, indicating where the well is to be dug or drilled. (I have witnessed such an operation myself and can attest to having seen the hazel branch shiver and bow, although I was not around for the well-drilling. I do know, however, that many people who are not ordinarily superstitious believe in dowsing as scientific fact.) Besides

Witch Hazel-Hamamelis virginiana

exploiting its supernatural powers, the witch very likely used her witch hazel for less dramatic results when she steeped the leaves and branches and used the astringent infusion as a wash for skin irritations and bruises, insect stings, or poison ivy, or a tea against diarrhea.

If the witch were of the black variety, and therefore a reliable source when an effective poison was needed, she would be sure to have in her garden the ingredients of a draught that would satisfy a Borgia. One of these botanicals would undoubtedly be deadly nightshade, which, in the Middle Ages, was thought to be the favorite plant of the Devil. The botanical name for this plant is *Atropa belladonna*. In Greek mythology, Atropos was one of the three goddesses of fate. While her two sisters were in charge of spinning the thread of a person's life and determining its length, it was Atropos who finally cut the thread and so ended the person's life—with the assistance, it is said, of the black berries of the nightshade. One of the constituents of the nightshade berry is the alkaloid atropine, which, if taken in sufficient quantity, accomplishes the work of Atropos by producing complete motor paralysis followed by delirium, stupor, and death, usually by asphixiation.

The latter part of the botanical name, *belladonna,* comes from two Italian words meaning "beautiful lady," and refers to the custom among Italian beauties of using the juice of the berries to dilate the pupils of their eyes to achieve a luminous, mysterious expression. The pupil-dilating effects of belladonna have also been used by eye doctors to facilitate examinations.

Related chemicals are found in two other plants that, along with belladonna, are members of the botanical order *Solanaceae:* datura and henbane. The latter was the favorite plant of the witch goddess Hecate. The former, which is a common weed all over North and South America, is also known as jimsonweed, a reference to a rather ignominious moment in American history when a company of British soldiers who had been dispatched to quell an uprising in the Jamestown colony ate some jimsonweed and—so the story goes—went on an eleven-day bender courtesy of datura's hallucinatory and narcotic effects.

A third member of this botanical family was the most feared weapon in the witch's arsenal: European mandrake. Some say the name is derived from two Sanskrit words meaning "sleep-producing substance," referring to its use as an anesthetic and sedative since ancient times. Others say that the name refers to the shape of the root, which is forked and resembles human legs. Both explanations are plausible, although Gerard, ever the skeptic, tartly

European Mandrake

observes that it "in truth, is no otherwise than in the roots of carrots, parseneps, and such like, forked or divided into two or more parts, which Nature taketh no account of."

* * *

Mandrake would have been a likely ingredient in any love philter the witch might concoct, since it has a reputation as an aphrodisiac and fertility plant. It was also reputed to be hard to find and perilous to gather, although Gerard reports, "I my selfe and my servants also have dug up, planted, and replaced very many," and presumably lived to tell the tale. Here is his tongue-in-cheek summary of the current mandrake theories:

> That it is never or very seldom to be found growing naturally but under a gallows, where the matter that hath fallen from a dead body hath given it the shape of a man; and the matter of a woman, the substance of a female plant; with many other such doltish dreames. They fable further and affirme, That he who would take up a plant thereof must tie a dog therunto and pull it up; otherwise if a man should do it, he would surely die in short space after.

To complete her collection of deadly botanicals, the witch would probably also grow foxglove and monkshood, the latter named for its hood-shaped purple flowers. Another name for monkshood is wolfsbane, referring to its use as an arrow poison by wolf hunters. An arrow dipped in monkshood surely would be the bane of any wolf it struck, for the plant contains aconite, one of the most powerful poisons known, causing death within a few hours.

The interesting thing about nightshade, henbane, datura, European mandrake, foxglove, and monkshood is that, although in large doses each is deadly, in smaller doses all were powerful therapeutic drugs. Most of them have been used in medicine for centuries. As late as 1917, Dr. A. D. Bush, in his *Materia Medica* based on the ninth revision of the U.S. *Pharmacopoeia*, writes that aconite extracted from monkshood "has been called 'the therapeutic lancet.' " He notes, "Its power over the circulation, respiration and transpiration renders it of great value in all afflictions characterized by high, resisting pulse, dry, hot, skin, and elevated body temperature." Bush goes on to recommend aconite for treating a variety of disorders including acute infections of the throat and respiratory organs, peritonitis, surgical fever, rheumatism and neuralgia, diarrhea, menstrual suppression, and cardiac problems. The list of uses for atropine, extracted from belladonna, is even longer, ranging from treatment of the common cold and constipation to typhoid, scarlet fever, and cardiac failure. Before penicillin was discovered, both atropine and aconite were the physician's main weapons in combating life-threatening infections. To this day, both drugs are still used in homeopathy.

Henbane, datura, and European mandrake, which contain chemicals similar to atropine, also had their uses in medicine. Nefertiti and Cleopatra used mandrake as a sedative. Before ether and chloroform were discovered, European mandrake was used as a general anesthetic in European surgery. For a time, henbane was also used for general anesthesia, and more commonly as a hypnotic and sedative for acute mania, tremors, coughs, and bowel and urinary problems. Datura was used as a sedative and the leaves were smoked to relieve asthma.

One poisonous plant in the witch's garden has been important in medicine since the time its therapeutic use was discovered by a Shropshire witch. Leaves of the foxglove, also known as witch's glove because of the shape of the purple flowers, yield glucosides used to make digitalis, a heart tonic and diuretic that has extended the life span of countless cardiac patients.

Another digitalis source the witch was likely to have on hand was toads. For centuries toad venom has been used in Chinese medicine for treating cardiac disease. As you may recall, the skin of toad was a favorite ingredient in the infamous brew that boiled and bubbled in the witch's cauldron, which she consulted on behalf of prophesy-seeking clients and before she hopped on her broomstick for a nocturnal jaunt. I had always assumed that the toads were added for local color—until I learned that toad skins contain a hallucinogenic substance.

In fact, most of the witch's favorite poisons contain mind-altering drugs. Some, such as mandrake, datura, and henbane, were thought to be aphrodisiac as well—so of course one or more of these would be used in concocting a love potion. In Central Europe, nightshade has been used as an inebriant by those who couldn't afford the price of alcohol, while in Egypt, at least as far back as two thousand years before Christ, mandrake was added to beer to enhance its effects.

Witches used psychoactive plants for a variety of occasions that required an alteration of consciousness. Monkshood, a powerful sensory, cardiac, respiratory, and spinal depressant, when used externally paralyzes the sensory nerves and produces a sensation of numbness and tingling. After smearing an ointment containing monkshood on their broomsticks, witches would have a sensation of flying. By burning incense and anointing herself with a cream containing monkshood or some other mind-altering drug, a witch could persuade herself that she was changing into an animal, another popular pastime among sorcerers. Those witches who participated in orgies were no doubt assisted by psychoactive drugs of one sort or another.

In addition, and most important, psychoactive botanicals enabled the witch to achieve the state of ecstasy and trance that allowed her to commune with the spirit world and foretell the future. The practice of using mind-altering substances to transcend ordinary consciousness is rooted in ancient religious

There is an Egyptian document of c. 2000–1800 B.C., which tells of the wrath of the lion-goddess Sehmet, who, according to this text, came into being as an aspect of the cow-goddess Hathor, to wreak chastisement on the people of Seth. She could not be stayed when her work was done, however, and so the gods, to save mankind, caused their slave girls to brew seven thousand jars of beer, which they infused with powdered mandrake, to make it resemble human blood. And in the best part of the night, we read, "this sleeping draught was poured out until the fields were flooded four spans by that liquid. And when the goddess appeared in the morning (as the blazing morning sun) she beheld this inundation: her face, reflected in it, was beautiful. She drank and, liking it, returned to her palace drunk. And it was thus that the world of mankind was saved.

From Oriental Mythology
    by Joseph Campbell

and magical ceremonies practiced all over the world. In shamanism, which may have been the first religion to use drugs for such purposes, the priest- or priestess–physician ingests hallucinogenic plants to heighten the level of receptivity to portents from the gods—portents that can be interpreted and used for healing the sick and predicting the future. As early as 2000 B.C., Hindu priests ingested *soma*, an elixir that anthropologists believe contained *Amanita muscaria*, a psychoactive mushroom. In ancient Greece, priests and priestesses at oracular shrines burned laurel leaves, henbane, or marijuana to release their powers of prophesy. Even today, in the Native American church, the eating of peyote is central to religious observance.

The role of psychoactive plants in the development of world religions is a fascinating story, and much too long and complicated for more than passing mention here. Suffice it to say that the powers of magic, healing, and prophesy attributed to the witch are by no means an anomaly, but instead part of a tradition that may be older than written history, reminding us that body and spirit are inextricably bound to one another and sustained by the health of our planet—a relationship we ignore to our peril.

Part Two

The Herbal Pharmacopoeia

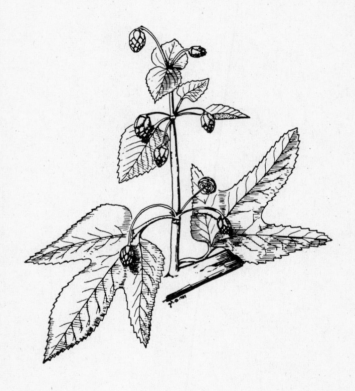

Chapter 3

The Kitchen Pharmacy: How to Use Herbs

Strictly speaking, an herb is a nonwoody plant that withers after flowering. In practice, though, the definition of an herb is very elastic and includes any member of the plant kingdom that can be used for medicine, seasoning, or scent. Such plants range from the humble mold that was the original source of penicillin to sweet grasses once used to freshen the air of courtroom, church, or castle to the leaves, seeds, or bark of certain trees used to season food, provide a stimulating beverage, or treat a medical disorder.

An herb is a tiny, powerful factory that manufactures a complex of chemicals—acids, alkalies, and essential oils—that produce various effects in the human organism. Some dull the sense of pain, others tone and energize the organs, a few are poisonous to insects, animals, or humans. Increasingly, scientists are investigating these chemicals and how they interact with human biochemistry. When used in a pharmaceutical preparation, the particular active ingredient that has the desired medicinal property is isolated, extracted from the herb, and refined so the dose and strength can be regulated. When you take an aspirin tablet, for example, you know exactly how many grains of salicylates you are getting. When you drink a tea made from a plant containing salicylates, the natural chemical originally used to make aspirin, you have no way of knowing exactly how strong the dose is; that will depend on the soil in which the plant grew, the stage of development the plant had reached when it was harvested, and how the herb was stored. On the other hand, because the pharmaceutical drug is refined, certain natural chemicals that modify or reinforce the active ingredient in the plant are lost. Meadowsweet, for example, which contains salicylic acid, also contains mucilage and tannin, which coat the stomach lining and protect it from the irritation and upsets some people experience when taking aspirin.

Because most herbal preparations work gradually, we may be tempted to overuse them in the mistaken belief that they are harmless. However, certain ingredients can have adverse effects, ranging from allergic reactions to actual poisoning in sensitive individuals.

Before you use a new herb, make note of its various properties. This is especially important for pregnant or nursing women. Pennyroyal tea, for example, is useful in treating headaches, nervousness, and colds; it also causes the uterus to contract, which can cause miscarriage. Other herbs may be emetic, laxative, or even toxic, and these effects can be passed on to a baby through its mother's breast milk. An astringent herb such as sage can reduce the flow of the milk. Generally speaking, when pregnant or nursing it is best to avoid taking herbs except in the tiny amounts one uses in condiments.

Although the majority of natural chemicals in the raw herb are beneficial, some herbs should not be taken in large doses or over long periods of time. For example, prolonged use of yarrow or St. John's-wort can make the skin sensitive to light; Chinese ephedra causes a temporary rise in blood pressure, and, more disturbing, some herbs have carcinogenic properties.

Comfrey, one of the first herbs to be investigated for the presence of carcinogens, contains pyrrolizidine alkaloids, a group of natural chemicals found to cause liver cancer in laboratory rats. Coltsfoot, an old folk remedy for coughs and other respiratory problems, also contains pyrrolizidine alkaloids and in clinical tests has been shown to cause lung and liver lesions in rats. Safrole, which makes up 70 to 80 percent of the oil extracted from the root bark of sassafras, a popular folk remedy and flavoring agent, also produced cancer in laboratory rats. Formerly used to flavor root beer, sassafras oil was banned from use in 1960. Traces of safrole or estragole, a related chemical, are found in nutmeg, star anise, mace, cinnamon, black pepper, tarragon, basil, fennel, and calamus.

Tannin, present in Chinese tea and many medicinal herbs, has caused liver cancer when injected into rats; there is a high incidence of oral cancer in those countries where betel nuts, which are high in tannin, are chewed regularly.

Scientists view these findings from various perspectives. Some point out that laboratory animals, which may or may not be biochemically similar to humans, are exposed to highly concentrated doses of suspected carcinogens. In some tests they are fed exclusively on the substance for long periods of time; in other tests the suspected carcinogen is injected or applied directly to the skin. Normal human exposure does not usually approximate these conditions. As the American Council of Science and Health has observed, "There is usually little or no confirmatory evidence from direct observation on humans to show that a substance in question is a *human* carcinogen." Other scientists agree, although they do not rule out the possibility of a particular substance causing cancer in susceptible individuals.

Another perspective from which such findings might be viewed takes into account the fact that nearly everything we eat, pure or processed, contains toxic chemicals that occur naturally. Some of these chemicals are carcinogens, and the list of foods that contain them includes beets, spinach, radishes, cabbage, turnip, kale, bracken fern, celery, parsnips, parsley, mushrooms, and, in some instances, milk, cereals, nuts, and peanut butter.

Bruce Ames, a biochemist who has done pioneering studies of naturally occurring carcinogens in foods, advises a well-balanced and varied diet as the best way to reduce the possibility of getting a high concentration of one carcinogen and to gain the benefits of anticarcinogens, which are also present in foods and perhaps more widely distributed than scientists have yet discovered. (You will read more about anticarcinogens in a later chapter.)

It may seem by now that there are a lot of drawbacks to using herbs, which are supposed to be so good for you. In most instances, however, herbs provide far safer alternatives to synthetic chemical drugs, which may have unpleasant or even dangerous side effects. Herbal preparations have been used in medicine and in folk remedies for centuries because they work, and people who use herbs properly suffer no ill effects. The thing to bear in mind is that in taking botanicals, one is still dealing with chemicals—in some cases, very powerful ones—so herbs should be used as carefully as any synthetic chemical drug a doctor has prescribed for you.

Never regard any herbal remedy as a replacement for the services of a physician. *If your symptoms persist, see a doctor.* If you have a serious medical problem, get medical advice before you attempt to doctor yourself. Physicians who practice homeopathic or holistic medicine do prescribe herbal remedies for their patients. (Local herb societies and publications devoted to alternative medicine are good sources for information about locating such physicians, or see the "Resources" listed at the end of this book.)

Most people who use herbs, especially city dwellers, will probably get them from a health food store or a shop that specializes in herbs. Mail-order suppliers are also listed in the resource section. Growing herbs in a garden, a window box, or in a planter indoors is a very satisfying and economical way of providing yourself with a reliable supply of fresh herbs. So is gathering them in the wild.

If you do gather wild herbs, make sure that the area where you harvest is as chemical-free and wholesome as your vegetable garden. Do not harvest from lawns or fields that have been treated with weed killers, or from areas close to highways, where the lead from gasoline fumes tends to concentrate. Similarly, while gathering rose hips while ye may, make sure that the roses haven't been sprayed with pesticides. Also, be very sure of the identity of the plants you are gathering. Many excellent field guides are available, and one should accompany you on your walks. The ones I find most useful are illustrated with color photographs or paintings—the larger the better, because you can see more details. Guides which show the flower in detail are particularly helpful.

Obviously, before foraging on private property, common courtesy demands that you ask the owner's permission. And courtesy toward nature demands that you do not gather any plant that is a member of a rare or protected species.

When you are using an herbal preparation for the first time, it is best to start with the lowest possible dose—about one half-teaspoon to a cup of water will do for most herbal teas; you may increase the dosage to one teaspoon per one cup when you are assured the herb is safe for you. When treating children and the elderly, use about half the adult amount. One traditional formula for children is to add twelve to the age and divide that number by the age, then give that fraction of the adult dose. Thus, for a two-year-old child, the formula would be: $2 + 12$ divided by $2 - 7$, or $1/7$ the adult dose.

Herbal preparations come in various forms. The most common, and usually the safest, is the *infusion*, which is prepared in the same way that you make ordinary tea. Use one teaspoon of the herb part (usually the leaves, sometimes also the flowers) to one cup boiling water. Steep in a covered glass or enamel container for at least ten minutes. Doses range from a teaspoonful or two of the infusion every few hours to a wineglass or a cup full. Sweeten with honey if you like. Sweetening is not necessary for most purposes, and should be avoided when using an herb for the first time, as honey masks the taste.

A *decoction* extracts minerals and salts from roots, bark, or seeds that do not readily yield their properties to steeping. Boil the plant part in water—about half an ounce of the herb to one pint water—for about ten minutes. Boiling does destroy certain vitamins and other volatile ingredients, but you can restore them by adding green parts of the plant to the decoction when you have removed it from the fire and infusing the mixture for ten minutes. Strain and use as you would an infusion.

Juicing the flowers and leaves of plants will preserve vitamins, especially vitamin C, which is destroyed by heat. Chop the plant into small bits and press out the juice, then add a little water and press out the remaining pulp. A garlic press is a handy tool for this operation. The vitamin content deteriorates if the juice is allowed to stand, so only prepare as much juice as you will use immediately.

A *cold extract* will release some of the mineral content and preserve heat-sensitive vitamins. Prepare as you would an infusion. Use about one ounce of the plant part to a pint of cold water and let the mixture stand overnight; then strain and use.

Bitter-tasting herbs, such as boneset, or unpleasant-smelling herbs, such as valerian, are most easily taken in the form of *powders,* which are packed into gelatin capsules. The latter can be purchased in some pharmacies or herbal outlets. To make a powder, pulverize the dried plant part with a mortar and pestle; seal the powder in the capsule. Size 0 capsules hold about ten grains; size 00 capsules hold about fifteen grains. *Capsules* are compact and spare you the nuisance of infusing or decocting when you are traveling.

Tinctures are another convenience for travelers, because they are ready-made and very concentrated. The basis for a tincture is alcohol, which, being a preservative, will allow you to keep the herb for a long time. Preparing a tincture is a good way to extract the properties of fresh herbs and preserve the qualities of dried herbs that you use only occasionally but wish to keep on hand. Some ingredients, such as essential oils, which are not soluble in water, can be extracted by using alcohol. To prepare a tincture, add one quarter to one ounce of the powdered herb to eight to ten ounces of a relatively tasteless spirit, such as vodka. Depending on the proof of the alcohol, add enough water to make a 50 percent alcohol solution. Seal the bottle and let the mixture stand for two weeks, shaking it once or twice a day. Strain out the herbs and the tincture is ready to use. Dosage ranges from a few drops to a teaspoonful.

Cuts, wounds, bumps, bruises, and skin irritations are treated most effectively with a *poultice,* a mass of heated herbs laid directly on the skin. Fresh herbs should be crushed or pounded to release their healing properties; dried herbs should be soaked in water to soften them. Spread the herbs over the affected area, then cover with a warm, moist cloth. Keep the poultice warm by dipping the cloth in hot water whenever it cools; leave on for about twenty minutes. When the injured area is fairly small, the most convenient poultice is an herbal tea bag that has first been moistened and softened with boiling water. When using garlic, mustard, pepper, or other substances that may irritate the skin, wrap the herb in a cloth rather than lay it directly on the skin.

A *fomentation* is a cloth or towel soaked in a hot infusion or decoction and applied like a poultice.

A *cold compress* is similar to a fomentation, only the liquid is cold.

Salves and ointments keep the skin soft and moist, protect it from the air, and release their healing properties over a long period of time. The traditional base for ointments was lard, lanolin, or other animal fat. Today the most common base is petroleum jelly, but you could also use olive oil, adding enough white emulsifying wax or beeswax to harden. The simplest method is to mix one part powdered herb to four parts hot Vaseline or lard, then allow to cool and congeal. The more traditional and probably better method is to make a very strong decoction, boil it down, strain, then simmer with fat or oil until the water has evaporated. For a creamy consistency, add about one teaspoon beeswax to the hot oil. A woodstove, if you have one, is wonderful for making salves because it allows you to simmer the mixture very slowly for a day or two and thus obtain a more concentrated extract. A drop or two of benzoin or balsamic resin is antiseptic and will keep the oil from becoming rancid.

Herbal baths offer a wonderful way to relax, quiet jangled nerves, soothe the kinks from aching muscles, and relieve skin irritation. A long soak in a hot tub is a traditional cure for insomnia; adding sedative herbs will further nudge you into a good night's sleep. A hot bath followed by a cup of herbal tea with a pinch of cayenne added is a time-honored cold cure that helps sweat out toxins. Adding herbs to the bath is helpful in treating certain medical disorders because the skin absorbs the healing properties of the herbs. Rheumatism, bladder and kidney infections, and respiratory problems have been treated by herbal baths for centuries.

The *sitz bath* is helpful in treating bladder and urinary infections and for easing menstrual cramps. Only a small amount of water is used in a sitz bath. You can fill a wash basin or a small tub, or run a shallow bath in a full-sized tub; the water should come no higher than your navel. Those who prefer not to douche will find that the sitz bath is a good way to treat vaginal infections. It is also very soothing to hemorrhoids. Adding an astringent herb such as witch hazel to a warm sitz bath, followed by a brief immersion in cold water, helps shrink the inflamed hemorrhoidal tissue.

Vapor baths open the pores and respiratory passages. Inhaling the steam from a pot of simmering water to which aromatic herbs such as mint or eucalyptus have been added breaks up congestion from cold or sinus problems.

The smallest bath, of course, is the *eyebath,* in which infused or decocted herbs are used to soothe inflamed and tired eyes. Using an eyecup is the more civilized method, but if both eyes are affected and you don't mind getting soused, you can immerse your entire face in a bowl or basin of water containing the strained infusion or decoction.

The final method of using herbs, which goes back to the fifteenth century, is *distilling,* which extracts and concentrates the essence of herbs and flowers for medicinal or cosmetic purposes or for making alcoholic beverages.

If your distilling project is fairly modest—for instance, you want to make a quart of witch hazel or even some stronger stuff—you can make do with what you have on hand in the kitchen. According to that master of resourcefulness Euell Gibbons, all you need is a deep kettle with a domed lid. This container must be made of stainless steel or flameproof glass or crockery; otherwise your brew may be toxic. Fill the kettle with a gallon (more or less) of water, then set a bowl containing the plant parts above the water on a rack or on fireproof material, such as a brick. Invert the dome over the pot and fill the dome with cold water, which you must constantly replenish so the condensation beneath won't evaporate. The distillate then gathers under the dome and drips into the bowl of herbs or flowers. The recipe Gibbons used for witch hazel was four cups dry, crushed leaves to half a gallon of water; your brew is ready when you have two cups of liquid in the bowl. For other mixtures, you can experiment with the proportions.

Home Distillation

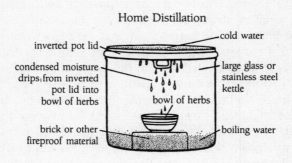

inverted pot lid
cold water

condensed moisture drips from inverted pot lid into bowl of herbs
large glass or stainless steel kettle

bowl of herbs

brick or other fireproof material
boiling water

In former times, herbs were known as *simples,* which was also the name for preparations made with a single herb. *Compounds* are preparations containing more than one ingredient. While simples are fine if your ailment is uncomplicated—a headache, for example, or a touch of indigestion—a compound will serve you better when you have a cluster of symptoms, such as the aches and pains, stomach upset, or congestion and fever of a cold or flu. Certain herbs can enhance the effects of others, or neutralize unpleasant side effects. Before deciding what to use, consider your symptoms. Is your headache caused by tension? A sedative combined with a salicylate-containing herb will help—unless the stress and pain are accompanied by excessive menstrual flow, which will increase if you take salicylic acid. Similarly, you do not want an astringent if you have a dry, scratchy cough; a stomachic that is also laxative if you have diarrhea; or an herb that raises blood pressure if yours is higher than normal. As I mentioned earlier, herbs are made up of a complex of chemicals and can be used for treating a variety of symptoms affecting more than one organ. This is a virtue if you are using peppermint for a stomach upset accompanied by a headache, but risky if you have high blood pressure and use a vasoconstrictor such as Chinese ephedra for the sniffles. In the Glossary that follows, you will find a listing of the various herbs and their properties. Study it well; use each herb as a "simple" before you attempt a compound. If you are in doubt about any herb, use an alternative one, especially if you have allergies. Most of the herbs listed in the Glossary are relatively harmless; the listings for those that are toxic or have adverse side effects include warnings. Some of the herbs discussed in the historical section (chapters 2 and 3) are very toxic. Although they can be dramatically effective in the hands of an experienced herbalist, I strongly caution you against experimenting with them. There is much truth to the old saying "He who attempts to treat himself has a fool for a doctor." Nevertheless, learning the ways of nature puts you in touch with an ancient wisdom that is as essential to our contemporary well-being as it was to that of our distant ancestors, who first learned healing from the woods and fields thousands of years ago.

ANNOTATED GLOSSARY

Acid. A sour ingredient in plants that in concentrated form acts as a caustic, inhibits production of acid, and stimulates alkaline secretions. Examples: acetic, citric, benzoic.

Alkaloid. A bitter, nitrogenous ingredient in plants; has the effect of neutralizing acids, inhibits alkaline secretions, and stimulates acid secretions. Examples: atropine, caffeine, cocaine, codeine, quinine.

Alterative. Gradually alters the course of disease by improving digestion, absorption, and elimination. Beneficial in chronic ailments. Examples: burdock root, chickweed, dogwood, ginseng,

goldenseal, yellow dock, sarsaparilla, wild Oregon grape, spikenard.

Anthelmintic. Destroys or expels intestinal worms; usually administered by enema or with a purgative. Examples: butternut bark,
betony, birch, Queen Anne's lace, fern, aloe, thyme, garlic, onion,
mugwort, papaya, pumpkin seed, tarragon, catnip, woundwort.

Analgesic/Anodyne. Relieves pain by either blocking sensory nerves
or depressing the central nervous system. Examples: wintergreen,
meadowsweet, willow, poplar. (All contain salicin, the raw material for aspirin.)

Anaphrodisiac. Reduces sexual desire or potency by acting on the
nervous or circulatory system. Examples: bark and catkins of black
willow, tobacco.

Antidote. Alters the chemistry of a poison and renders it harmless.
For example, tannic acid combined with digitalis forms a compound that is relatively insoluble, so it is not readily absorbed;
aconite and atropine are antagonists, each counteracting the effect
of the other.

Antispasmodic. Prevents or relieves spasms or cramps by stimulating
or depressing the nervous system. Examples: peppermint, nerve
root, dill, angelica, valerian, lady's mantle, pasque flower, skullcap, passionflower, chamomile, imperial masterwort. *Warning:*
Don't use masterwort with heavy menstrual flow.

Astringent. Contracts tissue and arrests mucous secretions. Used externally to correct oily skin, check bleeding, reduce inflammation,
internally as a douche for vaginal infections or to control diarrhea,
catarrh, and bronchial and pulmonary discharge. Includes herbs
that contain gallic or tannic acids. Examples: white oak bark, witch
hazel, stem and root of pomegranate, red rose petals, blackberry
leaves, woundwort.

Antiseptic/Detergent. Destroys or inhibits putrefactive bacteria; used
externally on wounds to prevent infection, internally for putrefactive bacteria in stomach, intestines, lungs, and other organs. Examples: sphagnum moss, goldenseal, garlic, agave, blueberry,
clove, echinacea, eucalyptus, heather, Iceland moss, lavender, mus-

tard seed, myrrh, nasturtium, olive oil, onion, sandalwood, sweet gum, willow, wormwood.

Aperient. A mild laxative that acts by stimulating the bowels (see **purgative**). Some act by adding fiber, thus increasing the bulk of stools. Except in drastic cases, use instead of purgatives. Examples: asparagus, boneset, borage, licorice, burdock root, marigold, hibiscus, cucumber, dandelion, elder, apple, prune, fig, psyllium seed.

Cardiac. Affects heart action. There are three categories. *Sedatives* reduce force and frequency of heart action and are used to control palpitation and overstimulation. Most are cardiac poisons. Examples: digitalis, aconite. *Stimulants* increase the force and frequency of pulse. Examples: atropine, cocaine, caffeine. *Tonics* stimulate the cardiac muscle, causing longer, slower contractions. In large doses they cause irregular heart action and possibly death. Examples: digitalis, black cohosh, hellebore, lily of the valley, mistletoe, wahoo, woodruff, wormwood. *Caution:* **Do not use any of these drugs without medical supervision.**

Carminative. Expels gas from intestines by increasing peristalsis. For this reason, carminatives may also act as laxatives. In general, aromatic herbs are carminative. Examples: cinnamon and other spices, cardamom, dill seed, fennel, ginger, mustard, pepper, peppermint, anise, wintergreen, chamomile, caraway, garlic.

Cholagogue. A laxative that acts by increasing the flow of bile into the intestines, may cause green or "bilious" stools. Examples: artichoke, burdock root, marigold, chicory, dandelion, elder, fern, garlic, lavender, linden, yarrow, mint, mugwort, olive oil, radish, yellow dock, gentian, aloe vera, rhubarb.

Demulcent. Soothes and protects mucous membrane, relieves inflammation. Examples: common mallow, marshmallow, tragacanth, acacia, licorice, almond oil, olive oil, comfrey, barley, slippery elm, fig, ginseng, hollyhock flowers, Iceland moss, corn silk, mullein, plantain, daisy.

Decoction. Herbal preparation made by boiling plant parts in water. Primarily used to extract active ingredients from tough parts such as roots, barks, seeds.

Diaphoretic/Sudorific. Stimulates perspiration. Useful for "sweating out" a cold, bringing down a fever, eliminating toxins. Examples: angelica root, boneset, yarrow, willow bark, meadowsweet, poplar, wintergreen, asparagus, lemon balm, ginger, violet, calendula, chamomile, elder.

Digestive. Aids digestion. Many culinary herbs have this property. Examples: anise, cayenne pepper, chervil, chive, garlic, bay leaf, mustard, papaya, mint, caraway.

Diuretic. Increases flow of urine, removes fluid from tissues, promotes elimination of waste, maintains action of kidneys, dilutes urine. Useful in kidney disorders, arthritis, and cardiac disease. Examples: water buchu, cayenne pepper, juniper berry, uva-ursi (bearberry), corn silk. All of the preceding are renal stimulants and may irritate the kidneys, so use sparingly. Other diuretics include dandelion, meadowsweet, parsley, strawberry, cleavers, sarsaparilla, lemon juice, hops, cranberry, celery, cucumber, mallow, watercress.

Emetic. Causes vomiting. Useful in treating some types of poisoning. Examples: ipecac, mustard, salt, fresh alder bark, hot boneset tea, lobelia.

Emmenagogue. Promotes menstruation. Examples: angelica, lemon balm, basil, pennyroyal, caraway, vervain, imperial masterwort, parsley, rue, lovage, motherwort, sumac. *Caution:* **Avoid using during pregnancy or excessive menstruation. Many emmenagogues not listed here are toxic in varying degrees.**

Emollient. Soothes skin by softening and relaxing tissue and protecting it from air. Examples: olive oil, almond oil, aloe vera, cocoa butter, marshmallow, comfrey, slippery elm, fig, hollyhock flowers, linden bark, mallow.

Expectorant. Modifies and promotes expulsion of mucus from broncho-pulmonary passages. Examples: garlic, mallow, myrrh, anise, betony, caraway, chervil, chickweed, eucalyptus, fennel, fenugreek, violet, horehound, hyssop, licorice, mullein, nasturtium, onion, parsley, peach leaf, plantain, pleurisy root, sage, spruce gum, yerba santa, wild cherry bark.

Febrifuge/Antipyretic. Reduces or eliminates fever. Because the function of a mild fever is to kill disease-causing microorganisms, it is best to let such a fever run its course. The safest fever remedies are those that lower body temperature by sweating. See **diaphoretic/sudorific**. Other useful herbs are: borage, brooklime, buck bean, colombo, red currant, dogwood bark, European centaury (use weak infusion, strong decoction is emetic, strong infusion diaphoretic) everlasting, feverweed, garlic, hops, lady's mantle, imperial masterwort, ginseng, horehound, yarrow, olive, sage, sumac, red elder, white oak, yerba santa, desert tea *(Ephedra),* mahuang, also Chinese ephedra (Ephredra Sinica). *Warning:* **Avoid ephedra if you have high blood pressure.**

Galactagogue. Increases milk secretion. Examples: anise, fennel, jaborandi, borage, caraway, dill, milkwort, nettle, apple juice.

Hemostatic/Styptic. Stops bleeding. Examples: shepherd's purse, alder bark, club moss, comfrey, great burnet, knotweed, yarrow, stinging nettle, plantain, tormentil, witch hazel.

Hepatic. Acts on the liver. Examples: asparagus, dandelion.

Hypnotic. Promotes sleep. Examples: valerian, hops in tea or pillow, tarragon. *Warning:* **Do not use valerian for more than two weeks; do not use tarragon with excessive menstrual bleeding.**

Infusion. Herbs steeped in hot water and either taken internally or used externally as a wash for wounds and skin conditions.

Laxative. Promotes emptying of the bowels by stimulating movement of the intestinal tract. Use only when absolutely necessary; overuse creates dependency and reduces kidney secretions. Senna is effective, but causes griping. Gentle laxatives include apple, asparagus, chickweed, fig, damiana, hibiscus, olive, peach leaf, plum, raspberry, fresh blueberry, sorrel, tamarind, walnut bark, wild Oregon grape, daisy.

Parturient/Oxytocic. Stimulates uterine contractions and facilitates childbirth. Examples: birthwort, blue cohosh, cannabis, ergot. *Caution:* **Do not use without medical supervision; do not use any of these herbs if you are pregnant.**

Pectoral. Relieves congestion in chest and lungs. Examples: almond oil, everlasting, ginger, loosestrife, mullein.

Poultice. A mass of crushed, warmed herbs applied directly to the skin in order to draw out impurities or to soothe.

Refrigerant. Lowers abnormally high body temperature; a cooling drink on a hot summer day. Examples: alpine cranberry, barberry (also a laxative), red currant, hibiscus, citrus juices, maidenhair fern, mint, raspberry, red sumac berry, tamarind, gentian.

Rubifacient. Increases circulation, reddens skin. Examples: horseradish, juniper berry, cayenne pepper, mustard, thyme.

Sedative/Nervine. Soothing to nerves. Examples: birch leaf, blind nettle, celery, feverweed, goldthread, hawthorn, hops, lavender, lettuce, New Jersey tea, passionflower, peach leaf, pennyroyal, periwinkle, wild cherry bark, witch hazel, skullcap, valerian, blue vervain. *Warning:* **Do not use pennyroyal with pregnancy or heavy menstrual flow.**

Simple. A single herb or a preparation made with a single herb.

Sialagogue. Stimulates salivary glands, aids digestion. Examples: cayenne, mustard, currant, European centaury, ginger, lemon, rhubarb.

Stomachic. Gastric tonic that increases appetite and promotes digestion. In general, most aromatic oils, bitter herbs, and culinary herbs are stomachic.

Styptic/Hemostatic. Arrests bleeding by contracting blood vessels when taken internally or by forming blood clots when applied externally. Examples: tannic and gallic acids, vegetable astringents, witch hazel, shepherd's purse, bennet, bistort, blind nettle, horseweed, loosestrife, milfoil, sanicle, goldenseal, woundwort, myrrh.

Tonic. Strengthens and invigorates specific organs or the entire system. In general, foods with high vitamin and mineral content. Also: ginseng, fo ti teng, gotu kola, sarsaparilla, poplar bark, willow bark, quassia, European centaury, peach leaf, sage, gentian, chamomile.

Tincture. A preparation made by steeping herbs in alcohol; especially good when properties of the herb are not water-soluble. Dosage is usually measured in drops.

Vulnerary. Heals wounds. Examples: aloe vera, amaranth, calendula, club moss, sphagnum moss, comfrey, echinacea, mullein, plantain, lemon, onion, goldenseal, slippery elm, myrrh, sweet gum, yerba santa, woundwort.

Chapter 4

Civilization and Its Discontents: Ancient Remedies for Nervousness, Fatigue, Pain, and the Doldrums

As you read in the last chapter, botanicals that affect the nervous system in some way have been chewed, inhaled, sipped, or used in ointments since earliest civilization. At one time or another, humankind has used stimulants, depressants, and hallucinogens for purposes that were sacred or profane, recreational or medicinal. The list of psychoactive plants affecting the nervous system in some way is long and diverse, ranging from coffee, tea, and tobacco to the coca plant and the opium poppy, all used medicinally by various cultures.

Until the twentieth century and its range of wonder drugs, the most prescribed remedies were painkillers and sedatives, which helped the patient rest and sleep so the natural healing process could take its course. Opium has the most extensive history of use both in Oriental and in Western medicine. In Europe, opium and its derivatives have been used throughout history except during the Inquisition, when all psychoactive drugs were banned by the Catholic church. Even then, midwives and herbalists infused poppy flowers and leaves to treat insomnia and mashed the flowerheads for poultices to ease pain, in contrast to the barber-surgeons who formed the medical establishment and used leeches, blood-letting, and unanesthetized surgery to deal with illnesses. In extreme cases, a priest might be called in to exorcise the demon or burn the witch believed responsible for the patient's affliction. It was the monk or the witch (usually also the local midwife and herbalist) who offered the most effective remedies at that time, however. In the witch's garden grew plants containing aconite, atropine, or opium, all of them powerful therapeutic drugs and painkillers, while the monastery garden was home to more wholesome alternatives not associated with witch or devil or used for poisons, love potions, or drastic alterations of consciousness.

Among the monks' botanicals were those that could safely be used as home remedies to relax the nerves, allay pain, and promote sleep. One of these was probably a plant used in ancient Egypt, Greece, and Rome, and which today is the source of Valium, our most widely prescribed tranquilizer. *Fragrant valerian* is a perennial that grows wild all over Europe and in the northern and western parts of America. Even if you are not acquainted with valerian's uses, you have probably encountered it in health food stores or herbal outlets where, unless tightly sealed in bottles, it announces its presence as soon as you walk in the door. The odor, which is quite strong, to me resembles unwashed feet, or perhaps the effusions of an aroused tomcat. When Gerard wrote his Herbal, the poor people of northern England used dried valerian root in "counterpoisons and medicines preservative against the pestilence." It was held in "such veneration amongst them, that no broths, potage or physicall meats are worth anything if Setwall [a common name for valerian] were not at an end [of the meal]." Culpeper recommends a teaspoon or two of the tincture or the powdered root for "hysterical affections, trembling headache, spasms, epilepsy, and dullness of sight." For centuries the tincture was used as a sedative on the Continent. Since I imagine the taste of valerian would be as obnoxious as the aroma, tinctures or powders would be the preferable way of taking it. I have found capsules of dried valerian very helpful in treating insomnia, and certainly less harmful than taking Valium, which can be addicting. Valerian is a very powerful botanical, however; an overdose can bring on vomiting and diarrhea, and extended use can cause depression. And no sedative, whether made from a plant or a synthetic chemical, should be used for longer than a week or two, nor should any sedative be used for a persistent nervous condition without the advice of a doctor.

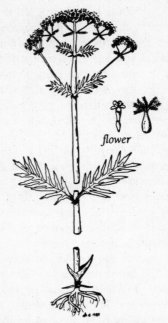

flower

Fragrant Valerian-Valeriana officinalis

The unpleasant odor of valerian comes from valeric acid, a constituent of the volatile oil that also contains the natural chemicals valerine and valerol. Valerol is also present in hops, source of another time-honored remedy for nerves and insomnia. A climbing vine found growing in the wild, hops are bitter, astringent, sedative, and antibacterial. In folk medicine the scaly, cone-shaped fruits have been used as a poultice for wounds and inflammations, sipped as a bitter to stimulate the appetite, and sewn into pillows to court sleep. Early in this century, a fluid extract of hops was an official pharmaceutical used as an alcohol substitute for treating delirium tremens. Brewers have used hops for centuries to kill the wild yeasts that can give an off-flavor to beer. Recently, when it was observed that workers in the hop fields became drowsy while harvesting, the fruits, which are the medicinal part, were studied in the laboratory where tests confirmed their sedative qualities.

Hops flourished in the arid New Mexico mountains that first summer I lived there, and I did have occasion to drink the tea. I can well understand why it might be used as a bitter. After a few discouraging encounters with hops in my teapot—hops in home-brewed beer were quite another matter—I could also understand why hop pillows might have been the more popular method of enjoying their tranquilizing effects. Inhaling the valerol in the hops apparently does the trick. To make this old-fashioned insomnia cure, sprinkle the hops with alcohol and sew them into a pillow or sack. You will want to refresh the contents of your pillow every so often because long exposure changes the valerol in hops to odorous valeric acid. Your nose will inform you when it's time for a change.

Hops-Humulus lupulus

As far as I am concerned, any advantage to taking either valerian or hops in tea is surely a negative one; the unaccommodating aroma or flavor will soon persuade you to seek a more congenial nightcap. The ingredient for such a beverage was likely a favorite of both monk and midwife, who would have prescribed it for cramps, spasms, headaches, and nerves as well as stomach upsets. This herb is safe to give to children; it is the one that so comforted Peter Rabbit after his harrowing adventure in Mr. McGregor's garden. For centuries chamomile tea has been a popular tisane on the Continent, where chamomile is a perennial wildling. The name means "little apples" in German and refers to the delicious aroma that wafts from the teapot—soothing in itself. Although I am very fond of this lovely tea, I have discovered that it doesn't return my affection, but instead produces mild nausea. The bad reaction, I think, comes from chamomile's single drawback: the pollen in the flowers, which are used for tea, can produce allergic reactions in people (such as myself) who are sensitive to ragweed, which is closely related to chamomile. So if you, too, are a ragweed sufferer, it would be wise to experiment cautiously, using only a quarter-teaspoon to a cup of water at first.

Wild or German Chamomile- Matricaria chamomilla

The majority of herbs used for medicine, seasoning, or scent belong to one of three botanical families. The *Umbelliferae,* or carrot family, is characterized by umbrella-shaped flowerheads composed of tiny flowers. Members of this family, which includes dill, parsley, coriander, and wild carrot, are used for flavoring both food and medicine. The *Compositae* family, which includes chamomile, marigold, wormwood, and dandelion is used primarily for medicine. The third, which is the largest family, is used for seasoning, medicine, and scent. This is the *Labiatae,* or mint family, and includes, besides the mints, thyme, sage, savory, lavender, basil, and rosemary. The leaves of these plants have a strong, penetrating fragrance and have been used as strewing herbs since ancient times. Some, such as balm and hyssop, have biblical associations, and most were grown in monastery gardens. You can also find *Labiatae* growing in the wild, where they are easily identified by their square stems and opposite, pointed, crinkled leaves, which release a pungent aroma when crushed.

Just about all the members of the mint family are beneficial to the nervous system, acting as painkillers and antispasmodics. They are frequently added to herbal mixtures to reinforce the medicinal properties or improve the flavor. Peppermint is my favorite member of this or any other family. It was also a favorite of the early American colonists, who drank it as a replacement for the Chinese tea they had eschewed during their troubles with England. A stimulant and tonic rather than a depressant, mint tea has a

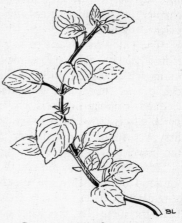

Peppermint-Mentha piperita

penetrating warmth when hot and is refreshingly cooling when iced. Besides being an enjoyable beverage, peppermint is a wonderful home remedy for stomachache, gas pains, and menstrual cramps, as well as nerves and insomnia. The menthol in crushed peppermint leaves makes a cooling poultice to ease stiff and aching muscles, stomach cramps, and headache. Improving the flavor is gilding the lily, but I do like it even more with the fresh leaves of lemon balm added—a natural combination since they grow side by side on my windowsill. Being botanical cousins, mint and lemon balm have a similar chemical makeup, although lemon balm is a tranquilizer while peppermint is not.

Pennyroyal, a mint that grows in fields, woods, and on mountain slopes as far west as the Rockies, was treasured by the American Indians, who drank it as a carminative and sedative, for headache, and to sweat out a cold. Squaws used it to bring on menstrual periods. Because pennyroyal stimulates uterine contractions, they drank several cups each day to prevent conception, or, that failing, to produce an abortion. For this reason, pennyroyal should never be used by pregnant women. The oil is also a good flea repellant, and anyone who doesn't think this application is appropriate for a chapter on nervous complaints has never lived in a household plagued by fleas.

The followers of catnip, as everyone knows, are not limited to Homo sapiens, although people can use it as they would the other mints for relaxation and pain. Back in the sixties and seventies, catnip was rolled into marijuana cigarettes by aficionados, who claimed it enhanced the high. Interestingly, a romp in the catnip patch affects cats similar to the way cocktail parties affect humans— first as a stimulant and euphoriant, then as a depressant—so maybe the flower children were onto something after all.

Although most of the plants in monastery gardens were grown for food or medicine, there was often a corner dedicated to the Virgin Mary, where flowers grew. One of these would surely have been the plant that bears her name: rosemary. In pagan times the rosemary was used to crown Greek virgins before they were sacrificed on the altar. Later, when incense replaced human sacrifices, the fragrant branches of rosemary were often burned. In *Hamlet*, Shakespeare immortalizes rosemary for remembrance. Rosemary has been used in funeral processions for centuries, and was often buried with the corpse—a custom that has survived to this day in some parts of England. Medieval scholars applied to rosemary quite literally for remembrance, wearing the fragrant garlands while they studied in the belief that it would aid the memory. Rosemary is, in fact, a stimulant, quickening the digestive processes and improving circulation, so there may have been some factual basis for the custom. Since rosemary is also poisonous except in the tiny amounts used as seasoning, it was generally used as a garland instead of taken internally.

The strongest sedative and antispasmodic in the mint family is found in skullcap, named for its purple or blue helmet-shaped flowers. A resident of Canadian and northeastern U.S. wetlands, skullcap contains scutellaine, which is extracted by pharmaceutical companies for use in sedatives. The American Indians used skullcap as a diuretic and emmenagogue as well as an antispasmodic and sedative. Reputed to be strong enough to deal with convulsions, skullcap, I have found, is an excellent remedy for nervousness and insomnia.

Another plant that is frequently used in over-the-counter pharmaceuticals for nervousness and insomnia is passionflower. Not a member of the mint family, passionflower is a climbing vine that grows wild in the American South and Southwest and in South America. Priests who accompanied the conquistadores to South America named the plant in honor of Christ's passion on the cross. I have found an infusion of equal parts skullcap and passionflower to be a wonderful relaxer when I am under stress. However, the chemicals in these two plants are powerful, and not recommended for extensive or intensive use.

A third plant often specified for nervous conditions is nerve root, a member of the orchid family more commonly known as lady's slipper. Bearing a yellow, slipper-shaped flower, nerve root is a rare and endangered American species, so don't gather it in the wild. You can buy it from herb dealers or order the seeds from a company that specializes in wildflowers. Good for tension, hysteria, cramps, delirium tremens, and other muscle spasms, nerve root is said to be hallucinogenic in large doses.

As I have already mentioned, just about all varieties of mint are good for relieving pain as well as nervousness. The oils of many of these plants, particularly peppermint, are used externally for toothache and headache. Other plants effective in relieving headaches are those containing methyl salicylate, salicylic acid, or salicin, which is converted to salicylic acid in the body. All are chemically similar to aspirin and used for the same purposes.

Willow bark, which contains salicylic acid, has been used for pain, fever, and inflammation for over two thousand years. The way to prepare it is by a cold extract. Either soak one tablespoon of bark in a cup of water overnight and drink cold, or soak the same amount of bark for two to five hours and bring to a boil.

An Herbal Pharmacopoeia

Wintergreen, a creeping evergreen shrub that grows in woodlands as far south as Georgia, is familiar to children, who like to nibble the leaves for their fresh, minty flavor; in Maine, where I grew up, we called this plant checkerberry. Wintergreen oil contains methyl salicylate, the flavorful, therapeutic element. The leaves do not yield this oil unless they are distilled or soaked in alcohol, however. Dose for a tincture is five to fifteen drops. The oil can also be applied externally to relieve aches and pains. This oil is very concentrated and can irritate the skin, so apply it sparingly. Meadowsweet, a perennial that grows wild in damp meadows as far south as Ohio, also contains salicylic acid and can be taken in an infusion, a teaspoon or two

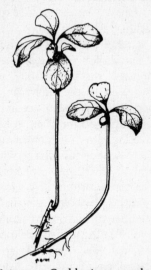

Wintergreen-Gaultheria procumbens

to a cup boiling water. Possibly the most effective remedy for headache is feverfew, a member of the chrysanthemum family occasionally found growing in the wild but usually cultivated. The aspirin of the eighteenth century, feverfew has been used since at least the time of Plutarch, who mentions it in his writings. Gerard and Culpeper prescribed it for depression. For some years, feverfew, along with other remedies for pain and fever, was replaced by aspirin. In the 1980s, however, research done in Wales and England indicated that feverfew may be our most effective remedy for migraine. I shall have more to say about these new findings in the next chapter.

While substances classed as sedatives have important uses in medicine ranging from mild sedatives to anesthesias, nerve stimulants, which speed up electrical impulses so people taking them experience heightened alertness and increased endurance, are more often used casually as a part of daily life. Most Americans, when feeling the need of a stimulant, look no further than their coffeepot, and they feel not a twinge of guilt for indulging in a bit of caffeine. In seventeenth-century Europe, though, when coffee was first brought from Arabia, where it had been used in Muslim ceremonies for eight hundred years, the use of coffee was prohibited by the Catholic church, which regarded anything that came from the East as wicked. In the Orient and certain European countries, most notably the British Isles and Russia, the teapot would be the source of caffeine. In China, where this evergreen shrub was first grown, tea had important medical applications and religious associations. Chinese physicians prescribed tea to relieve fatigue, delight the soul, strengthen the will, and repair the eyesight. Taoists, who believed tea was an ingredient in the elixir of immortality, ascribed the origin of tea to Bodhidharma, a Buddhist saint. After spending nine sleepless years in meditation, Bodhidharma, the story goes, at last succumbed to sleep. Upon awakening, he so repented his lapse that he cut off both his eyelids to prevent it ever happening again. The eyelids fell to the ground, took root, and grew into the tea plant. Centuries later, in Japan, Zen monks gathered before the image of Bodhidharma to sip tea from a single bowl, a ritual which later developed into the tea ceremony. In Brazil, Argentina, and other Latin American countries, yerba mate, or Paraguay tea, is the preferred stimulant and is brewed with great ceremony. Other botanical stimulants are chocolate, which contains theobromine, and coca leaves, which Peruvians and other inhabitants of South American mountains have chewed for centuries to boost their energy and endurance. The source of cocaine, one of the plant world's most powerful stimulants, coca was held sacred by the Incas, who prayed to the spirit of coca before setting off on journeys and used it in funerals and other religious ceremonies. As you might expect, when the conquistadores introduced coca to seventeenth-century Europe, the Catholic church promptly condemned its use. Interestingly enough, two centuries later, the Pope himself endorsed coca-based Mariani Wine, an elixir that was all the rage around the turn of the

An Herbal Pharmacopoeia

last century. Tobacco, which contains nicotine, is also a stimulant, and the plant was sacred to the American Indians who used it for both medicinal and religious purposes.

Because stimulants such as these act immediately upon the nervous system, allowing the user to stay awake for long periods and accomplish feats of physical endurance without taking in much food (most stimulants also suppress the appetite), they must have been vitally important to cultures where hard work was a necessity. Their effects undoubtedly seemed truly magical to those who used them; small wonder they were worshipped as deities. Even today, in urban, success-oriented societies, stimulants ranging from caffeine to cocaine are very much a part of the culture.

Not all stimulants work merely on the nervous system. Some also invigorate the glandular system. A few Oriental botanicals, known as tonic herbs, are believed to have rejuvenating powers that border on the mythical. The most venerable of these is ginseng. Used for over five thousand years in China, the forked root of this rare plant is highly prized as a panacea and restorative, stimulating the nervous and glandular systems, which in turn regulate the functions of the other body systems. In ancient China, ginseng was worth its weight in gold and consequently was usually reserved for important dignitaries and the well-to-do. Preferring shady forests and hillsides where it grows very slowly, gin-

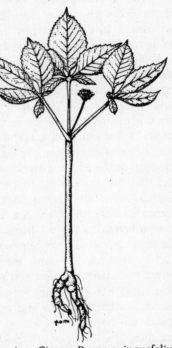

American Ginseng-Panax quinquefolius

seng is difficult to find in the wild, so most of it is cultivated. The wild variety is considered more potent, however, and therefore more prized. In America, wild ginseng can still be found in the woods of Kentucky and in the Catskill Mountains of upstate New York. Native Americans decocted the root to relieve nausea and vomiting and also used it as an aphrodisiac, for which it has legendary powers. Ginseng root, powdered ginseng, and ginseng elixirs are sold in Korean markets as well as in health food stores.

Should you manage to obtain fresh ginseng, you can use all parts of the plant, either by chewing small portions about the size of a kernal of corn every two hours as many Chinese do, or by infusing the leaves and decocting or making a tincture of the root. The dose for an elixir is a teaspoonful two or three times a day.

Another remarkable Oriental tonic is fo-ti-tieng, known to Chinese medicine as "Long Life Elixir." According to Richard Lucas, author of *Nature's Medicines,* fo-ti-tieng attracted worldwide attention upon the death, in 1933, of the Chinese herbalist Li Chung Yun, who had used the herb daily during his exceptionally long life. According to Chinese government records, Li Chung Yun lived for 256 years. The leaves and seeds of fo-ti-tieng supposedly have an energizing effect on the nerves, brain cells, and ductless glands. Some consider the herb to be the woman's answer to ginseng, rejuvenating the female hormonal system as ginseng does the male.

The last herb in the triumvirate of Asian tonics is gotu kola, a botanical relative of fo-ti-tieng that grows in India and on certain islands of the Indian Ocean. This herb is reputed to have rejuvenating and life-extending properties similar to ginseng. It is also believed to revitalize the brain and improve memory. Researchers have found that while gotu kola is stimulating in moderate doses, it is sedative in larger ones. They have also found it to be anti-inflammatory and wound-healing.

I can't say whether or not my memory and brain function have improved upon using gotu kola, but I do add half a teaspoon to an herbal mixture I drink every day. When I am trying to wean myself from coffee, I add a teaspoonful or two of gotu kola to a mixture of black tea and hibiscus. My energy level and alertness seem to remain fairly constant throughout the day, rather than fluctuating between jolts of energy and periods of fatigue, which happens when I drink coffee. Guests to whom I have served this tea find it pleasantly relaxing and quite tasty.

In the preceding chapter, I referred to plants that have been used for religious or magical purposes. Many of these botanicals are hallucinogens, which alter the consciousness so that priests, seers, and sorcerers could actually see the spirit world with which they communed. Besides peyote, which was considered a deity by certain Indian tribes, and the *Amanita muscaria,* which has been used by shamanic tribes, primitive peoples have used a variety of other psychedelics, including the iboga plant of the Congo, the yage vine of Colombia, and, in certain parts of Mexico, morning glory seeds.

Morning glory seeds have also been ingested for recreational purposes, as have datura, henbane, belladonna, nutmeg, and, of course, marijuana leaves, although in America they are usually smoked. Thujone, present in sage leaves, is said to be chemically similar to THC, the inebriating substance in marijuana. Traces of hallucinogens are also to be found in the oils of dill, anise, parsley, fennel, and sassafras, but I imagine that one would have to ingest such a quantity of these herbs as to get pretty sick before even getting mildly high. It is possible, though, that even these herbs have served as experiments for what seems to be a basic human need—to somehow change the way we experience the world in order to escape the ordinary or to pursue a spiritual goal.

Chapter 5

A Daisy for Your Migraine, a Dandelion for Your Liver, and the Miracle Bulb of the Pharaohs for a Healthy Heart

As I thumbed through herbals, one term that always puzzled me was *blood purifier*. Of what, I wondered, should the blood be purified? Somewhat enlightened by Varro Tyler's *Honest Herbal*, which observes that *alterative* and *blood purifier* (used interchangeably in the older herbals) were euphemisms for syphilis cures, I turned to *Potter's Compend of Materia Medica Therapeutics and Prescription Writing*, based on the ninth revision of the U.S. *Pharmacopoeia* and published in 1917. The author, A. S. Bush, defines alteratives as:

Agents which alter the course of morbid conditions, modifying the nutritive processes while promoting waste, and thus indirectly curing many chronic diseases. Mercury, iodine and arsenic are the typical alteratives, the first breaking up new deposits, the second stimulating the absorbant circulation, and the last acting like the first on pulmonary deposits, and being almost specific to the chronic diseases of the skin. Those who denounce the term alterative as "a cloak for ignorance," have never been able to replace it by any more definite designation for a group of agents whose effects upon disease are facts of clinical medicine.

The alteratives Bush lists were indeed used in "syphilitic affections," but they were also used for other life-threatening infections such as pneumonia and malaria, which today, along with syphilis, are treated with antibiotics.

Around the second century B.C., Galen, the Greek physician, observed that the arteries carried blood, not air, as had been formerly supposed. William Harvey demonstrated the workings of the circulatory system to his medical colleagues in the seventeenth century, but not until the nineteenth century was it discovered that germs, not impure blood, caused disease. Before that time, the prevailing theory was that blood was a vital but mysterious fluid that somehow determined the health of the entire organism. Leeches were commonly applied to most afflictions on the theory that reducing the amount of blood would affect a cure. (For certain conditions, such as blood clots, this unsavory remedy probably worked; recent research has shown that certain chemicals in the leech's saliva are anticoagulants.) Meanwhile, herbalists used "blood-purifying" roots and leaves based on the belief that disease was caused by a toxic condition and could be treated by encouraging the body to eliminate the toxins. Contemporary herbalism, Oriental, homeopathic, holistic, and other forms of alternative medicine still operate on the theory that toxins and blockages of energy are the underlying causes of disease. Some contemporary physicians, like their ancient ancestors, recommend proper diet, massage, sweating, acupuncture, and herbs that encourage the body to eliminate waste as the most effective ways of restoring health.

Several of the minerals alteratives used in Dr. Bush's time, such as mercury, iodine, and arsenic, are highly toxic and have deservedly fallen into disfavor, along with certain vegetable alteratives such as daphne and bloodroot, which are drastic irritants. (The latter, though, is still used in pharmaceuticals.) The common factor among all these poisons is that they stimulate the digestive organs to eliminate waste and the sweat glands, the liver, and the kidneys to eliminate toxins through sweat, feces, or urine. Hence, the various organs would be purified and the patient's condition gradually altered—for the better, one would hope, although each of these drugs can kill as well as cure.

Dr. Bush also lists two herbs that were "official" (i.e., listed in the US *Pharmacopoeia*) at the turn of this century. Both are safe to use, and still considered by herbalists to have a high degree of alterative power. One is Oregon grape, a member of the barberry family that grows in the mountains of the Pacific Coast. A favorite bitter tonic of the California Indians who used the root in decoctions and tinctures for failing appetite and general debility, Oregon grape has a long history in Western medicine as a tonic and blood purifier and

Spanish Sarsaparilla-Smilax officinalis

will be discussed more fully in Chapter 8, which covers the gastrointestinal system.

The other alterative is sarsaparilla, a traditional spring tonic and the basis for a soft drink popular until a few decades ago and still on the market. Although Bush, following the prevailing medical view of his time, dismisses sarsaparilla as having no therapeutic value, more recent research has discovered that the root contains hormonal substances that regulate the reproductive glands and stimulate the immune system. Once the organs of elimination are working prop-

An Herbal Pharmacopoeia

erly, sarsaparilla stimulates the body to get rid of tissue wastes by releasing them into the bloodstream, where they are carried to the kidneys and from there to the bladder to be excreted in the urine. Devil's claw, an indigenous African remedy, has a similar cleansing effect on the body, described more fully in Chapter 5, which discusses the skeletal system.

According to some writers, burdock, figwort, blue flag, and yellow dock help clear out tissue waste as well as fatty deposits. Stinging nettle, an excellent blood builder because of its high iron content, helps the body excrete harmful excess acid. Nettles grow wild all over the world and are free for the taking. Because they affect several or all of the body systems, nettles and most of the other herbs mentioned in this chapter will appear again and again in later chapters, where you will learn more about their considerable curative powers.

Two other herbs with venerable reputations as alteratives are ginseng and Chinese licorice root, for centuries the cornerstones of Chinese medicine because of their ability to restore vigor by stimulating the endocrine system, which in turn regulates the workings of the other body systems. Chinese licorice root, which is reputed not to have the side effects of Western licorice (see below), is known in China as the "grandfather of Chinese herbs," the "great adjunct," and the "great detoxifier." Esteemed as a tonic and longevity herb, Chinese licorice root is used in herbal recipes to harmonize the other ingredients and counteract unfavorable side effects. It is believed to regulate the blood sugar level, sharpen concentration, relieve pain and congestion, and increase vitality by improving glandular function. I add about a quarter-teaspoon to my daily herbal potion (recipe on p. 81) and have noted that when I leave out the licorice my elixir does not seem to work as well.

Although not classified as alteratives, herbs that build the blood do gradually restore health and vitality. Yarrow was used for this purpose by the American Indians, who made decoctions of the whole plant for use as a blood builder and drank hot infusions of the leaves to stimulate the liver and decoctions of the roots to stimulate the kidneys. Yarrow is also an ingredient of my daily potion because of its astringent and blood-building properties.

Researchers now believe that potent blood builders can be found in the roots of all plants. It has long been known that a substance similar to hemoglobin (a constituent of red blood cells that contains iron and transports oxygen to the tissues) in animals can be found in the roots of nitrogen-fixing plants such as beans, lentils, clover, and alfalfa. Recently, scientists in Australia, France, and West Germany have found evidence suggesting that hemoglobin may be universally distributed throughout the vegetable as well as the animal kingdom. So maybe all those maternal exhortations to eat our turnips and carrots were on target after all.

Affairs of the heart, as they relate to high blood pressure and cholesterol, are everybody's concern these days as accumulating evidence links the health of our circulatory system to diet. Drugs such as cholestyramine and colestipal are frequently prescribed to lower levels of blood cholesterol. Recently, researchers have found that one tablespoon of psyllium seeds, which come from a plant related to plantain and are used in bulk-producing laxatives such as Metamucil, taken daily, can lower blood cholesterol by 15 percent. Bile acids, which are chemical derivatives of cholesterol, are ordinarily secreted into the intestines, where they are reabsorbed into the blood stream. Psyllium seeds act on the bile acids much as the drugs do; they bind the bile acids so they are excreted.

High blood pressure, another life-threatening disorder, is sometimes treated with reserpine, a tranquilizing drug based on an extract from the Indian rauwolfia tree. Mild forms of the disease can sometimes be treated successfully with a diet that includes herbs rather than synthetic chemicals, which can have serious side effects. Garlic, for example, may help lower blood pressure—without side effects. One of the most useful plants in the herbal pharmacopoeia, garlic has been used for over five thousand years to treat or prevent diseases as various as dysentery, typhoid, whooping cough, tuberculosis, and cancer. In ancient Egypt, the bulb was so revered that slaves working on the great pyramids went on strike until their daily ration of it was restored. During the Middle Ages, people ate garlic to avoid bubonic plague and used it to disinfect burial grounds.

The use of garlic tincture to lower blood pressure has been

known to modern medicine at least since the 1920s. John Lust's recipe for tincture is half a pound of peeled cloves steeped in a quart of brandy for two weeks and taken as needed, five to fifteen drops at a time. Rumors of garlic breath, to my mind, are greatly exaggerated, but if you wish to take precautions, a helping of fresh parsley ought to preserve your social acceptability.

One common cause of high blood pressure is fluid retention by the kidneys, which increases the volume of blood, causing the heart to pump more forcefully and encouraging an accumulation of excess fluid in the body tissues, a condition aggravated by the use of salt. Diuretics are commonly prescribed to deal with this condition. Several herbs have long histories of use as diuretics: an infusion of buchu, a South African shrub used by the Hottentots for centuries; the oil, spirits or tincture of juniper berry; cayenne pepper tincture; infused or decocted bearberry leaves; and corn silk infused or in liquid extract. These herbs act by irritating the urinary-genital membrane; they should be taken very sparingly because they may cause inflammation. Gentler diuretics, which can be taken safely, are cranberry juice, which is also excellent for urinary infections; dandelion, which for centuries has been used to treat kidney and liver ailments; meadowsweet, which contains salicylic acid and can be used instead of aspirin; parsley, strawberry, cleavers, which also are reputed to help people lose weight, sarsaparilla, lemon juice, hops, celery, cucumber, and watercress.

If you are taking a diuretic, be sure to eat foods such as parsley, dried apricots, prunes, figs, and sunflower seeds, which are high in potassium; use of diuretics causes a loss of potassium which the body needs to maintain electrical stability in the cells and regulate heart rhythms.

A second cause of high blood pressure is constriction of the blood vessels, which causes a resistance to blood flow, thus forcing the heart to pump harder. The berries and flowers of hawthorn, the shrub or tree beloved by witches, have long been used in European medicine for heart and circulatory disorders. A member of the apple family, hawthorn is said to dilate the blood vessels, regulate the heart action, and lower blood pressure when taken regularly. Herbalists consider hawthorn a mild heart tonic that strengthens aging heart muscles and helps prevent arteriosclerosis. Because of its sedative properties, hawthorn has also been prescribed for nervous heart conditions.

Hibiscus may also be useful in treating high blood pressure; a mild laxative and diuretic, it has been shown to lower blood pressure in dogs. This lovely flower is often added to herbal tea blends because it adds a rosy hue and pleasantly tart flavor.

Earlier in this chapter I referred to common licorice and its undesirable side effects. The sweet taste of licorice comes from glycyhrizin, a natural chemical that raises blood pressure and produces lethargy, headache, retention of water and sodium, and potassium loss. If you are a licorice lover and experience any of these symptoms you can easily reverse them by cutting down on your consumption of licorice.

In the previous chapter I mentioned a few of the powerful poisons that grew in the witch's garden but were also used medicinally in smaller doses. The aconite in monkshood and the digitalis in foxglove are cardiac sedatives that reduce the force and frequency of heart action and are used to control palpitation and overstimulation. Aconite was an official drug early in this century and digitalis is still important in medicine. Atropine and related chemicals, which are present in belladonna, henbane, datura, and mandrake, are stimulants that increase the force and frequency of heart action. Cardiac tonics stimulate the cardiac muscle, causing longer, slower contractions. In large doses they cause dangerously irregular heart action, which may even be fatal. Varying amounts of cardiac tonics are found in foxglove, hellebore, lily of the valley, mistletoe, and wormwood. In the hands of an experienced herbal physician, all of the herbs can be very useful in heart conditions, but these potentially lethal drugs should *never, never* be used for self-medication.

Diabetes, a serious chronic disease, is a condition in which the pancreas does not produce enough insulin to control glucose levels in the blood. The usual method of managing diabetes is with insulin treatment. In its early stages, though, diabetes can sometimes be controlled by diet. The globe artichoke is a good addition to this diet because the starch it contains is in the form of inulin, which is not converted to sugar as other starches are. Artichoke heads steeped in wine are also considered an excellent diuretic and also helpful in preventing arteriosclerosis. Oddly enough, the tuber of the Jerusalem artichoke, which is botanically unrelated, also contains the starch inulin. This delicious food, which grows wild and resembles sunflower, a member of the same family, can be easily grown in any climate. The raw tubers have a crisp texture and nutty taste; I use them in salads and as a substitute for water chestnut in Chinese dishes. Cooked, the Jerusalem artichoke tubers resemble potato, although sweeter and without the mealy texture.

Chicory-Cichorium intybus

Dandelion, a botanical relative of the Jerusalem artichoke, is a very beneficial food for just about any toxic condition. All parts of the dandelion are good for you, from the buds, which resemble globe artichokes in flavor and use, to the blossoms, which can be made into a sweet, golden, and extremely potent wine (not, alas, recommended for diabetics), to the leaves, which are high in carotene, vitamin C, and iron. The root, which can be roasted and ground for use as a coffee substitute, acts as a tonic and stimulant, encouraging the glands and organs of elimination to excrete toxins; it is also diuretic and good for the liver.

Chicory, a botanical relative of dandelion, can also be enjoyed as a cooked or salad green. The roasted ground roots make a delicious coffee substitute or additive, with medicinal uses similar to dandelion's. According to Varro Tylers' *Honest Herbal,* the dried and roasted root contains a digitalis-like chemical.

Recent clinical studies show that sage tea, especially when taken on an empty stomach, reduces the blood sugar level in diabetics. Rodale Press, in its booklet "The Good Fats," mentions that recent studies by Dutch doctors show that diabetics who were not dependent on insulin treatments could utilize their own insulin more effectively if they added purslane to their diet. Tea made with blueberry leaves or Chinese licorice is also said to reduce blood sugar level, as do yarrow and nettles. However, teas are not as dependable as insulin and may have a toxic effect on the liver if taken over long periods of time.

Although it has not been regarded as such until a few years ago, migraine is an affliction now regarded as a blood disorder. The attacks are triggered by a variety of causes, principally stress and tension, environmental factors such as glaring or flashing lights, and eating certain foods, notably chocolate, beef extracts, yeast, and fatty dairy products, especially cheese. The attack begins when blood platelets (disk-like bodies in the blood that assist clotting) clump together, releasing serotonin and producing prostaglandins, hormone-like substances. Experts now believe that these chemicals cause the blood vessels to contract and restrict the blood flow, then expand, causing the intense headache pain.

The usual way of treating migraine has been to lie down in a dark room and wait until it passes, but exciting research points to new, dramatic relief for migraine sufferers. Chemicals known as sesquiterpene lactones, isolated from an herb similar to the daisy, have been found to inhibit both phases of the migraine attack: the aggregation of platelets and their release of serotonin and manufacture of prostaglandin. At Chelsea College in London and at the London Migraine Clinic, patients treated with this herb experienced lasting relief from their symptoms.

The herbal heroine of this drama is feverfew, which was used like aspirin during the eighteenth century to relieve pain and reduce inflammation and fever. Little used after aspirin became popular, feverfew fell into disuse until the 1980s, when it became the subject of scientific research. Before its temporary banishment, feverfew had a long history of medical use, dating back at least as far as Plutarch.

Gerard prescribed it for melancholy and vertigo; Culpeper used it for depression, uterine cramps, and suppressed menstruation. In folk medicine it has been used to soothe insect bites, relieve hayfever, and produce abortion.

Taking feverfew daily over an extended period of time builds resistance to migraine attacks. The recommended dose is one large or three small fresh leaves a day, or a teaspoonful of the dried leaves infused in a pint of water. Like other members of its botanical family, feverfew can produce allergic reactions in sensitive individuals, the most common reaction being soreness and inflammation of the mouth, tongue, or lips. Other symptoms are itchy skin, increased menstrual flow, and indigestion.

Feverfew-Chrysanthemum parthenium

I was inspired to investigate feverfew upon listening to a friend describe her migraine attacks, which apparently afflict several female members of her family. Since my friend has experienced allergic reactions to a number of things, I advised her to take only a quarter-teaspoon of feverfew to a cup of water daily for the first week, then, if she had no adverse reaction, to increase her daily dose gradually. Since she has started taking feverfew, my friend has experienced one mild headache and one full-fledged attack, which came about when she was returning, quite reluctantly, from a vacation. The symptoms disappeared as soon as she reached home. Since then, although she has been in very stressful situations that in the past would have triggered a severe migraine, she has been free of symptoms.

Will feverfew become the aspirin of the 1990s? Although my knowledge of feverfew has so far been limited to one friend's experience and reading a very persuasive account of its miraculous powers, I certainly wouldn't hesitate to recommend it.

The more I read about the history of disease, the more it seems related to the history of civilization and its discontents. My friend, because she is my friend, may have been influenced as much by the placebo factor as by the actual chemicals in feverfew. The herbs mentioned in this and the previous chapter act on conditions that are certainly influenced by the state of our emotions. Herbal remedies are more likely to be dispensed or recommended by practitioners or friends who are interested in our personal welfare, and that has probably been so ever since the first shaman made the first foray into the unknown to bring back a life-giving remedy to an ailing neighbor. Perhaps it is the wish as much as the leaf that makes the cure.

Chapter 6

Long Live Lydia Pinkham, Culpeper's Spring Tonic, the Sorcerer's Herb, and Other Good News for the Reproductive System

For two or three years, autumn was not a happy time for me, not only for the usual end of summer reasons, but because the uterine fibroids I have had for nearly twenty years started acting up. The symptoms were excessive bleeding, sometimes every other week, with inevitable debility of strength and spirit. Doctors theorized, tested, sonogrammed, biopsied, threatened surgery or prescribing hormones—estrogen when they thought it was menopause, progesterone when they thought it wasn't. Neither recommendation was appealing. Hysterectomy, a common procedure in my mother's time, is a drastic measure, despite the reassurances of (usually male) gynecologists. (One recommended it as a form of birth control!) Estrogen is by no means safe, as recent studies linking estrogen with breast cancer indicate, and the facts aren't in about progesterone's safety. A less risky side effect of hormone therapy is weight gain, and I didn't much like that, either.

Wasn't there something I could take that was more natural? I asked the young doctor who had just scraped tissue from my uterine wall for what seemed like a century of intense pain. (He apparently thought it "unnatural" to use an anesthetic.) He disappeared for a moment, presumably to consult a textbook or a colleague, then returned. "No," he told me. Nevertheless, I returned home, thumbed through my herbals, and decided to try a certain formula before I succumbed to the doctor's prescription.

A month after I began taking the formula, my periods returned to their normal cycle and duration, my vitality was restored, and my spirits lifted. Whether this would have happened without the herbal formula I really can't say. However, I have since given my formula to other women with similar problems and they reported improvement. The formula: one teaspoon sarsaparilla; one teaspoon red clover; one half-teaspoon yarrow; one half-teaspoon squaw vine; one half-teaspoon gotu kola; one quarter-teaspoon licorice root.

Sarsaparilla, as you read in the preceding chapter, is an alterative, cleansing the body of waste; as such, it can be very helpful when used for a chronic condition such as fibroids. Sarsaparilla also reputedly contains a material similar to progesterone, the hormone prescribed by my doctor to regulate the menstrual cycle. (Hormones in plants regulate reproduction, growth, and survival, just as they do in humans.) Jethro Kloss, who wrote *Back to Eden,* a modern bible for some herbalists, extols the virtues of red clover, which he claims dissolves benign and malignant tumors. Yarrow, recommended to regulate excessive menstrual flow, is also a tonic and blood builder. Used by American Indian women after childbirth, yarrow, along with iron, helps restore strength after excessive bleeding. Squaw vine is tonic to the uterus and corrects scanty, suppressed, or excessive menstrual flow. James Duke, in his *Handbook of Medicinal Herbs,* reports that American Indian women also took squaw vine for easy child-birth and notes that a mixture of squaw vine, lobelia, raspberry leaves, and wild yam has been used to prevent miscarriage. In India, gotu kola is used as a blood purifier and stimulant. It is also said to have an energizing effect on the brain cells and to prolong life. Licorice is an ingredient in Lydia Pinkham, an herbal compound still sold today, which my mother and maybe your grandmother used for "female complaints." As I noted in Chapter 5, Chinese licorice root is tonic and regulates the endocrine system.

Although I have benefited from my formula, I must stress that I only used it after a series of tests indicated that my problem was indeed fibroids and not a more serious condition. Excessive bleeding is also a symptom of cancer of the endometrium, the lining of the uterus, and any woman who bleeds heavily should be checked by a doctor immediately.

Other herbs that help control excessive bleeding are comfrey, which I have found very helpful but use only occasionally because it may be carcinogenic; shepherd's purse, a vasocontrictor, good for internal and exter-

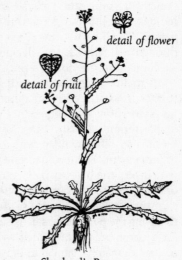

detail of flower

detail of fruit

Shepherd's Purse-
Capsella bursa-pastoris

nal bleeding, provided you don't have high blood pressure; and birthroot, also known as trillium or wake robin. Used by the American Indians, trillium grows in the mountains—a fact that may be helpful to know if you have an emergency while hiking or camping. Amaranth, an herb found in the wild and also cultivated for its handsome red flowers and its seeds, has been used for centuries to control excessive bleeding and hemorrhage. In ancient Greece, amaranth was a symbol of immortality; in the New World, the Incas mixed the seeds with human blood or honey and made them into cakes, which they offered as a sacrifice to the gods. Amaranth can be taken in infusion or eaten as a steamed or boiled vegetable.

Excessive menstrual flow can be exacerbated by vigorous exercise, alcoholic drinks, and herbs that stimulate uterine contractions or contain salicylates, which act as anticoagulants. Staying off your feet as much as possible for the first day of your period may prove helpful.

Another common female complaint is listed in herbals under the rather vague term "vaginitis," an inflammation of the vagina. Frequently the problem is a yeast infection, which comes about when the normal bacteria that keep the vaginal tract healthy are overcome and outnumbered. Birth control pills, antibiotics, stress, poor dietary habits, and a rundown condition are all contributing factors. To prevent or relieve a yeast infection, be sure to include yogurt in your diet when you are taking antibiotics; yogurt with active cultures acts to restore the healthy flora in your vaginal tract. Fermented foods such as cheese, wine, beer, Chinese tea, sugar, and starches, which are converted to sugar in the digestive process, all promote or aggravate yeast infections. The best treatment is douching with antifungicide solutions. A 50 percent solution of fresh aloe vera gel liquified and blended with water kills both yeast cells and the nasty little protozoa that cause trichomoniasis. James Duke, in his *Handbook of Medicinal Herbs,* notes that some of his readers report good results from drinking an infusion of pao d'arco and douching with a solution of one teaspoon pao d'arco soaked overnight in a quart of cold water. My own observation is that extended use of the tea is more effective than the douche. Drinking infusions of echinacea also seems to help. The external remedy I have found most helpful is the powdered root of goldenseal. A powerful antiseptic used for treating skin diseases and inflammation of the mucous membrane in the mouth and eyes, goldenseal offers immediate relief in yeast infections and trichomoniasis. The latter can be treated with a twice-a-day hot sitz bath made with one tablespoon of the powdered root to one quart water. One teaspoon goldenseal to one pint water can be used as a douche. If the yeast infection has advanced and produces sores on the vaginal sheath, a solution of one teaspoon goldenseal to one cup water applied with cotton several times a day should heal the sores in a day or two.*

Other herbs recommended as a douche for vaginitis include peppermint, white oak bark, yarrow, white pond lily root, myrrh, witch hazel, and birthroot. Oak, yarrow, witch hazel, and birthroot are astringent, good for cleansing and for checking discharges; the others are antiseptic.

Delayed or tardy menstruation has a variety of causes and should also be treated only after you have consulted with a doctor. Poor nutrition, anemia, overly strenuous exercise, and of course pregnancy can all interrupt the menstrual cycle. Adequate rest, sensible exercise, and a well-balanced diet rich in iron should all be on the agenda.

Hot baths and hot drinks may be sufficient to "bring down the courses," as the old herbalists used to say. Herbs that improve menstrual function include fresh juice of aloe vera, formerly an official remedy, which, according to Dr. Bush, "determines blood to the pelvic viscera"; black haw, also official at the turn of the century, which may improve flow by relieving pain and irritation; squaw weed, a perennial wildling known as "female regulator" and another ingredient in the Lydia Pinkham compound; squaw vine, mentioned earlier in this chapter; and black cohosh, a major ingredient in the Lydia Pinkham compound. According to James Duke, laboratory studies on mice and rats show that black cohosh acts as a sedative and tonic. In homeopathic doses black cohosh is used to treat the female system for both excessive and suppressed menstruation and for certain difficulties of menopause and childbirth. Beware, though: prolonged or excessive use can irritate the uterus.

Menstrual cramps sometimes accompany suppressed menstrua-

*Needless to say, neither yeast infections, which can be a symptom of more serious conditions such as candida or diabetes, nor trichomoniasis, which can be communicated to one's sexual partner, should be treated by any of these home remedies unless you consult with your doctor first. Nor should you resume sexual activity until the infection clears up.

tion, especially when it is caused by abrupt changes in climate or cold and exposure. To prevent cramps you might adopt the Chinese practice of avoiding iced or very hot drinks during your menstrual period. The drop in blood calcium level that occurs about a week before menstruation can cause cramping of the uterine walls when flow begins, so it is important to take extra calcium during this time.

Some emmenagogues (herbs that bring on menstruation) are also good for cramps. Culpeper prescribed "sitting over the steam of a decoction of feverfew." Motherwort, a member of the mint family, is emmenagogue and calmative, also good for cramps. So is mother of thyme, a species of wild thyme and a member of the mint family. A very good mixture is a strong infusion of spearmint, peppermint, German chamomile, and lemon balm, which relaxes muscles, eases cramps, and stimulates flow. Actually, this is an all-purpose mixture, good for fever and respiratory ailments, restlessness, and insomnia— and it tastes delicious. As you might expect, the antispasmodics, sedatives, and analgesics discussed in Chapter 8 also relieve menstrual cramps.

Emmenagogues act in one of two ways. The herbs discussed above work indirectly by toning the glandular and reproductive system, building the blood, or improving circulation to the pelvic area. Others, which work by stimulating uterine contractions, have also, in large doses, been used to produce abortions, and in smaller doses to prevent conception. As to the wisdom of such practices, Dr. Bush's observation is as good as any I have found:

The chief oxytoxics [from Greek words meaning "quick childbirth" or "abortion"] are ergot [a rust fungus that grows on rye and barley], savin [juniper], and pilocarpine [jaborandi], but any violent purgative, or gastrointestinal irritant, may produce abortion by reflex action if the patient is one who aborts easily.

It is in this way that all the volatile oils act as abortifacients, also tansy, Colocynth [species of bitter cucumber], Pennyroyal, and many other drugs used by women for that purpose; all of which are dangerous to the woman's life, in doses large enough to excite uterine action. As for the physician who prescribes

An Herbal Pharmacopoeia

such agents for the purpose indicated, he would stand on a par with a drunken husband who kicks his pregnant wife in the abdomen. Both operators initiate uterine contractions in the same manner, viz., by reflex action by a powerful impression upon the woman's system, made in the one case, by an irritant boot with a brute behind it; in the other case by an irritant drug with a scoundrel behind it.

Herbs that have traditionally been used to prevent conception are motherwort, used by Chinese women for over two thousand years, and Mexican yam, the original source of the birth control pill. Soybeans may also contain steroids related to antifertility hormones. At present, researchers are studying gossypol, extracted from cotton seeds, as a male antifertility drug. Studies indicate that gossypol can cause sterility and potassium depletion, and can shrink the testicles—so it may be a while before such a drug appears on the market.

Infertility and miscarriage are other problems that have been treated with herbs since prehistoric times. Conception and pregnancy require a well-balanced diet; especially important are foods rich in vitamin E, which maintains both male and female reproductive systems. Wheat germ oil and raw wheat germ are excellent sources of this nutrient, which is often lost when grains are processed to make flour. Alfalfa is rich in vitamin E as well as vitamins A and C, and vitamin K, which helps prevent miscarriage. All parts of the dandelion are high in vitamins and iron. The roasted and ground root is an excellent coffee substitute and said to reduce the craving for alcohol and caffeine, neither of which is recommended for pregnant women. A decoction of star root (also called star grass), taken a mouthful at a time several times a day, is considered one of the best preventives for miscarriage. Black haw, a botanical relative of the cranberry and official early in this century, was used to regulate the menstrual periods and prevent miscarriage.

Perhaps the best-known tea for pregnancy and childbirth is red raspberry leaf, which I became acquainted with twenty-five years ago when I read Dr. Grantly Dick Reade's *Childbirth Without Fear.* This manual by a British obstetrician was the first complete primer of natural childbirth and was widely read by expectant mothers when I was awaiting the birth of my older son. Reade gave the tea to his obstetrical patients during labor and observed that it seemed to make childbirth easier. Since that time I have read about raspberry leaf in just about every herbal that discusses pregnancy and childbirth; it seems to be one of the staples of folk medicine. The tea was taken with cream to allay morning sickness and during the last six weeks of pregnancy to prevent miscarriage and assure an easy delivery.

Small doses of goldenseal are recommended for nausea during pregnancy. I am somewhat skeptical about this claim because I find the tea quite bitter and rather nauseating to drink. Peach leaves are also recommended for nausea or morning sickness. My personal favorites are a weak infusion of Chinese tea with milk, or peppermint, which is wonderful for sweetening a sour stomach and expelling gas.

When a woman gives birth for the first time, the labor is likely to be a long one. During the Middle Ages midwives commonly urged ergot to stimulate contractions; the practice had apparently fallen into disuse by Culpeper's time, because he makes no mention of it. Blue cohosh, used by the Indians, was also probably the choice of colonial midwives and is still used by herbalists today. *Caution:* **Neither of these herbs should be used without medical supervision.**

Breast-feeding a baby is one of the joys of motherhood—and one of the best ways to protect the infant from infections, intestinal disorders, and respiratory disease. A welcome side effect of nursing is that the uterus returns more quickly to its normal size, and so, as a result, will you.

Several herbs are recommended for increasing the flow of milk, including fennel seeds boiled in barley milk, anise seeds boiled in water, and decoctions of the seeds of dill, caraway, or coriander. Since these herbs are also stomachic and carminative, they may help prevent colic. Long ago, when I was nursing, my galactagogues, although not strictly herbal, were vegetable in origin: cider and stout beer, an old country mainstay of nursing mothers, even those who were ordinarily teetotal. The effect was almost instantaneous.

For sore nipples, as for most skin conditions, aloe vera is a healer par excellence. Squaw vine berries mixed with cream or oil are also said to be very effective. Another remedy—and for me, at least, the best—is one that you are likely to find only in rural areas, especially dairy country. Manufactured by a small firm in Vermont, this marvelous preparation was introduced to me by a New Hampshire woman who had known it since her childhood on a farm. The preparation, marketed under the no-nonsense trademark Bag Balm, was applied to the cow's udder with near miraculous results. This woman had seen udders deeply lacerated by barbed wire healed almost overnight. After a single application I was convinced, and I used the lanolin-based salve on everything from chapped hands to wounds. When it was empty, the pretty green tin, decorated with the head and udder of a cow, became a great conversation piece. The last I heard, Bag Balm was still being manufactured and available in some pharmacies or animal feed stores.

Until fairly recently, premenstrual tension and menopause were given scant attention by the male-dominated medical profession, who often dismissed the symptoms as imaginary. We know now that either condition, caused by hormonal changes, can produce symptoms that are quite real.

As I mentioned earlier, blood calcium levels drop prior to menstruation and can cause irritability, nervousness, and depression. Extra calcium is important before and during menstruation, as is vitamin C, which may be drained by menstruation. Tension and irritability can be relieved by the herbal sedatives listed in Chapter 4. Water retention can be avoided to some extent by eliminating salt and relieved by diuretics listed in Chapter 9, on the urinary system.

Headaches, common to both the menstrual cycle and menopause, can be relieved by any of the salicylate herbs such as willow, wintergreen, and meadowsweet. If the headaches are usually stubborn, as they can be during menopause, try feverfew.

At all stages of the reproductive cycle and continuing into later years, vitamin E is a friend to both men and women, contributing to the health of the circulatory and reproductive systems. Rosetta Reitz, in her book *Menopause,* recommends a combination of 800 international units of E, 2,000 to 3,000 milligrams vitamin C, and 1,000 milligrams calcium for hot flashes, reducing the intake of vitamin E to 400 international units after the hot flashes have subsided. Medical writer Barbara Seaman advocates ginseng and vitamin E as an alternative to estrogen. Night sweats, which often come with hot flashes, can be relieved by sage tea, which suppresses perspiration. According to Varro Tyler, medical experiments conducted in 1939 indicated that sage also has estrogenic activity. However, sage also contains thujone, which is toxic to a degree, so use judiciously.

A mixture I have found very helpful in relieving menopause symptoms is a half teaspoon each of motherwort, spearmint, red clover, squaw vine, dong quoi, gotu kola, and sarsaparilla, and one quarter-teaspoon licorice infused for ten minutes in one cup boiling water. While the herbs are steeping I boil a piece

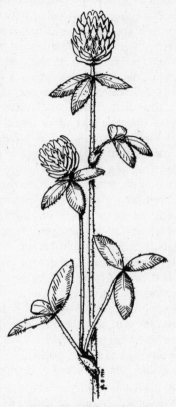

*Red Clover-*Trifolium pratense

of black cohosh root equal in size to one half-teaspoon in one third of a cup of water and add this to the infusion. The dose is one cup a day. I buy all of these herbs at Aphrodisia, which you will find listed in "Resources," at the back of this book.

Sarsaparilla is a tonic for the male as well as the female reproductive system. Introduced into Europe in the mid-sixteenth century as a syphilis cure, sarsaparilla has been alternately extolled, ignored, then rediscovered. Culpeper's recipe for English sarsaparilla, "an excellent Spring drink for renewing the blood and enlivening the juices of the body," calls for two ounces each of dandelion root, burdock root, and inner bark of elm infused overnight in boiling water, then boiled over a slow fire with the addition of "Spanish Juice" (perhaps wine?), then strained. The dose is three cups per day. In the 1940s, researchers discovered that sarsaparilla contains three hormones: progesterone, which triggers menstruation; cortin, an adrenal hormone; and testosterone, a male hormone that produces the male secondary sexual characteristics and influences sexual potency and physical strength. Testosterone has been used successfully in treating the early stages of hair loss, diseases of the blood vessels, and angina.

As you read in the preceding chapter, ginseng has legendary powers as a panacea and restorative. The major herb in Chinese medicine for at least five thousand years, ginseng was so highly valued in China that competition for the forked root led to several wars with neighboring Tartars. At one period in its history, exporting ginseng from China was a capital crime. The ancient Greeks called ginseng "the herb of the sorcerers," believing it had magical powers. Centuries ago in India, medical practitioners claimed that ginseng bestows on males the strength of the horse, the mule, the goat, the ram, and the bull. American Indians used the wild ginseng that grew on the hillsides as a digestive, a corrective for female disorders, and a love potion.

Wild ginseng is said to be more potent, but it is in short supply: the plant takes six years to mature and is very particular about its environment, requiring shade, adequate drainage, and, according to Richard Lucus, a soil that is naturally radioactive. Wild ginseng hunters, he tells us, set off at night to find it because the radioactive content makes it glow in the dark. They would shoot arrows at the ghostly light emitted from the leaves, then return the next day to dig up the roots where the arrows had fallen. Most of the world's cultivated ginseng supply comes from Korea; the "red" variety is considered the most stimulating.

All parts of the plant are infused or decocted for indigestion, coughs, and respiratory ailments, general debility, sexual "indulgences," and impotence. Chinese men take the herb to prolong their sexual potency into old age. It is believed that the plant is tonic to the endocrine system, activating the hormones and promoting health, vitality, and youthfulness. Not surprisingly, ginseng has a venerable reputation as an aphrodisiac.

Another vitalizing agent with which men of all ages should cultivate an acquaintance is the pumpkin seed, a traditional folk remedy in Eastern Europe and the Balkans for preventing and curing prostate disorders. In those parts of the world where pumpkin seeds are eaten freely throughout life, prostate disorders are rare. The seeds are packed with phosphorous, iron, B vitamins, protein, and unsaturated fats. They are excellent sources of zinc and lecithin, which contribute to the health of the prostate. In Russia, sunflower seeds, which are also rich in zinc and lecithin as well as protein, iron, and vitamins, are believed to have similar powers.

No chapter on the reproductive system would be complete without some mention of aphrodisiacs. Ever since courtship progressed beyond a knock on the head with the caveman's club, people have consumed any number of things, some of them pretty weird, in search of the perfect sexual stimulant.

Certainly a well-nourished and exercised body and an alluring partner are the best stimulants for romance. So is an absence of tension and the presence

Coriander: the powdered seeds given in sweet wine doth make me prone to the venereal act but yet too much used is evil. For that it bringeth men to a frenzy and raging with themselves.
Thomas Hyll

of sufficient energy. Depressants and stimulants are often used for such purposes, but they can work against you: coffee nerves aren't exactly a turn-on, and the drunken porter in *Macbeth* had the last word on alcohol when he said it increases the desire but kills the performance.

An Herbal Pharmacopoeia

Plants that are considered aphrodisiac have either some nutritive value or volatile oils, or they affect the neuromuscular system. Certain euphoriants such as ergot (the original source of LSD), marijuana, opium, coca, datura, and mandrake have all been used as aphrodisiacs. All of these are risky to use, however, because they are either illegal or poisonous.

Aromatic oils such as peppermint, anise, clove, and wintergreen, applied directly to the genitals, do produce a warming, tingling sensation that can be very erotic. They are also slightly anesthetic and may help maintain an erection.

The following herbs are reputed to be aphrodisiac: yerba mate (probably because it's a stimulant); damiana (the once or twice I tried it, we fell asleep—period); fennel seed (try the tincture); ginseng (maybe it works better for men); saw palmetto; yohimbe (said to cause tingling in the genitals); kava kava infused and refrigerated for at least twenty-four hours; coriander gathered in the last quarter of the moon and steeped in wine; cubeb berries; the root of joe-pye weed; cardinal flower; blue lobelia; saffron; eryngo herb; mustard, horseradish, peppers, and most spices, which cause tingling in the urogenital tract. A cream containing a mixture of celandine poppy, cow parsnip, savory, peppermint, and plantain is said to help women overcome frigidity.

Truffles, a rare and expensive fungus which grows underground, are much sought after by human and by pigs, which have remarkable ability to sniff them out. According to a New York Times article, West German researchers have found that truffles contain a substance that is synthesized in the testes of both boars and men. Later findings showed that the musklike scent of this natural chemical has an aphrodisiac effect on both sows and men, which may explain the predilection for truffles in both species.

Do they work? Since all these herbs have ancient uses, apparently they do—at least for some people. And the ritual of sipping or anointing using these herbs is itself a sensual pleasure, an aphrodisiac as potent as any herb.

Chapter 7

Kitchen Cures for the Common Cold and Other Respiratory Miseries

Long ago, when I was growing up, I used to enjoy a few days of winter invalidism, which were ushered in by a hot toddy made with sugar, hot water, lemon juice, and a dash of Four Roses whiskey. I savored the langorous days in bed, away from school (the best part), glued to the radio catching up on the most recent adventures of *My Gal Sunday, Stella Dallas, Backstage Wife,* and *Just Plain Bill.* In the evenings, our family doctor, an osteopath, came by to give me "treatments," which consisted of massage, spinal manipulations, and silly jokes. Back then, I thought colds were vastly underrated as a perfectly good excuse for a holiday from the rigors of mathematics and sentence parsing, a yielding to the voluptuousness of soap opera, comic books, and, later, trashy novels and vast quantities of grape juice. Even when I got older, I viewed colds as not so much a nuisance as permission to retire from the world for a few days of daydreams and such like activities, which serve no practical purpose except to remind us that we don't, after all, always have to be accomplishing something.

Unfortunately, all this changed when I grew up and had to take on duties that don't allow for much slack time—and viruses have become more relentless, exotic, and mean. What was once only a few cozy days in bed can become, for some, weeks or even months of wretchedness. Over-the-counter remedies aren't much help, since the little energy we have left over from fighting the germs has to be used to withstand the dizziness and drowsiness those remedies bring. So if you, too, must be up and doing instead of lounging around, here are a few of the ways various peoples have dealt with our universal affliction.

The culprit in most respiratory infections is mucus. We need a certain amount of this slippery secretion to lubricate and protect the membranes lining the eyes, nose, mouth, and other body cavities, and for body fluids manufactured by the reproductive and other glands. Too much mucus, however, clogs the respiratory passages and makes our digestion sluggish. And because mucus is sticky, it becomes a breeding place for germs.

In the autumn, when the brisk air sharpens our appetites, we tend to eat more stick-to-the-ribs foods, such as starches, meats, eggs, and dairy products—all of them mucus-producing. This may be one reason why we tend to get sick during the cold months. An obvious preventive is to limit our intake of the mucus-producing foods; another is to take in herbal teas and foods that dry up excess mucus or help the body to expel it.

Possibly one of the oldest plants for this use is the gingko, which has been around for about three hundred million years and continues to thrive, even in cities, because of its ability to resist pests and pollution. Extracts of the fan-shaped leaves have been used in Chinese medicine for over five thousand years for heart and lung problems, coughs, asthma, and acute allergies. Scientists are currently studying the gingko leaf for use in treating asthma, toxic shock, Alzheimer's disease, and circulatory disorders, and for making organ transplants safer, while Chinese people continue to boil the seeds and drink the decoction to dry up mucus in the lungs and intestines.

Stinging nettles are said to be an excellent corrective for excess mucus. In spring, the tender tops of nettles can be steamed or boiled for a delicacy that is rich in iron and vitamins. The flavor of this leafy green is somewhat like spinach, but more subtle. Wear leather gloves when you gather this plant to protect your skin from the stinging hairs (which are not a problem when the nettles are cooked or dried). Gather a quantity so you can dry the leaves and use them for tea in autumn and winter. Dill, peppermint, saffron, yellow dock, and gotu kola, used either fresh as seasoning or dried and brewed as tea, are said to help soften mucus so it can be eliminated along with other body wastes.

In traditional Chinese medicine, "warming" herbs and spices are taken at the first sign of a cold. Ginger is most often used for this purpose. A good mixture is a decoction of ginger root, cinnamon stick, coriander seed, and clove. Add lemon after you take the mixture from the fire and sweeten with honey.

But ye juice of it, doth take away the dimness that is in the eyes, and drie up the rhumes. But the seed being dranck is good for such as breed melancholye, and for ye dysureticall and for the flatulent. It causeth also many sneezings, being drawn up by the smell, and the herb doth the like. But the eyes must be shut whilst ye sneezing holds. Somme also doe not eat it, because being chewed, and set in the Sunne, it breeds little worms. But the Africans have entertained it, because they which eate it and are smitten of a Scorpion, yet remaine without paine.

From Greek Herbal *by* Dioscorides, Englished *by* John Goodyer A.D. 1655

The cold preventive I most enjoy is one I invented because I happened to have the ingredients growing on my kitchen windowsill. To three cups homemade chicken soup (or one package dry soup mix and three cups of water) add four garlic cloves, five or six fresh basil leaves, and one tablespoon fresh or one and a half teaspoons dried of each of these herbs: marjoram, thyme, dill, parsley, and chervil. Then add a pinch of cayenne pepper. Simmer for ten minutes and eat the entire portion while it is as hot as you can stand it. The parsley, garlic, thyme, and chervil will expel mucus; garlic, thyme, and cayenne are antiseptic; the basil, marjoram, and cayenne stimulate perspiration and help you sweat out toxins; and the chervil and cayenne are stimulants, which build resistance. A bowl of the vitamin-rich soup once a day helps me ward off colds and flu—and recover more quickly if the cold is already established.

Another excellent cold preventive comes from D. C. Jarvis's *Folk Medicine*. Jarvis made a study of the old-fashioned remedies used in the Vermont countryside where he practiced medicine, and he was particularly impressed with the curative powers of honey and cider vinegar. We become sick, he theorized, when our acid-alkaline balance is disturbed. Honey and vinegar, he claimed, restore that balance. His formula, which is one of my favorite remedies, is one tablespoon each of honey and vinegar in a cup of hot water. I add a pinch of cayenne

Cone Flower-Echinacea angustifolia

pepper (to help me sweat out toxins), then bundle up warmly and drink the mixture every two hours. If I treat a cold this way in its early stages I can usually avoid getting sick.

Fresh garlic is also a tried-and-true cold preventive. Keeping a fresh garlic clove in the mouth between cheeks and teeth is said to keep a cold from developing. How acceptable this practice may be to one's co-workers is another story.

The most reliable way to prevent colds, flu, and other viral infections is to build up immunity to them. An herb that is being widely used and studied nowadays for its effect on the immune system is echinacea, or coneflower, a daisy-like plant native to the American West and Midwest; its purple petals droop from a darker purple central disk to form a cone. Echinacea shows antiviral activity that is similar to the body's own supply of interferon, a protein manufactured by the cells in response to virus invasion. Currently, echinacea is prescribed by holistic physicians for wounds and ulcers, including herpes influenza and conditions such as chronic fatigue syndrome for which no specific treatment exists. Echinacea is apparently safe to use and has no side effects. Although resistance is not something that can be measured with any degree of accuracy, I have found that this past fall and winter when viruses seemed to be particularly vicious and widespread, I have managed to escape heavy bouts of the flu by taking about half a teaspoon of powdered echinacea on a daily basis.

Fever is nature's way of killing disease organisms; unless you have an exceptionally high temperature you should allow it to run its course. The best way to treat a mild fever is by taking a diaphoretic, which stimulates sweat and allows the body to throw off toxins. Evaporation of moisture on your skin will reduce the temperature gradually. Hot boneset tea, which is called "turkey flower" in parts of New England, is one of the best diaphoretics. You will want to sweeten the tea with honey, because it is very bitter. A warm infusion of elder flowers or linden blossoms is very good for colds, sore throat and fever, especially when mixed with peppermint and hyssop. Yarrow and the bark of spruce, hemlock, and pine are also diaphoretic.

If the fever persists or is very high, you can bring it down with a tea made from the salicylate-containing herbs such as willow, wintergreen, or meadowsweet. Because of its quinine content, Peruvian bark, a source of quinine, is one of the best infusions to use for a cold or bringing down fever. *Warning:* Do not take more than a cup or two a day, and do not use at all if you are pregnant, because quinine stimulates uterine contractions, which can bring on a miscarriage.

Vapor baths are wonderful for breaking up lung or sinus congestion. For immediate relief, lean over a pot of boiling water to which a handful of eucalyptus, peppermint, and wintergreen leaves are added, and drape a towel over your head to keep in the vapors. For nighttime relief put a few drops of the oil of one or more of these herbs in a vaporizer.

A hot bath to which aromatic herbs are added helps relieve the aches and pains of colds and flu. A pine-needle bath is said to increase the body's supply of white blood cells, which fight infection. Decoctions of spruce, hemlock, eucalyptus, thyme, and horehound help break up mucus and relieve coughs.

A few of my favorite cough remedies are a strong tea made from red clover sweetened with honey and a formula recommended by Dr. Jarvis, which I have found works on the most stubborn coughs. To make this delicious cough syrup, boil a whole lemon for ten minutes. When it is cool enough to handle, roll the lemon back and forth on a hard surface, then squeeze the juice into a pint of honey. Add one teaspoon glycerin and use as often as needed.

Roasted onions were esteemed by Culpeper and his fellow herbalists and by the American Indians. Culpeper's cough remedy consisted of roasting onions on the embers of a fire until soft, then mixing them with honey, sugar, and oil. The Indians roasted onions, then squeezed out the juice and mixed it with red clover syrup and honey. For bronchitis, they covered the patient's chest with a raw onion poultice kept warm with a sack of hot ashes. The Indians also ate a gruel of cooked onions for colds—a practice that was adopted by European settlers, who hoped it would help them survive the miseries of winter.

One of the very best remedies for coughs and colds is yerba santa, an evergreen that grows in the mountains of California and Oregon. Two or three of the fresh leaves or a teaspoon of dried leaves infused in a cup of boiling water is sufficient for a daily dose. Take a tablespoon at a time as needed, half a cup at bedtime. Other cough remedies used by both European and American Indian herbalists are wild cherry bark, licorice root, slippery elm, and skunk cabbage. Then there is garlic, which has so many medicinal as well as culinary uses that it could well be the one herb to take along if you expect to be stranded on a desert island. The antiseptic quality of garlic is excellent for combating colds and flu; its expectorant quality relieves coughing. Simply grate a garlic clove or two, mix it with about a teaspoonful of honey, and take as needed. Richard Lucas in *Nature's Medicines* reports that a poultice of finely chopped garlic applied to the soles of the feet, which have been anointed with petroleum jelly or similar greasy substance to prevent blistering, has brought spectacular relief from whooping cough. Early in this century, physicians in Ireland and America experimented with both internal and external applications of garlic and found it exceptional for treating tuberculosis.

Ginseng, the panacea of Chinese medicine, is also good for coughs. When taken at the onset of a cold it is said to build resistance; the tea sweetened with honey is said to relieve coughs.

When a cold settles in your chest, you need relief not only from coughs but from congestion. Plasters were used for breaking up bronchial congestion until the beginning of this century. These were made of paper, muslin, kidskin, or chamois skin impregnated with camphor, mustard, menthol, or similar rubifacient, which stimulated circulation in the underlying muscles or internal organs. Today the plaster has been replaced by various over-the-counter preparations such as Tiger Balm, Ben Gay, or Vick VapoRub. Most of these preparations contain camphor, an oil obtained from a tree related to cinnamon, and menthol, obtained from peppermint. Tiger Balm also contains the oils of clove and cajeput, a botanical relative of myrtle. You can make your own plasters by mixing equal parts of camphor and menthol with five parts olive oil, dampening a piece of cloth with the mixture, then covering with another cloth and keeping the area warm. Plasters are also good for easing muscular stiffness and soreness.

The raw, scratchy feeling of a sore throat is eased by mucilaginous herbs (which soothe inflamed tissue) such as marshmallow root, psyllium seeds, Irish moss (a seaweed you can buy from herbal suppliers), and linseed. The astringency of white pond lily root and fennel, used in a gargle, helps shrink the inflamed tissue. Horehound and thyme have been used for centuries for sore throat and also, because they are expectorants, for coughs. The latter is also antiseptic.

A spoonful of honey, which is both antiseptic and soothing, is also wonderful for easing sore throat caused by a cold or the voice strain singers often experience. To make lozenges for sore throat and coughs, soak three quarters of a cup horehound and a quarter of a cup thyme in one cup water overnight. Strain, then squeeze as much juice from the leaves as you can. Add one cup honey to the water in which the leaves were soaked and boil until the mixture forms a hard ball when dropped in water. When the mixture has cooled slightly, spread it on an oiled baking sheet; before it hardens, cut it into pieces about the size of a half-teaspoon.

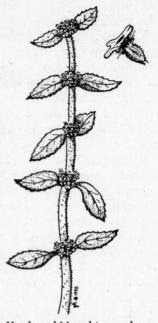

Asthma and hayfever are usually caused by allergies but are sometimes triggered by stress. Avoiding the allergens whenever you can, getting lots of vitamin C, preferably in the form of fresh raw fruits and vegeta-

Horehound-Marrubium vulgare

bles, and eliminating or at least limiting your intake of mucus-producing foods may lessen the intensity of the attacks. Chewing honeycomb has also helped some people recover from asthma attacks.

In the chapter on the nervous system, I mentioned that chamomile tea can produce side effects in people who are allergic to ragweed. Some people, however, can actually benefit from daily doses of this allergen. After drinking several cups of chamomile tea every day all winter, my old friend Charles found that when summer and allergy season rolled around he had managed to immunize himself; he got through the season symptom-free, although many people were having a particularly bad time with allergies that year. When Charles reported this, I remembered that many years ago a Kentucky herbalist had told me of a similar remedy: a daily teaspoonful or two of honey obtained from flowers that grow within a ten-mile radius of where one is living. This probably wouldn't be as helpful to one who has an itch to travel, but even then, one could benefit from honey made from those plants that grow universally or have close botanical kin that do.

If coughs, sneezes, or sniffles do plague you, the best herb to use is ma-huang, or Chinese ephedra. A relative of the American plant desert tea, ma-huang contains ephedrine, a potent alkaloid used in pharmaceutical medicines for colds, asthma, and hay fever. The most noticeable effect of ephedrine tea is that it quickly dries up mucus. An overdose can leave you feeling cotton-mouthed, so do not take more than four cups during a twenty-four-hour period, and don't take it more than every four hours. *Warning:* **Ma-huang also causes a temporary rise in blood pressure, so don't take it if you have hypertension.**

Although all of the remedies I have described so far have apparently worked for cold and flu sufferers for centuries, I'm still convinced that the best one of all is the one I mentioned at the beginning of this chapter: rest. Sickness is often an indication that we have been driving our internal machinery too hard. At times, when I've been feeling dragged out from what seems to be a very long flu season, I've found an instant cure in the company of good friends. In these days when the Puritan work ethic seems positively maniacal, friendship is often the need we most neglect—and to our peril, for it may be the most powerful remedy of all.

Chapter 8

Artichoke, Dandelion, Asparagus, and Other Gourmet Feasts for Digestive Health

Of all the systems of the human body, perhaps none is so immediately affected by our emotions as the gastrointestinal. Our language reflects this. When we are nervous we have "butterflies in the stomach" or a stomach "tied up in knots." Medical terms such as *anorexia nervosa* and *irritable bowel syndrome* suggest their link with the nervous system; gastric ulcers, spastic colon, and colitis are known to be directly influenced by stress.

Related to the stress factor, which we often can't avoid, are lifestyle and dietary habits, which we can change. Herbal medicines are not a substitute for a healthy lifestyle, but an adjunct to it, and as physicians all the way back to Hippocrates have observed, all medicines work much better in conjunction with a common-sense regimen of fresh air, exercise, and a diet rich in fruits and vegetables.

Consider the liver, for example. This hardworking gland performs over five hundred functions involving digestion, excretion, and storage of vitamins and minerals. The largest gland in the body, it is a detoxifier, purifying the blood and regulating blood chemistry; it produces bile, which helps fat digestion, and stores glucose, which affects the blood sugar level. An overload of alcohol, which is high in sugar as well as toxic, or rich, greasy foods can damage the liver and lead to a host of troubles that range from unpleasant—sluggish digestion and elimination—to dangerous—high cholesterol, gall-stones, hepatitus, or cirrhosis. Clearly, avoiding such excesses is the best way to prevent liver disorders. Certain herbs also have a long-standing reputation for helping protect the liver when we are well and restore it to health when we are sick.

One of the most plentiful—and palatable—herbs for liver complaints is the dandelion. A rough translation of the botanical name, *Taraxacum officinale,* is "the official remedy for disorders." Like the reigning favorite of the social season, this sunshine-colored weed has for centuries danced through the annals of herbal medicine—desirable, useful, and infinitely cheering. In Maine, where I grew up, and no doubt in many rural areas to this day, dandelion enthusiasts sally forth in early spring to gather the young leaves for potherbs and salads. Dandelion greens are cooked like spinach—steaming is best—and dressed with bacon grease (not very healthy, but tasty), butter, or olive oil. In Maine it was customary to add a dash of vinegar to dandelion and

Dandelion-Taraxacum officinale

other greens, doubtless an old practice dating back to a time when lemons and other citrus fruits were a rarity in the north.

When the dandelions blossom, they provide the makings for another rural treat—dandelion wine, which is one of the most potent and ambrosial of homemade inebriants, as sweet and delicately golden as a springtime afternoon.

In addition to its treasures of health-giving nutrients, the dandelion also contains bitters, which encourage the appetite and aid digestion, and enzymes, which stimulate the liver and kidneys in particular and the metabolism as a whole. Dandelion is also one of the most important chologogues (botanical or chemical drugs that increase the flow of bile and improve the functions of stomach, liver, and gallbladder).

The most potent concentration of dandelion's medicinal wealth is stored in the root in early spring. You can either boil or steam the roots as you would parsnips or carrots, or roast a quantity of them in the oven until they are brown and brittle, then pulverize for a coffee-like beverage.

Radishes are an old folk remedy for gallbladder symptoms, although they are not recommended when the intestines and stomach are inflamed. The remedy John Lust sets forth in *The Herb Book* is three to four ounces of radish juice taken before breakfast. The amount should be increased gradually to fourteen ounces a day, then reduced to three or four ounces after a week or two; treatment should be continued for at least three weeks.

Another superb food with chologogue properties is the globe artichoke. Dr. Rudolph Fritz Weiss, in his book *Herbal Medicines,* reports that recently an antitoxic substance, cynarin, has been isolated from the artichoke and found effective in treating gallbladder symptoms. Cynarin also regenerates the liver and lowers cholesterol, a substance researchers have found to be instrumental in forming gallstones.

The globe artichoke is a member of the thistle family. One of its relatives, the milk thistle, contains silymarin, chemically similar to the cynarin in artichokes. Studies published in 1983 indicate that silymarin is one of the best remedies for liver complaints, especially hepatitis. Weiss observes that silymarin stabilizes the liver cell membrane, preventing toxins from entering and damaging the cells. Although silymarin cannot cure acute hepatitis, if taken at the acute stage of chronic hepatitis it can relieve symptoms and arrest further deterioration of the liver cells.

Weiss recommends an infusion of milk thistle seeds, one teaspoon to one cup boiling water, sipped before breakfast, lunch, dinner, and bedtime, at the onset of a liver complaint. Twenty drops of the tincture, taken on the same schedule, can be used instead. The infusion is improved, he says, by the addition of peppermint, also a chologogue.

One of the most dramatic uses of silymarin, Weiss goes on to say, is in treating poisoning from the *Amanita verna* mushroom. Commonly known as the Destroying Angel, this snow-white, deadly mushroom kills liver cells and can be fatal to as many as 50 percent of the unfortunates who accidentally eat it. Little was available by way of antidote until it was discovered that if silymarin was given within forty-eight hours after the mushroom was eaten, the drug would prevent the amanita toxin from entering liver cells and the patient would recover. Although the Destroying Angel doesn't make its way often to the family dinner table, it is occasionally gathered by wild-mushroom hunters who mistake it for a puffball or other white mushroom, and it is comforting to know that an antidote to amanita poisoning does exist.

Another herb currently being studied for treating serious liver disease is *Colchicum autumnale,* more commonly known as meadow saffron. In appearance, colchicum resembles the autumn crocus *(Crocus satiuus),* source of our culinary saffron—hence the somewhat confusing botanical name. The bulb, or corm, of colchicum yields the toxic chemical colchine, which has an ancient history in Western medicine, more fully discussed in Chapter 10, which is about the skeletal system. Cirrhosis, a degenerative liver disease most often caused by alcoholism, is characterized by fibrous tissue that prevents proper functioning of the liver. According to studies reported in the Harvard Medical School newsletter, colchine seems to block formation of collagen, the main constituent of the fibrous tissue. Tests so far have been limited, but researchers are hopeful that colchine will prove to be successful in combating cirrhosis, which is often fatal.

While it is known that most liver disease is a direct result of dietary or drug-related excess, peptic ulcers, which are sores on the mucous membrane lining the stomach, remain something of a medical mystery—although it is' known that acid stomach secretions, often triggered by stress, are often responsible for ulcer formation. Recent studies have confirmed that the most effective ulcer remedy is one that has been used for centuries in folk medicine for stomach upsets, tension, and insomnia, or simply as a pleasant teatime beverage—chamomile.

Meadow Saffron-
Colchicum autumnale

It has been known since the 1930s that the active ingredient in chamomile is the oil, which contains the chemical azulene, named for its blue color. More recent studies show that it is the entire complex of chemicals, found only in the whole flower, that gives the full effect of chamomile, and that these are tailor-made for the treatment of ulcers. As I noted in Chapter 4, chamomile is antispasmodic and sedative—excellent for counteracting stress. It is also anti-inflammatory and healing to wounds and lesions. In clinical tests chamomile has been found to inhibit ulcers in rats. Weiss observes, "Chamomile does not give merely symptomiatic improvement in these cases, but effects a cure, influencing the pathological process. It will however be necessary to give it in sufficient quantity for a sufficiently long period for the ulcer to have genuinely healed." He prescribes two teaspoons in a cup of water, sipped on an empty stomach for more complete absorption, one to be taken before breakfast, a second in the afternoon, and a third at bedtime. Relief, he notes, is quite rapid, and adds that chamomile's anti-inflammatory and antispasmodic qualities are also very effective in treating colitis, an inflammation of the colon. Because of its antispasmodic, anti-inflammatory, and antibiotic properties, chamomile is also highly effective in treating stomach upsets caused by tension or bacterial infections, and it has long been used for such in folk medicine.

Peppermint, my personal household favorite, has similar properties and similar uses in folk medicine. Adding lemon balm, which has a tranquilizing effect in small doses, is particularly agreeable when the stomach upset is caused by tension.

Stress and tension are also major contributors to a disorder that is unpleasant and occasionally life-threatening—irritable bowel syndrome. Irritable bowel syndrome is characterized by alternating bouts of constipation and diarrhea caused by fluctuations between too much or too little watery secretion in the intestines. Some of the preparations used to treat this condition are psyllium seeds, the main ingredient in bulk-producing laxatives such as Metamucil, and atropine, found in belladonna and other plants of the nightshade family, which is used in severe cases to inhibit bowel action. Nutmeg has been found to have an atropine-like effect on the bowels and has been used for centuries in Aryurvedic medicine for children's diarrhea.

The body sympathizes with or follows the affections of the soul, more in disease than in health; it acts as the soul feels, and hence the influence of the mind in modifying the operation of medicines. Vexation disturbs the functions of the stomach, attending the secretion and the gastric juices; and thus, by impairing the digestive powers, it becomes a very common cause by dyspepsia or stomach complaint. . . . Joy, on the other hand, acts as a powerful stimulant. . . . Confidence acts as a most powerful tonic on the whole animal frame.

From The Simmonite-Culpeper Herbal Remedies
W. J. Simmonite and Nicholas Culpeper

The root of tormentil, a wild European plant related to cinque-foil, is a powerful astringent long used in herbal medicine for alternating constipation and diarrhea. The fresh or recently dried rootstock is infused—one teaspoon to one cup water—for thirty minutes and taken by mouthfuls throughout the day. Cinquefoil, a creeping plant resembling the strawberry, also has a long, brown root that is very astringent. The bark of this root, Culpeper tells us, is used for "all sorts of fluxes" including diarrhea, nosebleed, and kidney ulcers.

Blueberries and apples are also good for both constipation and diarrhea. Blueberry leaves are astringent and help check diarrhea. The berries are laxative when fresh and antidiarrheal when dried. Apples are high in fiber, an important dietary item which, among other things, keeps us regular. The fruit also contains substantial amounts of pectin, which restores the function of the large bowel.

Tannin is astringent and helps dry up the watery secretions that cause diarrhea. Chinese tea has a high tannin content, as do herbs such as tormentil, cinquefoil, comfrey, witch hazel, plantain, white oak bark, rose petals, and the leaves of raspberries, strawberries, and blackberries. The last is a favorite old-time country remedy for diarrhea.

Because astringents shrink tissue, they are also excellent for a very uncomfortable affliction that is regarded with humor only by those who have never suffered from it. Hemorrhoids are actually varicose veins on the exterior of or just inside the anus. They frequently accompany pregnancy and childbirth and are aggravated by constipation, heavy lifting, stress, overindulgence in alcohol, and a sedentary lifestyle. Approximately 50 percent of people over forty suffer from hemorrhoids at some time or other. Over-the-counter remedies don't really do much for hemorrhoids except lubricate and soothe them temporarily. Warm sitz baths offer some relief, but the only thing that really works, I have found, is a strong astringent. After years of suffering acute hemorrhoid attacks, I had gotten to the point where surgery seemed the only recourse. Fortunately, before I submitted to the operation (which I understand is quite painful), I encountered a doctor who suggested a remedy that has worked for me and for other people I have suggested it to: a solution of 50 percent distilled witch hazel, an astringent, and 50 percent ice water to help constrict the blood vessels. A cold compress of this solution, applied for at least ten minutes once every hour or two, worked. I found this treatment particularly effective when I alternated the witch hazel compresses with cold compresses drenched in a strong solution of Chinese tea and comfrey—two teaspoons each to a cup of water. The tannin in the tea and in the comfrey forms a protective film over wounds; the allantoin in the comfrey is a cell proliferant, which speeds healing; and the mucilaginous property of comfrey is very soothing.

Two or three days of this intensive witch hazel, tea, and comfrey treatment, I am happy to report, leaves me free of pain. Occasional flare-ups treated with witch hazel (either the distilled witch hazel sold at drugstores or a strong infusion of the leaves) are quite brief and more annoying than painful. The secret is frequent application and cold compresses.

Some people also report considerable relief from hemorrhoids by drinking tea made from tormentil root. I imagine that compresses would also be very helpful, due to the high tannin content.

Constipation, although sometimes stress-related, most often is the result of insufficient fiber in the diet, infrequent exercise, and, less commonly, a sluggish liver. As with any gastrointestinal complaint, you should consult a doctor if the condition persists, because the underlying cause could be serious.

There are various types of laxatives ranging from those that soften stool and produce bulk, such as psyllium seeds or flax seeds and foods high in fiber, such as asparagus, beans and lentils, prunes, figs, and most fruits and vegetables, to purgatives, which stimulate peristalsis (movement of the intestines) and also liquid secretions of the intestinal canal. Purgatives such as American mandrake, castor oil or senna leaves, which are used for severe constipation, are very taxing to the heart and kidneys and should be used rarely if at all.* Never take laxatives of any sort if abdominal pain or tenderness are present or if you are pregnant or nursing.

*The American Indians sometimes used the root of American mandrake, or mayapple, which is not botanically related to European mandrake, as a drastic purgative. The two mandrakes do, however, have this in common—both are highly toxic.

For most purposes, a gentle laxative should suffice to restore bowel function. Eliminating meat, eggs, cheese, and chocolate, and eating cucumber salad, asparagus, or artichokes dressed with olive oil and garlic are very pleasant ways of dealing with constipation. Dried fruits are also very good. Herbal teas to try are those made with flax or psyllium seeds, dandelion root, licorice, hibiscus, or sarsaparilla. Aloe vera gel, which is soothing to the gastrointestinal tract, is also gently laxative. However, be sure to use the fresh gel—the bottled variety you buy in health food stores is purgative. Aromatic herbs and spices such as mint, caraway, fennel, cinnamon, clove, garlic, or jasmine petals can be added to encourage movement of the intestinal canal and prevent cramps. By encouraging bowel action, these herbs also help expel intestinal gas.

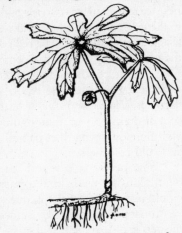

American Mandrake or May-apple— Podophyllum peltatum

Dyspepsia, or indigestion, is a common nuisance that afflicts most of us at one time or another. The cause can be as obvious as overeating or indulging in indigestible foods, rich desserts, or fried foods, or it can be simply a result of our body systems not working as well as they did when we were younger.

Generally speaking, most of the herbs we use for culinary purposes also aid digestion—a sound reason for using herbs liberally in cooking. Fenugreek, for example, which is popular in Middle Eastern cooking, is to this day prescribed by herbalists for dyspepsia, anorexia, and general debility. Herbs are often used in aperitifs to stimulate appetite and in after-dinner liqueurs to settle the stomach. You may have enjoyed the interesting flavor herbs such as calamus, angelica, anise, fennel, caraway, peppermint, or gentian impart to one of these beverages. Certain confections also contain digestive herbs—good for nibbling after a heavy meal. Such old-fashioned treats include candied ginger or angelica or "comfits" of candied coriander seeds, and candies made with anise, licorice, peppermint, cinnamon, or nutmeg.

Certain enzymes in pawpaw, papaya, and pineapple are potent digestives, particularly of protein. The fresh fruits are more effective, but since these are not always available in the market, many people drink tea made from the papaya leaf instead.

The traditional remedy for people convalescing from an illness or feeling run-down and listless is a tonic containing bitters. Bitters stimulate the appetite and digestion by increasing the flow of saliva and gastric juices. An important bitter traditionally prescribed in European medicine is the root of a familiar autumn flower, the gentian. Official in American medicine into the early twentieth century, gentian does not contain tannin, which can be constipating. Culpeper's recipe for Infusion of Gentian Root calls for two teaspoons sliced gentian root, two teaspoons dried orange peel, and four tablespoons dried lemon peel infused for four hours in one pint water. The dose is four tablespoons taken three times a day.

Hibiscus or Flower-of-the-Hour-Hybiscus trionum

Another bitter that has been used since antiquity is wormwood, the major ingredient in absinthe, an alcoholic drink that was the rage in Paris during the nineteenth and early twentieth centuries. Oil of wormwood, which is released in the distilling process, is poisonous to the central nervous system and can cause madness and even death, so it is no longer used in alcoholic spirits. However, Weiss points out that wormwood is a well-proven stomach and gallbladder remedy that can be safely used for short periods of time if it is infused, a process that does not release the toxic oil.

Oregon grape, mentioned in Chapter 5, bears clusters of dark blue fruits resembling grapes—hence the name. This plant was a favorite of the California Indians, who decocted the root as a bitter tonic; it was later introduced in Western medicine and was official until the late 1940s. The average official dose was thirty drops of the fluid extract. It is best to start with small doses of this plant— about ten drops—since it irritates the gastrointestinal system and acts as a purgative in larger doses.

The active ingredient in Oregon grape root is berberine, which is also found in goldenseal; an astringent bitter, it is a popular home remedy for constipation, stomach problems, and nausea during pregnancy. Its popularity is clearly due to efficiency and not flavor, which, to my palate, is horrid. Like Oregon grape, goldenseal is an herb to take with caution; an overdose can be purgative and extended use may cause constipation. John Lust recommends one teaspoon of the powdered root to one pint boiling water, taken cold, one or two teaspoonfuls at a time, three to six times a day.

Less common for adults than for children are intestinal worms, the eggs of which can be transferred to children's mouths after they have been playing in the dirt. As the name suggests, wormwood is a vermifuge traditionally used to expel worms from the intestinal tract. A strong infusion of the flowering tops of wormwood was taken by the teaspoonful. The leaves of mugwort or southernwood, botanical relatives of wormwood, are also considered to be vermifuges.

Bitters in general were often prescribed by herbalists because, Culpeper observes, "they often prove noxious to those animals and remove that debility of the digestive organs by which the food is not properly assimilated, or the secreted fluids poured into the intestines are not properly prepared."

As a rule, children do not like bitters, however, and some of the traditional vermifuges such as tansy, wormseed, and male fern are toxic to the host as well as the parasite. Culpeper used lavender seeds boiled in milk to expel worms, while the ancient Egyptians,

Babylonians, and Greeks used garlic. The most appealing worm medicine, however, is one that came to the attention of the American medical community in 1850. Dr. Bush listed it as official in 1917; *Potter's New Cyclopedia of Botanical Drugs and Preparations* listed it in 1956. The remedy is safe and enjoyable—pumpkin seeds. A good quantity of the seeds—about half a cup—should be eaten after fasting. Because pumpkin seeds paralyze the worms but do not kill them, the dose should be followed by a strong laxative or enema to clean the intestines thoroughly.

The health of the gastrointestinal system is crucial to our overall health and well-being. Happily, though, there are many delicious ways to keep it in good working order. You will find more ideas for eating and drinking to your good health in Chapter 15, "Herbs in the Kitchen."

Chapter 9

For Urinary Health: Madder, Saw Palmetto, and Refreshing Drinks and Salads

In the dry plains, deserts, and arid mountains of the world, where water is scarce and the climate dehydrating, urinary problems are fairly common. Cold, damp regions not only foster arthritis and rheumatism but are equally hard on the kidneys, encouraging excess accumulation of minerals and acids in the blood, which eventually make their way to the urinary system. So it is not surprising that peoples all over the world have experimented with the local flora to find ways of dealing with disorders of the urinary tract.

Kidney disorders range from relatively minor problems such as painful or insufficient urination, bedwetting, mild bladder and kidney infections, or gravel in the kidneys, to kidney stones, which can be excruciatingly painful, and kidney damage resulting from serious chronic conditions such as diabetes or severe cardiac or rheumatic disorders.

The main function of the kidneys is to filter waste products from the blood, and the best way to keep them healthy is to drink plenty of fluids in order to flush out the toxins, excess minerals, and harmful acids that can accumulate and form gravel and stones. Certain beverages are particularly good for the kidneys. One of the best is cranberry juice, which is wonderfully refreshing on a hot summer day. Besides being rich in vitamin C, cranberries also contain quinic acid, which helps deter the formation of kidney stones. Even orthodox medical doctors prescribe cranberry juice in addition to antibiotics when treating kidney infections. Black currant juice, tart and refreshing, is also good for the kidneys, being a diuretic that stimulates kidney function.

Some foods, too, are diuretic and keep the kidneys in good working order. These include cucumber and watermelon, particularly the seeds, carrots, watercress, nettles, dandelion, chicory, chervil, leeks and onions, asparagus, juniper, celery, and parsley. Garden, meadow, or green sorrel *(Rumex acetosa)*, a member of the buckwheat family, and sheep sorrel *(Rumex acetosella)*, which is smaller but very similar, are common wayside plants in New England and were traditionally eaten like spinach for "spring cures." Sorrel is di-

fruit

Common, or Garden, Sorrel-
Rumex acetosa

uretic, laxative, and astringent, said to be helpful in dissolving gravel and stones. I like to add a few tart, refreshing leaves to salad. *Caution:* Large amounts of sorrel can irritate kidneys and cause poisoning. The seeds of juniper, celery, and parsley have been used for

An Herbal Pharmacopoeia

centuries in treating urinary complaints. Parsley or juniper seeds, however, are not recommended for pregnant women because they may cause miscarriage; celery seeds and asparagus can irritate the kidneys and should not be taken when the kidneys are inflamed.

The herbs most commonly prescribed for urinary disorders are diuretics, which promote urination either by raising the blood pressure for a short time or by stimulating the kidneys. Diuretics are used in certain cardiac and rheumatic disorders in which excess fluid accumulates in the tissues, in conditions that call for flushing harmful substances from the kidneys, and for kidney and bladder infections.

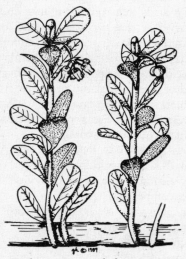

Bearberry-Arctostaphylos ura-ursi

The diuretics used most often are classified as irritants because they act by irritating the mucous membranes of the genito-urinary system. As the name implies, they should be used with caution. Excessive amounts can cause inflammation, painful urination, or blood in the urine. The list of irritant diuretics official in American pharmacology until 1917 includes juniper berries, usually taken as an oil or a spirit similar to gin; corn silk from Indian maize, long used by the American Indians for bladder and kidney infections; pipsissewa, a creeping woodland plant native to northern climates; buchu, a South African plant used by the Hottentots; and the leaves of bearberry, a creeping plant that grows in the mountains. Bearberry was a favorite herb of the American Indians, who called it *kinnickinnick,* a name they used for tobacco. They smoked the leaves as either an additive to or a substitute for tobacco and also exploited the high tannin content of the leaves for tanning leather. Bearberry leaves are used to relieve chronic accumulations of uric acid, believed to be a factor in rheumatism; to ease pain caused by kidney stones and gravel; for chronic cystitis or bladder inflammation; and to prevent bedwetting. Varro Tyler notes that bearberry leaves are a urinary antiseptic only if the urine is alkaline, so acidic foods should be avoided when taking bearberry. He adds that the intake of tannin, which is released in hot water, can be avoided by soaking the leaves in cold water for twelve to fourteen hours. Bearberry leaves darken the urine; overuse (more than two or three cups a day for longer than a week or two) can have a toxic effect.

Another favorite diuretic of the American Indians was goldenrod, which they used to strengthen the bladder, to relieve colic, and improve the taste of other medicinals. Goldenrod is rich in bioflavonoids, which assist vitamin C absorption.

The birch is well known. It is under the dominion of Venus, and of course is diuretic. The juice of the young leaves, or the distilled water of them, or the sap procured by boring a hole, is good against scurvy, dropsy, and in all cutaneous disorders, outwardly applied. A strong decoction of the leaves is good to wash sore mouths, and to break the stone and remove gravel in the kidneys.

Culpeper and Simmonite

Perhaps the most painful kidney affliction, particularly for males, is the formation and passing of kidney stones, which are composed of minerals not dissolved and passed out in the urine. Why kidney stones are formed in some people but not in others is still something of a mystery, but the preventives most often recommended are cranberry juice, nettle leaves, and all parts of the dandelion. Culpeper writes that Spaniards in his time ate a piece of columbine root before breakfast to break up stones. He also recommends birch leaf tea and hawthorn berries. For stone and pain in the kidneys he advises one ounce each of the seeds of parsley, fennel, anise, and caraway along with half an ounce each of the roots of parsley, burnet, saxifrage, and caraway. These seeds and roots are boiled in one quart of water until it reduces to one pint. One-third of this strained decoction is taken three times a day.

Weiss recommends a decoction of madder root to help pass kidney stones. A Mediterranean plant with a long, reddish-brown rootstock, madder is a traditional remedy for urinary problems. Drinking madder tea does have a side effect that can be rather alarming when one is not prepared: once used for coloring fabric, madder yields a red dye that colors the urine so it resembles blood.

The berries of saw palmetto, a small palm tree that grows in Georgia and Florida, are said to help pass kidney stones by increasing the flow of urine and easing the spasms that contribute to the pain of passing the stone. Saw palmetto acts as a sedative on the urinary tract and was included in the 1910 edition of the U.S. *Pharmacopoeia* for treating prostate disorders, irritable bladder, and urinary incontinence. To prevent bedwetting, Weiss recommends Saint-John's-wort, the bark of sweet sumac, or twenty drops of gentian tincture morning and evening. For the irritable bladder some elderly women experience and the prostate disorders that affect elderly men, he prescribes a combination of saw palmetto, sweet sumac, pumpkin seed oil, and hops. Pumpkin seeds are excellent for preventing prostate disorders and are discussed more fully in chapters 6 and 8. More recently, willow herb has shown promise as a remedy for prostate disorders; several institutes are now investigating the plant.

Needless to say, serious kidney ailments are not a matter for self-diagnosis or self-medication. Although herbs can be effective when prescribed by an experienced physician, they should not be taken as a replacement for or a supplement to conventional medical treatment unless you first consult with your doctor. Some diuretics are quite powerful and may not be compatible with other prescribed medications.

Earlier in this chapter I pointed out some of the dangers associated with certain diuretics such as parsley, celery, and juniper seeds. An even more serious danger of excessive use of diuretics—true also of laxatives and of severe diarrhea—is that in eliminating excessive amounts of water the body also loses potassium, which can cause the heart cells to become electrically unstable. As a result, the heartbeat becomes irregular, which may lead, in extreme cases, to heart failure. To restore the electrolyte balance, Weiss recommends the following mixture: one teaspoon each peppermint and fennel seed, one liter water, one half-teaspoon salt, one quarter-teaspoon bicarbonate of soda, one quarter-teaspoon potassium chloride, two teaspoons glucose. Drink as much as possible for a couple of days.

For mild bladder and kidney infections and relatively minor problems such as urinary incontinence sometimes experienced by the very young and the very old, some of the herbs I have mentioned above are safe to use and helpful. Many of the herbs used by the American Indians were already firmly established in the folk medicine of various cultures. The reason is self-evident: they worked. It is now the task of medical researchers to find out how and why.

Chapter 10

Arthritis, Gout, and Other Skeletal Disorders: New Findings About Old Remedies from Tribal Africans, Hippocrates, and the Queen of Hungary

The skeletal system is not generally something to which we pay much attention unless we strain a muscle or break a bone, or until our stiffening joints and imperceptibly dwindling limbs begin to warn us that we are aging. Paying attention to diet and exercise helps slow the skeletal aging process, but sooner or later—and, for some unfortunate people, far too soon—some form of arthritis, our most disabling chronic illness, catches up to most of us.

The causes and cure of arthritis are still largely unknown, although accumulation of uric acid is a major suspect, along with decreased calcium supply and inefficient utilization by the body. Inflammation, pain, and stiffness in the joints are the main symptoms, and the initial treatment is hot baths and hot packs to relax muscles and ease connective tissue and aspirin to reduce inflammation and pain.

Diuretics, a folk remedy for arthritis, are still used by herbal practitioners to stimulate the elimination of uric acid. Horsetail, or shave grass, a rush-like plant that to some observers resembles a well-groomed horse's tail, is considered an excellent diuretic for arthritic conditions because it is believed also to strengthen connective tissue. A primitive plant that is jointed, like asparagus, and often grows beside streams, horsetail is also known as scouring rush because its high silica content renders it abrasive and suitable for scouring kitchen utensils. It is a useful plant when you are camping. Dioscorides and Galen used it as a dressing for wounds; Gerard recommended it for nosebleed and asthma. Some writers, however, warn that horsetail has caused poisoning, probably due to the silica content, so do not use it internally unless it is prescribed by an experienced practitioner.

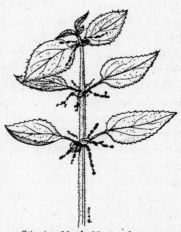

Two herbs, however, that you can take freely are dandelion and stinging nettle. The dandelion, as you read in previous chapters, improves the function of both liver and kidneys. The active ingredient in dandelion, taraxin, which is concentrated in the root, sup-

Stinging Nettle-Urtica dioica

posedly improves overall cell function and is very healing to the skeletal as well as other body systems. Weiss recommends a cup of dandelion root tea or two tablespoons of the juice of the leaves taken morning and evening.

Accidentally brushing against a nettle is a memorable experience if one's skin is not protected by clothing. The fine hairs that coat the leaves contain formic acid, which produces a fiery stinging sensation that can be relieved, it is said, by applying dock leaves to the area. In former times people who were afflicted with rheumatism or paralysis flayed themselves with nettles in an attempt to restore circulation and mobility—with some success, apparently. A less dramatic method of using nettles is to steep them in alcohol and apply the nettle spirit as a liniment for rheumatism, lumbago, and sciatica. Feasting on the young tops of nettles gathered in early spring (while wearing gloves as protection against stings) is not only a gourmet treat but good for most anything that ails you.

Two popular folk remedies that have recently come under scrutiny in the laboratory are devil's claw and feverfew. Devil's claw, a vine native to South and East Africa also grows in the deserts of the American Southwest. The blooming of its trumpet-shaped purple or yellow flowers is followed by the appearance of black, woody seed pods with two hooked, claw-shaped appendages at the ends. The active ingredients are mainly concentrated in the storage tuber. Devil's claw is listed in the British *Herbal Pharmacopoeia* as anti-inflammatory, analgesic, and diuretic, and is prescribed for rheumatism, arthritis, gout, and lumbago. Regarded as an alterative by herbal practitioners, devil's claw has been used for centuries to reduce inflammation and release tissue waste, presumably by way of the kidneys. Weiss reports that harpagoside and harpagide, the active ingredients in devil's claw (also found in common figwort and mullein leaf) show antirheumatic, analgesic, and anti-inflammatory effects in clinical studies and have been used successfully in treating arthritis, lower back pain, neuralgia, and headache. He adds that devil's claw also acts as a bitter tonic and lowers cholesterol.

Feverfew has been used in Western medicine at least since the time of Plutarch, who mentions it in his historical writings. A popular painkiller in the eighteenth century, feverfew fell into disuse with the discovery of aspirin but attracted the attention of medical researchers in the twentieth century when the wife of a Welsh physician got relief from both migraine and arthritis symptoms by eating sandwiches made with fresh feverfew leaves.

Jennifer Britt and Lesley Keen, in their book *Feverfew,* tell us that studies conducted in Nottingham, England, in 1985 indicate that feverfew relieves arthritis symptoms by "inhibiting the release of damaging materials from white cells in inflamed joints." They conclude that feverfew proved to be more effective in treating arthritis than the most potent drugs currently available. *One cautionary note:* **Feverfew should not be used during pregnancy, for it may trigger a miscarriage.**

A third folk remedy for arthritis is purslane, the sprawling plant with fat, succulent leaves that you met in previous chapters. Some authorities believe purslane originated in Asia, where it has been enjoyed as a leafy green vegetable for over two thousand years. Used in continental medicine since antiquity for urinary complaints and gout, purslane is now under intensive study because of its omega-3 fatty acids, which may prove useful in combating cancer and heart disease. Rodale Press reports that omega-3 oils, present

Devil's Claw or Unicorn Plant-
Proboscidea louisiana

in fatty fish and some plants, most notably in purslane, are achieving good results in treating arthritis patients in England. In addition to other virtues, omega-3 oils seem to inhibit the body's ability to produce inflammatory products, which cause the painfully swollen joints characteristic of arthritis.

A fourth remedy dating back to antiquity is colchicine, derived from meadow saffron. According to an article published in the Harvard Medical School Newsletter, colchicine was used in Egypt as early as 1500 B.C. and was a specific for gout at the time of Hippocrates, who wrote that the best natural remedy for gout was an attack of dysentery. The Greek physician was referring to the unpleasant side effects of colchicine, which produces nausea, vomiting, and diarrhea, and in large doses was a popular strategy in ancient Greece for disposing of one's enemies. In small doses, colchicine interferes with the inflammatory reaction to the tiny, needle-like crystals of sodium urate, which cause severe pain, most often in the big toe or sometimes in the heel, ankles, or instep. Although gout was formerly associated with long-term overindulgence in food and drink, it is now known to be caused by excessive amounts of uric acid that form crystal deposits rather than being eliminated by the kidneys. *Warning:* Colchicine is not a drug to be used for self-medication; it is poisonous to the central nervous system and the kidneys, and an overdose can be fatal.

Other traditional remedies for rheumatoid complaints include plants containing salicylic acid such as wintergreen, willow, meadowsweet, and aspen leaves; tea made with the shoots of yucca, a member of the lily family that grows in the desert and resembles a cactus; hot baths with chamomile or wild thyme added; arnica compresses; applications of the oils of juniper, calamus, angelica, or henbane; salve containing nutmeg; and hot packs of seeds gathered from hay flowers (sweet clover). Wild grain was also employed by the American Indians in vapor baths.

Horseradish is governed by Mars . . . the eating frequently and in quantities at table is good against rheumatism. As an external application in rheumatic affections, there are few remedies to compare with the juice of Horseradish. It will also relieve palsy.

Culpeper and Simmonite

Steam baths in general were a favorite remedy for many ills, and the Amerinds burned a variety of plants including the aromatic branches of sagebrush, juniper, and creosote bush.

Perhaps the most charming remedy of all is the famous Hungary water, reputedly given by a beggar to Elizabeth, Queen of Hungary, who suffered from paralysis. Supposedly the queen recovered the use of her limbs after they were rubbed every day with this miraculous fluid. The following recipe is recorded by Eleanor Sinclair Rohde in *A Garden of Herbs*:

> Take to every gallon of Brandy, or clean Spirits, one handful of rosemary, one handful of Lavender. I suppose the handfuls to be about a Foot long a-piece; and these Herbs must be cut in Pieces about an Inch long. Put these to infuse in the Spirits, and with them, about one handful of Myrtle, cut as before. When this was stood three Days, distil it, and you will have the finest Hungary Water that can be.

The oils of rosemary and lavender, which would be released in alcohol, are warming and stimulating and well-suited for a home-made liniment, which Hungary water actually is. Other ingredients for homemade liniment are the oils of camphor, peppermint, euca-lyptus, wintergreen, clove, and oregano, and tincture of cayenne pepper. If you prefer a mixture that is not oily, steep the leaves of the herbs and/or the ground spices in rubbing alcohol for a couple of weeks—about a handful of the leaves and a teaspoon of the ground pepper or cloves.

For strains and bruises, cold com-presses of arnica have long been a pop-ular remedy and are recommended by a variety of sources. Arnica grows in the mountains and resembles a small sun-flower, for which it is often mistaken. The medicinal properties—antibiotic, anti-inflammatory, and analgesic—of this plant are concentrated in the flower. Ar-nica is not to be taken internally, be-cause it irritates the gastrointestinal system and can be toxic. Some sources advise against using arnica if the skin is broken: it may cause a rash. Dr. Bush, however, writes: "Infusion of arnica, 20 parts of the flowers to 100 of water, is thought by some to be the best preparation for local use, as it never excites dermatitis,

*M*ore than a flirtation, almost a religion, the lily of the valley is celebrated on the first of May.
From Flowers and Fruit, *a collection of writings by Colette*

probably by reason of its being devoid of the Essential Oil and the insoluble principle arnicine."

Other folk remedies for sprains include poultices of comfrey or chopped raw onion, or a hot bath followed by a rubdown with spirits of juniper, angelica, calamus, or marijuana. Marijuana tincture, which was official early in the twentieth century, was often used as a painkiller and anesthetic.

In my opinion, the best way to reap the benefits of the herbs mentioned in this chapter is to grow them yourself. Not only are you assured of a continuous supply of herbs grown and harvested under optimum conditions, but you are engaged in one of the most cheering activities I know, one that does immeasurable good for the health of the spirit as well as the body. Waiting for the first green blades to push up from the earth in spring is surely one of the most optimistic of moments. To garden is to be constantly active. With so much life around us, how can we ever feel old?

Chapter 11

The Barefoot Doctor's Hair Restorer, a Favorite Herb of the Cherokees, and Other Folk Remedies for Skin Wounds, Infections, and Diseases

Beauty is not a characteristic we ordinarily require of a bodily organ—except for the skin. Our largest organ, a complex mechanism consisting of fat, blood vessels, glands, and nerve endings, the skin is our first line of defense against germs, chemicals, and extremes of heat and cold, a primary source of information about the environment, and the most visible indicator of our health and emotions.

As anybody who has binged on chocolate or french fries, or flushed, paled, or perspired when excited or distressed has discovered, the thin layer of cells that is our epidermis is the first to expose our otherwise secret emotions and our dietary sins. Nonetheless, the skin is relatively easy to care for, and the array of herbs that can heal most skin injuries and diseases is actually quite small. An ounce or so of arnica, comfrey, goldenseal, myrrh, oak bark, and shepherd's purse, and an aloe vera plant will serve for most purposes.

Aloe vera is one of my favorite household remedies. One plant that was no taller than my index finger when I bought it from my local supermarket a year ago is now too big to fit on my windowsill; another, grown from tiny cuttings, will provide enough gel for my first aid and cosmetic needs for perhaps a year. If I should burn myself when I am cooking, I need only slice off a section of leaf, split it open, and rub the gel on the burn. Relief is instant, and there

Aloe-Aloe vera

is no scarring afterward. The gel is also wonderful for sunburn. Mild cases heal overnight. So powerful is aloe vera's burn-healing property that it was used for treating radiation burns in World War II. The gel is also astringent and antibacterial—qualities I have appreciated in a variety of situations. A bit rubbed on my face tones, tightens, and freshens the skin; under my arms, it makes an excellent deodorant; liquefied, it can be used for treating yeast infections. I have also given the fresh gel to a friend who applied it to a wretched case of poison ivy; it dried up his itchy blisters in no time. Carol Kent Miller, in her book *Aloe Vera,* describes laboratory studies in which a 70 percent solution of aloe vera killed 91 to 97 percent of staph and strep germs. Also active against fungi, a 50 percent solution of aloe vera kills yeast cells and is effective in treating athlete's foot and herpes. In addition, the gel is said to be effective as an insect repellent and sunscreen. You will find other uses for aloe vera, which the American Indians aptly named "medicine plant," listed in Chapter 8, on the gastrointestinal system. Only the fresh gel is active against bacteria, so it is essential to grow the plant yourself. It is inexpensive, widely available, and very easy to grow; see Chapter 18 for details.

Another favorite household remedy is comfrey. A rather homely resident of damp meadows all over North America and Europe, the sturdy root and broad, hairy leaves of comfrey have been used since antiquity for lung and skin problems, including bleeding, and for setting broken bones. Comfrey, like many herbs, contains appreciable amounts of tannin, an astringent that forms a protective film over wounds, promoting healing. The plant is also high in mucilage, a slippery substance composed of sugars, which swells in water and soothes inflammation. The most important ingredient, though, is allantoin, which stimulates new cell growth. Currently used in medical practice for healing leg ulcers caused by varicose veins, allantoin is also a major ingredient in certain cosmetic skin creams used for restoring youthful freshness to the skin. According to Richard Lucas, comfrey has also healed cancerous growths on the skin.

Comfrey-Symphytum officinale

I witnessed an interesting demonstration of comfrey's healing powers a couple of years ago after I intercepted my older son, Toby, who was on his way to the drugstore to buy a tube of cortisone for his eczema. Toby has suffered from occasional outbreaks of eczema since infancy; this time it had settled on his eyelids in red, sore-looking patches. After relating a few things I had read about cortisone's unwelcome side effects, including possible cataracts, I persuaded him to give comfrey a try.

For the next two days, Toby made a cup of tea using two teabags of comfrey leaves, and steeped the tea for ten minutes. Three times each day, he drank the tea and used the cooled teabags as compresses on his eyelids, leaving them on for twenty minutes. By the end of the first day the inflammation had subsided; by the end of the second it was gone. He returned to college with a supply of comfrey and reports instant relief from eczema flare-ups by using what he refers to as my "witch cure."

Shortly after this modest medicinal victory, I began reading up on the troubling matter of carcinogens in herbs. As I wrote in an earlier chapter, comfrey contains pyrrolizidine alkaloids, which caused liver cancer in rats. Although there have not, as far as I know, been published reports of human cancers caused by ingesting comfrey, I would not advocate taking it internally on a regular basis. As for occasional medical use, people have used comfrey and other plants that may contain carcinogens for centuries with no ill effects. Generally speaking, cancer is caused by exposure to toxic substances over a long period of time. Moreover, it has been noted that the pyrrolizidine alkaloids, which are concentrated in the roots and young leaves in comfrey, are harmful only when liver enzymes alter them so they become toxic. Consequently, an external application of the leaves should have no harmful side effects. Personally, I limit my use of comfrey to external use and only for problems that can not be treated just as well by an alternative plant. One possible alternative is the comfrey produced by the Minnesota firm listed in "Resources," which claims to sell only alkaloid-free leaves which they grow themselves using a special process.

Another possible treatment for eczema, as well as psoriasis, is feverfew, which acts as an antihistamine when applied externally or taken internally. Insect bites can also be treated with feverfew.

Weiss favors compresses of decocted oak bark as the best treatment for eczema and psoriasis, presumably because the high tannin content helps to dry up the sores. In the Himalayas, eczema is treated with poultices of marijuana leaves.

With a cut or wound, the most immediate problem is to stop the bleeding, and the herbs to use are those that act to cause clotting of the blood. Shepherd's purse, a common weed that grows in fields and wastelands and bears a triangular pod shaped like an old-fashioned shepherd's purse, is considered one of the best herbs for staunching blood. Fresh leaves, or a poultice of dried leaves, can be applied directly to the wound. Lady's mantle, which grows wild in woods and fields, can be used in a similar fashion. Other readily available herbs useful in stopping bleeding are discussed in Chapter 14, "Herbal First Aid."

When treating wounds and sores, it is essential to use a substance that promotes healing and kills bacteria. Aloe vera, of course, does both; so do myrrh and goldenseal, which are astringent and antiseptic. The use of myrrh dates back at least as far as ancient Egypt, where it was used for embalming. Reputed to be one of the gifts the Three Wise Men gave the baby Jesus, myrrh was scarcely less precious during the time of the Crusades, when it became a major item of commerce. I have gotten extraordinary results by sprinkling dry, powdered myrrh directly on an open wound: about fifteen minutes after dusting myrrh on the raw, oozing surface, the wound dried up and a protective crust was formed which left no scar after the wound was healed. Powdered goldenseal root can be used in the same way. An ingredient in patent medicines a century ago, goldenseal was a favorite herb of the Cherokee Indians, who used it for a variety of purposes; today it is used in India for treating lip and mouth sores. Generally disregarded by the medical profession, goldenseal remains a popular folk remedy for treating both internal and external disorders, particularly those affecting the mucous membranes.

A chamomile poultice is anti-inflammatory and heals and soothes wounds and ulcers. Oil of chamomile, which acts as both an anti-bacteria and a fungicide, is said to be used in treating staph infections.

Echinacea, an antiseptic and antiviral, helps heal and disinfect cuts and wounds. Good when used in combination with goldenseal and myrrh, this humble weed of the western plains is also said to be effective against herpes. As with many herbs, when you are using echinacea externally, it's a good idea to drink the tea at the same time to reinforce the effect.

Other herbs that have traditionally been employed to heal wounds are marigold tincture, hops, sweet gum leaves, gotu kola, raw potato, and Saint-John's-wort. Garlic, and, in the West where it grows, creosote bush, are applied to kill skin bacteria.

Boils, in both popular and medical theory, are thought to be an expression of inner impurity, so the recommended treatment is to clean out the system with mild laxatives and "blood purifying" plants. The herbs recommended for such purifications are, as you might anticipate from reading previous chapters, our old friends the nettle and the dandelion. Sarsaparilla, another "blood purifying" herb, was popular in folk medicine for skin diseases—and its efficacy has been confirmed by clinical studies. The British *Herbal Pharmacopoeia* lists the rhizome of the white pond lily, which is astringent, demulcent, and antibacterial, as a poultice for boils.

For warts, which are caused by a viral infection, folk remedies include aloe vera, garlic, raw potato, green walnuts, and the white juice from dandelion leaves.

Most skin infections and allergies are accompanied by pain and itching. Currently, scientists are making some interesting discoveries about capsaicin, the pungent substance in red pepper. In one study, patients suffering severe pain after recovering from shingles experienced relief after applying cream containing capsaicin for a period of time. Apparently the peppery substance first stimulates then depletes substance P, a chain of amino acids released by the nerve endings and thought to be responsible for the pain. Capsaicin has a similar effect on histamines, which cause the inflammation resulting from allergies, first increasing, then decreasing their release— indicating that a dash of red pepper may help both itchy and painful skin conditions.

Finally, there is the skin condition that is more injurious to the pride than anything else: alopecia, or more commonly, hair loss. The causes of this condition are various—genetic, dietary, hormonal, chemical, emotional, or the result of an illness, but the results are the same: hair on the head and other parts of the body that thins, recedes, and may disappear altogether.

People go to great lengths and considerable expense to restore their crowning glory, often to no avail. Stimulating the circulation by massage can help in some instances. Rubbing the scalp with burdock root oil or an infusion of nettles is said to be helpful, but the most promising hair regenerator to date seems to be Dr. Zhao Zhangguang's 101 Hair Regeneration Liniment.

Dr. Zhao, who lives in Beijing, was formerly one of China's "barefoot doctors" and trained in herbal medicine. Dr. Zhao's formula, discovered by a combination of trial and error and serendipity, supposedly has a 90 percent success rate with the more than one thousand people who have used it. Zhao's secret is a careful blending of ginseng, the root of membranous milk vetch, Chinese angelica, a variety of aconitum, dried ginger, walnut meat, safflower, the root of red-rooted salvia, a psoralea, and alcohol. If you are patient, you could experiment with this combination, and you might come up with something that works. The less ambitious could wait until the product finds its way to America, as it very well may have done by the time this book is published.

At the beginning of this chapter I mentioned that the skin is one bodily organ we expect to be beautiful as well as healthy, and then went on to enumerate a few of the epidermal misfortunes that can befall us. Most of the time, though, we concern ourselves with keeping our skin soft, moist, and glowing. In the chapter on cosmetics, you will read about how some of the great beauties through the ages have contrived to do just this—without the dubious blessings of modern chemistry.

Chapter 12

Onions for Your Ear,
Flax for Your Eye,
and Twigs for Your Teeth

Dear to the hearts of the old English herbalists was a tiny herb "not above two handsful high," writes Gerard, with flowers "small and white, sprinkled and powdered on the inner side, [and] with yellow and purple spekes mixed therewith." The name for this herb—eyebright—refers to its reputation for preserving and restoring the eyesight, but possibly also implies that one needs bright eyes to find its modest and tiny flower, which is almost hidden by the surrounding leaves.

Gerard recommends powdered eyebright, an equal quantity of fennel, and a dash of mace for protecting the eyesight; used in poultices the mixture is said to clear dimming vision. Half a teaspoonful of the powdered herb mixed with one-fourth part powdered mace, taken before breakfast with a cup of wine would, he asserted, "taketh away all hurts from the eyes, comfort the memorie, and cleareth the sight." I'm not so sure that a cup of wine before breakfast would result in clearsightedness, but, if nothing else, this last recipe would seem to testify to the hardiness of the British constitution in those days—as well as to the leisurely ambiance of the times.

Herbalists still recommend eyebright compresses for eye inflammation, injuries, and styes, with eyebright infusions taken internally at the same time. Although it has not been established exactly how or why, they claim it works. For inflammation caused by infection, either chamomile or fennel, which are both anti-inflammatory and antimicrobial, are mixed with eyebright. Chamomile can be irritating if one has sensitive eyes or allergies and should not be taken if either of these conditions is present. Personally, I would rely on fennel, which I find very soothing and often use for eyestrain, an occupational hazard for those of us who spend our days reading and writing.

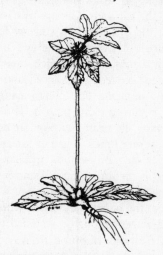

Goldenseal-Hydrastus canadensis

Goldenseal, as you read in the preceding chapter, was the favorite herb of the Cherokee Indians. A resident of shady woods and damp meadows, goldenseal is found in Connecticut and states southward. The plant bears a solitary greenish-white flower, followed by the appearance of an inedible berry resembling the raspberry. The name refers to small scars on the surface of the root, which resemble the seals people once used for fastening letters and documents. The root, which is the medicinal part, contains berberine, also found in Oregon grape; hydrastine, from which the plant receives its botanical name; and canadine, a yellow dye used by the Cherokees for coloring cloth. The root also yields tannic acid, which is astringent

An Herbal Pharmacopoeia

and healing. Antiseptic and healing to the mucous membranes, gold-enseal was used as a decoction for compresses applied to sore eyes (one teaspoon of the root to one cup water) and as a gargle for sore throat. The Blackfoot tribes favored the leaves and flowers of yarrow as an eyewash, while the Winnebagos made a decoction of the whole plant for earache.

If you have access to a garden, you can avail yourself of two remedies that have been used successfully in getting rid of styes— the fresh juice of parsley leaves or of marigold petals. If you don't happen to have a garden in your vicinity, try hot compresses of chamomile tea mixed with infusions of eyebright and fennel.

One nuisance we all have experienced at one time or another is getting some foreign material—grit, perhaps, or an eyelash—caught on the surface of the eye. A co-worker whose mother is Indian told me that his mother's strategy for dealing with this problem was to place a flax seed in the eye. I later read with great interest that a similar practice was once common in domestic medicine: A mois-tened flax seed was placed under the eyelid, which was then closed for a moment. The foreign matter would stick to the seed and could be removed along with it. The seeds of clary sage, or chia, a plant botanically related to sage, are both mucilaginous and were also used in former times to gather foreign matter from the eye.

A far more serious problem, which afflicts many people as they age, is the formation of cataracts, a thickening of the lens of the eye. The name for this condition, which can result in blindness, comes from the blurring of vision, which makes it appear as though objects were seen through a waterfall or cataract. Cataracts may be caused by faulty nutrition or the way food is metabolized in the body, by certain drugs such as cortisone, or by exposure to solar radiation, which can "cook" the lens. Before microwave technology had ad-vanced to the point where some of the harzards were removed, microwave ovens were also blamed for some cataract formation. The usual treatment for cataracts is surgery, which is said to be a rela-tively minor operation. My father, however, would be unlikely to agree with this estimation, having lost the sight in one eye after three operations—the first to remove the cataract and the next two to attempt to repair the irreparable damage caused by the first.

While herbal remedies abound for most disorders, reliable scientific literature yields relatively few for cataracts. These include supplements of vitamin C to prevent oxidation, thought to be an element in thickening the lens of the eye exposed to strong sunlight over a long period of time; bathing the eyes three or four times daily in a cooled infusion of rue and comfrey (one quarter-teaspoon each to one cup of water); and the eyebright treatments (with the possible exception of the wine cure) mentioned at the beginning of this chapter.

Glaucoma, which is caused by an accumulation of fluid behind the eyeball, can be relieved by smoking marijuana, which helps dry up fluids. Some glaucoma sufferers have even managed to obtain governmental permission to grow marijuana for this particular medical purpose.

While herbs used for eye conditions are relatively few, such is not the case for throat and mouth conditions, probably because the healing properties needed are astringents, antiseptics, and demulcents (soothing materials), which are widely distributed throughout the plant kingdom.

Garlic oil, which is antiseptic, can be taken internally to kill the germs that cause sore throat. A number of herbs, used either alone or in combination, are good to use for a gargle. Goldenseal and myrrh are astringent and antiseptic, serving to fight infection and soothe inflamed tissue. Tormentil and oak bark are also highly astringent, due to large amounts of tannin. Fennel and chamomile are antiseptic and anti-inflammatory. An ancient Chinese remedy is to use the spores of the puffball mushroom. The mucilaginous properties of both mallow and comfrey are very soothing—good to add to sore throat mixtures. Lemon juice, high in vitamin C and astringent, is an old-fashioned home remedy for sore throat and colds. All of these mixtures are much improved by the addition of honey, which is antiseptic and soothing.

You might want to experiment with herbal mixtures when you are making a gargle, including antiseptics, astringents, and demulcents for the full effect. Other herbs you might want to add are sage, an astringent that also helps clear the respiratory passages of mucus; hyssop, a member of the mint family frequently cultivated for medicinal purposes; and horehound, an old folk remedy for coughs, sore throat, and fever. Horehound candy is an old-fashioned treat that was formerly a staple item in drugstores and can still be found in some today.

For gum disease, astringents are often used to shrink the inflamed tissue, but use of herbs alone is not sufficient because herbs do not treat the underlying problem—an accumulation of plaque and then bacteria, which eventually causes the gums to pull away from the teeth. For seven thousand years and more, primitive peoples have had an interesting and inexpensive way of preventing this problem; the method is still used in Africa and southern Asia and in the American Ozark and Appalachian regions. The instrument involved is the "chewing stick." Chewing sticks are twigs or branches, about eight inches long, that have been washed and soaked in water or perhaps whiskey, then frayed at the ends to form brushlike instruments that are used for cleaning the teeth. The toothbrushing, which is very thorough and takes about ten minutes, removes plaque and keeps gums healthy. In countries where the use of chewing sticks is widespread, there is a low incidence of tooth decay and the teeth are retained longer. Cleaning sticks are commonly made of materials that are high in natural flourides, resins, and tannins; some are also antibacterial. The most popular materials for cleaning sticks are dogwood, witch hazel, and persimmon.

For those of us who live in cities and are unable to pluck a toothbrush from the wild, the best herbs to use for gum problems are goldenseal, myrrh, and garlic. Garlic kills bacteria in the gum pockets and also supposedly removes plaque—although it doesn't do much for sweetening your breath. Goldenseal and myrrh can be used as a dentifrice—I sprinkle powdered myrrh on my toothbrush, on top of the toothpaste. Some dentists now also prescribe myrrh tincture for patients with gum disease.

Other herbs that are used to "fasten the teeth" by treating the gums are ginseng extract, applied directly to the gum pockets; European goldenrod, chewed or decocted for a mouthwash; and the leaves and roots of the strawberry plant. Strawberry juice was used by the Iroquois as a dentifrice.

Over the years, a variety of folk remedies have been used to ease toothache, including the leaves of cedar, cypress, tulip tree, lemon balm, sage, calamus, sweet fern, and alder; cinquefoil, prickly ash (called "toothache tree") bark; garlic cloves; the roots of any California poppy; star anise seeds; and nutmeg oil. The most common household remedy today is clove oil, a good one because it anesthetizes the tooth. Peppermint oil does, too.

For chancre and mouth sores, an old New England remedy is the root of goldthread—also called chancreroot or mouthroot—a small woodland plant that grows as far north as Laborador and as far south as Maryland. In former times the root was steeped in an eggshell, perhaps to extract the calcium. Goldenseal, myrrh, and oak bark are also used for oral infections, the last for its astringency, the first two as antiseptics and astringents.

Although earache caused by hardened earwax is seldom a major medical problem, it can certainly ruin your day. When I was growing up, our household remedy was olive oil, gently heated and placed in the ear with an eyedropper. Other cultures have used the oils of safflower or sesame to soften the earwax. Adding crushed garlic to the oil serves to kill any bacteria. Pumpkin, papaya, and lemon juice have also been used as folk remedies in various cultures. Some authorities also swear by the virtues of a baked onion applied to the outside of the ear and held in place with some bandaging material.

The eyes, the ears, and the mouth, together with the skin, are our main sensory organs and provide our primary link with the outside world. Happily, nature is generous with plants for maintaining their good health. Some, such as the tiny eyebright, grow no farther than a nearby field; a few, such as yarrow, are as familiar as our own backyards; others, such as garlic, are as convenient to us as the kitchen pantry. These helpful remedies, so close at hand, remind us of our link to the natural world—even as they keep us healthy enough to enjoy it.

An Herbal Pharmacopoeia

Chapter 13

Garlic and Other Herbal Anticarcinogens

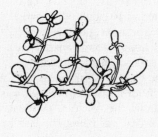

At the beginning of this book I mentioned some of the findings during the past two decades regarding carcinogens in foods. Less is known about naturally occurring anticarcinogens, but scientists are actively pursuing the study of herbs and other plants in hopes of finding new preventives and cures. Interestingly, some foods that contain suspected carcinogens also contain substances that may help fight certain forms of cancer. Comfrey, for example, used as a leafy green vegetable as well as a tea, contains chemicals that have produced tumors in laboratory rats; however, in studies conducted by the National Institutes of Health, other chemicals contained in comfrey, notably *beta sitasterol*, have proved active against some cancers of the glandular system and the lungs. Richard Lucas, in *Nature's*

Medicines, recounts a number of astonishing recoveries attributed to comfrey, from ulcerations and gout to a facial cancer.

I also mentioned that nitrogen-containing alkaloids, found in such highly nutritious foods as beets and spinach, are converted during digestion into nitrates, which are proven carcinogens. More recent evidence indicates that these nitrogen-containing alkaloids may also be anticarcinogenic. The American Council on Science and Health, for example, mentions that "a very recent report found an *inverse* relation between the incidence of stomach cancers and the nitrate/nitrite content of the patient's saliva." Also, studies being done on plants growing in the tropical rain forests of Costa Rica suggest that some nitrogen-containing alkaloids that mimic sugar may help prevent malignant cells from spreading to secondary sites in the body by interfering with their ability to form glycoproteins, essential nutrients in these cells.

In laboratory studies flavonoids, flavoring agents in buckwheat, peaches, cherries, and other stone fruits, berries, and other fruits and vegetables, were proved safe to eat; moreover, at a 1987 conference in France, new evidence came to light suggesting that flavonoids may actually be a new class of anticancer agents, protecting against viral infections and inhibiting the production and action of enzymes that play an important role in producing leukemia cells.

Bruce Ames, the California biochemist who led the inquiry into carcinogens in foods, advises eating a well-rounded diet as the most reliable way of avoiding cancer. Current evidence shows that a normal, well-balanced diet already contains substantial amounts of anticarcinogens: vitamins A (particularly beta-carotene), C, and E; purines, which are widely distributed in plant and animal tissue; and selenium, found in tuna, all show anticancer activity.

Garlic, one of the most useful remedies in the herbal pharmacopoeia, might well qualify as a panacea because of the wide range of disorders it can be used to treat. Recently, in an experiment at the Akbar Clinic, a private hospital and research center in Panama City, Florida, volunteers who were tested shortly after they ate garlic, either raw or in capsules, produced white blood cells that destroyed 159 percent more tumor cells than white cells taken from a control group who did not eat garlic. The results of this experiment would have been no surprise to Hippocrates, who prescribed garlic for uterine cancer. Use of garlic as a cancer treatment goes back at least as far as 1500 B.C., when it was listed in the *Ebers Papyrus*.

Purslane, which you have met again and again in these pages, may be another addition to the anticarcinogen list. Long used in folk medicine to treat inflammations, purslane contains generous amounts of omega-3 fatty acids. Primarily found in fish oils, omega-3 acids lower the risk of heart disease and may help prevent cancer.

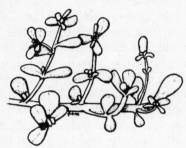

Purslane-Portulaca oleracea

Another herb that shows promise in treating or preventing cancer is Pao d'arco, long used as a folk remedy for Hodgkin's disease and leukemia, as well as cancers of the esophagus, head, intestines, lung, prostate, and tongue. Some constituents of Pao d'arco have been active against cancer in clinical tests. James Duke, in his *Handbook of Medicinal Herbs,* reports that he has received "many unsolicited testimonials of Pao d'arco cancer cures." National Institutes of Health researchers have also validated the status of tansy, another folk remedy, as anticarcinogenic. At the New York University Medical Center, two chemicals in Saint-John's-wort, a wild herb used for centuries in treating wounds, chest colds, and urinary complaints, has inhibited the spread of the AIDS virus in laboratory tests.

Herbs that are already being used to treat leukemia in children include mistletoe and Madagascar periwinkle. Other herbs that may inhibit the formation of cancer cells include *Maesa lanceolata,* an African shrub that produces orange berries containing maesanin, a substance similar to vitamin K, which also has antibiotic properties; plumyew; rattlebrush; coffeeweed, a poisonous legume that contains sesbanimide, a cancer inhibiter; and Pacific yew, which yields taxol, an anticarcinogen used in treating ovarian cancer. Researchers funded by the National Cancer Institute are studying avelaz, chaparral, gold-enseal, iscador, and winter tea.

For more information on this important subject you can consult *Plants Used Against Cancer: A Survey,* by J. L. Hartwell, published by Quarterman Press in Lincoln, Massachusetts, or write NAPRALERT, Program for Collaborative Research in the Pharmaceutical Sciences, College of Pharmacy, University of Illinois at Chicago, P.O. Box 6998, Chicago, Illinois 60680. Funded by grants from several government sources, NAPRALERT maintains a data base of information about the chemistry of plants, including antitumor activity. This information is available for a fee to scientists and industrial and academic institutions.

How long it will be before any of these herbs make their way into the mainstream battle against cancer is hard to predict. Many natural substances, such as laetrile, have been tried and proved in-effective. In the meantime, although the facts are not all in about what we should or should not eat, I am somewhat reassured by knowing that generations of hearty eaters have enjoyed, survived, and even thrived. Eating, after all, is the first basic drive we satisfy on coming into this world, and I suspect that our relationship to this life-giving act has much to do with how we get on in the world—in ways we may never fully understand.

Chapter 14

Herbal First Aid

It's 2 A.M. and the drugstore is closed, or you're on a camping trip and miles from civilization. Suddenly the baby has colic or teething pains, your stomach starts acting up, you cut yourself and the bleeding won't stop, or—too late—you discover there was poison ivy lurking in the leaves you raked this morning. Your medicine chest or knapsack doesn't offer much by way of remedy. What to do?

From where I sit writing this chapter, in a forest of pine and birch at the edge of a lake in Maine, where I live for part of the year, I can, without rising from my chair, spot remedies for headache, cramps and spasms, coughs and sore throat, insomnia, bleeding, stomach complaints, poisoning, and heart failure. A few yards away, in a clearing behind the cabin where I am staying, grow breath fresheners, wildwood teas, a remedy for diarrhea, and a sure cure for poison ivy. A less casual inventory than I am inclined to make right now would no doubt yield palliatives, if not cures, for just about every ill that flesh is heir to, as the American Indians discovered long ago.

Not everyone lives surrounded by woods and fields, but some healing plants flourish just about anywhere. They grow in vacant lots near my Brooklyn residence, even between the cracks in the pavements. If you have a back yard, you will surely find some growing there; for minor complaints, you may need to walk no farther than your kitchen spice shelf.

Perhaps the baby is crying. The most likely causes are colic or restlessness. The remedy could be one that only a few hours ago added a piquant touch to your fish or salad—dill. The name comes from the Saxon word *dillon*, meaning "to lull," and that is how Saxon mothers used this herb: to expel intestinal gas, soothe an upset stomach, or lull the baby to sleep. A decoction of dill seeds boiled in one cup water and fed to the baby by the teaspoonful every half hour is recommended by some herbalists for relieving colic and allowing the baby—and you—to rest. This decoction is also said to increase the milk flow in nursing mothers, so you might give it a try if hunger is baby's problem. In the Carribean, a decoction of anise seeds (one teaspoon to a cup of water) is used for the same purposes. *Warning:* Use only anise seed obtained from a trusted herb dealer, not star anise, which in some supermarket products may be adulterated and unwholesome or even poisonous.

My personal favorite for gas and indigestion grows at the edge of the lake a few yards away: peppermint. If you are camping in the woods, look for peppermint in wet places, particularly beside streams. The scent of the crushed leaves is unmistakable. Peppermint oil has the same medicinal properties as the leaves and is also antiseptic and pain-relieving, good to have on hand for cuts and wounds and also as an insect repellent. A few drops on a piece of cotton inserted into the cavity of an aching tooth will ease the pain, although oil of clove is better known as a toothache remedy. Like most aromatics, clove oil also corrects flatulence.

Goldenrod, peppermint, and wintergreen make tasty and aromatic wildwood teas. Chewing fresh wintergreen or peppermint leaves will freshen your breath and leave a clean, minty taste.

Ginger, like most of the herbs we use for seasonings, is also good for stomach upsets. If you season generously with herbs and spices, you can take advantage of their digestive properties.

Perhaps the most versatile member of the mint family, and sure to be on your spice shelf, is thyme. Its vagabond sibling, known familiarly as wild mountain thyme or mother of thyme, grows abundantly in the wild and can be easily recognized by its blue or purple flowers, which resemble mint blossoms, and the square stems and opposite leaves characteristic of mint. Each year, I always harvest a quantity of wild thyme, which grows in profusion near the Hudson River.

detail of flower

Thyme is one of those general practitioner plants, good for an assortment of minor medical emergencies. Like its mint-family relatives, thyme is calmative and carminative, good for colic and the jitters. Thymol, a constituent of oil of thyme, is a powerful antiseptic. Once used in hospitals

Mother of Thyme or
Wild Thyme-Thymus serpyllum

as a germicide, thymol is also used in toothpastes and mouthwashes. A strong tea made from the leaves of either wild or domestic thyme can be used as a wash for wounds and mouth infections and to expel worms.

Nor does this exhaust the uses of this versatile plant. You can also use thyme to treat diarrhea and indigestion. Taken hot, the tea will help you sweat out a cold, soothe a sore throat, and bring up mucus if the cold has settled in your chest; added to your bath water, thyme will ease the aches and pains of the flu and help you sleep. Mother of thyme, as the name suggests, has a long tradition of treating female complaints, especially painful menstruation.

Thyme is one herb, however, that must be treated with great respect. Never take it with fats, oils, or alcohol, which may cause the thymol to be absorbed and stored in the liver, kidneys, and lungs and cause poisoning. An overdose can irritate the urinary and respiratory systems; large doses can paralyze the central nervous system.

Another hardworking kitchen physician is one I have already discussed in earlier chapters: garlic. If you go camping, be sure to take a head of garlic along. Not only will it add distinction to your freeze-dried camping meals, it can be used for coughs, colds, sore throat, constipation, diarrhea and stomach upsets, as a disinfectant for cuts and wounds, and a quick source of energy.

If you don't have any garlic on hand, onion will perform most of the same culinary and medicinal functions. Wild onion is easy to find in woods and fields and is easily identified by its quill-like leaves with the shape and scent of chive. In spring you can snip off the tops for a camp stew; in autumn you can dig up the bulbs. Use a spoon for this operation so the tops won't break off without the bulb.

The American Indians used onions as a cure for croup, asthma, and earache. To bring down a fever, they laid slices of raw onion on the soles of the feet; to treat the flu, they covered the patient with raw onions, then wrapped him in a blanket—certainly an incentive to a speedy recovery. If you don't mind smelling like a tossed salad, you can also rub on the juice to repel insects.

When you feel a cold coming on, you can try a remedy that was popular with the Romany gypsies: basil tea, which has a warm, spicy taste with a hint of licorice. Your basil tea will be even more effective if you add a slice or a pinch of ginger, recommended by Chinese herbalists for the early stages of a cold because of its warming effect.

The cough remedy I referred to at the beginning of the chapter is white pine. American Indians drank tea made from the inner bark or from the young shoots of the tree to relieve cough and congestion. In the winter, when fresh fruit were in short supply, infusions of pine needles provided a much-needed source of vitamin C.

If you are hiking in California woodlands, you are likely to find two very powerful cough remedies close to hand. One is eucalyptus, which gives the California forests their characteristic fragrance. Eucalyptus leaves should not be taken internally, but you can boil them and inhale the vapor for instant relief of sinus and lung congestion. Yerba santa, which grows in the mountains, is one of the very best cough and cold remedies. You need only two or three leaves of this "holy plant" to make an infusion for coughs, colds, and fevers. If you are not a Californian, buy some of the dried herb to have on hand during cold and flu season.

While headaches, colds, and gastrointestinal upsets can be uncomfortable, they are usually not very serious and can go untreated, if necessary, until next day. Cuts and wounds, on the other hand, need immediate attention. If you live outside the city, it is likely that a very effective herbal bandage grows outside your door: plantain. The Indian name for this plant means "white man's footstep," referring to the fact that the first white settlers inadvertently carried the seeds to this country in their clothing or on the fur of animals. The English name may have been suggested by the spire-shaped seedhead that rises from

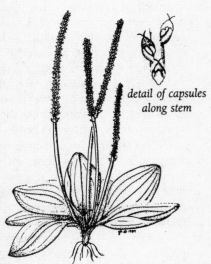

detail of capsules along stem

Common, or Broad-leaved Plantain— Plantago major

the center of the cluster of leaves and resembles that of the banana plant or plantain. There are three varieties of plantain: lance-leaved, hoary, and broad. The last is the most common, having dark green spade-shaped leaves ribbed with strong veins. Early settlers called plantain soldier's herb and laid it over wounds to help the blood coagulate. You can take advantage of the leaves' astringency by first bruising them to release the juice, then laying them over a cut or wound to stop the bleeding.

Even more powerful as a blood stauncher is yarrow, which has been used since ancient times. During the Middle Ages, knights tucked a few stalks in their helmets when they went off to a war. The various common names for yarrow, such as soldier's wound-wort and nosebleed, indicate the high esteem in which it has been held for many centuries all over the world. Yarrow is another herb you are likely to find growing in your neighborhood or in the vicinity of your campsite. The clusters of tiny white flowers resemble Queen Anne's lace, for which yarrow is sometimes mistaken.

For external bleeding, lay bruised yarrow leaves and flowers over the wound; the bleeding should stop immediately. Drink a cup of the hot tea (one teaspoon to one cup water) to stop a nosebleed or to sweat out a cold.

Another styptic and antiseptic that has been used by such diverse cultures as the Amerindians, the Chinese, and New England farmers where I grew up, is the dried puffball mushroom. The farmers used to keep a quantity on hand for cuts and wounds and applied the mushrooms to stop bleeding and prevent infection. This is very handy knowledge if you are camping in the woods. Fresh puffballs, which in some areas grow to be as large as basketballs, are usually easy to identify and perfectly wonderful to eat; however, before you consider using this gill-less mushroom, read the warning below carefully. Puffballs will add a gourmet touch to your camping meal if you are lucky enough to find them, and the dried mushrooms, which are antibiotic, could save your life if you are seriously injured. The Chinese use them for coughs, throat infections, and suppressed menstruation as well as bleeding.

Before you consider gathering mushrooms—or any other wild plant, for that matter—you must be very sure of what it is. Some plants, es-

pecially mushrooms, are poisonous; a few are deadly, even in tiny amounts, most notably the deadly Destroying Angel, which in its early stages, before the outer membrane ruptures, can be mistaken for a puffball. A field guide to wild plants or mushrooms, with detailed descriptions and color illustrations, is essential. Many such books are designed to fit into a pocket and have waterproof covers. Once you become experienced at identification, you can begin to build your repertoire of wild herb remedies. Take small amounts of any new plant with plenty of water. This will help you avoid a bad reaction.

Astringence can also be found in a wild member of the mint family which grows in profusion in woods, lawns, and fields. Woundwort is one of the common names for *Prunella vulgaris;* self-heal and heal-all are others. I have steeped one or two of the entire herbs and found the infusion an excellent wash for wounds. The astringency also relieves sore throat and diarrhea. The brew is also said to alleviate fits and expel worms.

An excellent plant to get to know, especially if you are hiking around bogs and wet country, is sphagnum moss. The American Indians and other indigenous peoples used sphagnum for baby diapers because it is antiseptic and absorbent. These properties also make sphagnum an excellent material for bandages. In fact, during World War II, English schoolchildren collected it for just this purpose. As late as 1950, a factory in Maine used it for stuffing baby mattresses.

Another extremely valuable plant to have on hand during a domestic or camping emergency is aloe vera, which I have discussed in previous chapters. Aloe vera grows in warmer regions of the Southwest and South, and it can easily be grown on your windowsill. Take along a blade or two when you go camping to use for cuts and burns. I have also seen it work wonders with poison ivy.

If sunburn is your problem and you don't have an aloe vera around, another very effective remedy is plain old supermarket tea. A strong infusion—a couple of teaspoons or teabags to a cup of boiling water—that is cooled and applied to the skin with cotton was our household remedy in my childhood. The tannic acid, which is used in pharmaceutical preparations for sunburn, is very soothing and promotes healing. Tea with milk was also our family remedy for stomach upsets and diarrhea.

Although we seldom think of it as life-threatening, diarrhea is one of those complaints for which we pray for instant relief. Astringents in general are good because they help dry up the watery discharge. The diarrhea remedy I referred to in my woodland inventory a while back is blackberry leaves. The leaves of raspberries, blueberries, and strawberries are also good, although the most effective cure, to which my children's pediatrician introduced me, is a meal of white rice and ripe bananas.

The root of the common Floure de-luce cleane washed, and stamped with a few drops of rose-water, and laid plaisterwise upon the face of man or woman, doh in two daise at the most take away the blacknesse or blewnesse of any stroke or bruse.

Gerard on iris

Poison oak or ivy rash is another affliction you can live with, but not comfortably. Happily, the palliative for this particular itch can usually be found growing in the neighborhood of the plants that cause it. This is jewelweed, the poison ivy cure that grows up the road a piece from my woodland retreat. When in flower, the plant has delicate orange blossoms spotted with reddish brown. The mature seedheads propagate by bursting open and casting their seeds for next year's crop, a phenomenon that has prompted its other common names: touch-me-not and snapweed. As with most herbs, the best time to harvest jewelweed is before it flowers, but since the flower is the most distinguishing characteristic, most people gather the plant when it is in bloom.

When Joe, the staff artist on an environmental education project I was working on, contracted a severe case of poison ivy on his hands just before a deadline, we decided to experiment with the extensive patch of jewelweed that grew nearby. After gathering a quantity, we washed the jewelweed and put the whole plant, flowers and all, in an electric blender with about a quarter of a cup of water

An Herbal Pharmacopoeia

to make a puree. Joe smeared a layer of the green paste on his hands, then packed the rest of it into ice cube trays, which he stored in the freezer. When he needed to re-new his poultice, he thawed one of the ice cubes. For the next two or three days his hands some-what resembled those of a swamp monster, smeared with green paste as they were, but the itch was notably soothed, and after a few days the rash was completely gone. So if you, too, are allergic to poison ivy or oak, you would do well to locate a patch of jewelweed and make up a batch to have on hand when the need arises. (A more fanciful use of jewelweed is one that is practiced in India: it is said to remove insanities of children oc-casioned by the influence of a ghost.)

Jewelweed-Impatiens biflora

My late friend Euell Gibbons, who was braver about such things than I, used to immunize himself against poison ivy every spring by eating three leaves every day for three weeks, beginning when the first tiny leaves appeared. He claimed this rash experiment, which he had learned of from loggers in the Northwest, allowed him to roam the woods as he pleased all year with nary a blister from oak or ivy. Personally, I wouldn't risk Euell's immunization method—people have been hospitalized after a brush with poison ivy—or recommend it to others, but I found his story interesting. Homeo-paths prescribe a similar prophylactic, immunizing sufferers with a dilute tincture of poison ivy, which is discontinued if the patient shows any sensitivity. If you want to boost your immunity, head for the homeopath rather than the dry patch.

To close this chapter on a more cheerful note . . . I read recently that in Yalta, Soviet doctors prescribe a walk through a "healing park" on the theory that breathing the air in the seven "therapy zones" of trees can facilitate healing. Perhaps this is the best reason of all for gathering herbs outdoors; the walk to where they grow may be as healthful as any tea.

First Aid Chart

Condition	Herbs to Use	Method of Use
Infection	Aloe vera, echinacea, chamomile, garlic, hops, goldenseal, myrrh, sweet gum, white pond lily, oil of peppermint, oil of thyme (see also Antiseptics in Glossary)	Use as a wash.
Bleeding	Shepherd's purse, yarrow, plantain, horsetail, dried puffball mushroom	Apply poultice of fresh leaves or dried leaves soaked in hot water that is allowed to cool. If bleeding persists, get medical attention.
Bruises	Arnica, bay leaf, comfrey, violet, calendula, Balm of Gilead, Saint-John's-wort, oregano, blue iris	Apply cold compress or tincture externally for about 20 minutes two or three times daily.

An Herbal Pharmacopoeia

First Aid Chart

Condition	Herbs to Use	Method of Use
Burns	Aloe vera, comfrey, calendula, witch hazel, white oak bark, red currant	Apply aloe gel or cold compress of other herbs; for severe burns seek medical attention immediately.
Colic, Gas	Fennel seed, dill seed, anise seed, peppermint, spearmint, angelica, lavender, lovage, marjoram, mullein	As a decoction or infusion to be drunk.
Constipation	Senna, cascara, cucumber, apple, prune, fig, hibiscus wild daisy (see also Aperient and Laxative in Glossary)	Fruits and vegetables to be eaten with meals or as a snack; herb teas to be drunk.
Diarrhea	Blackberry, strawberry, raspberry, or blueberry leaf; tormentil, garlic, Chinese tea, purple loosetrife, woundwort (see also Astringents in Glossary)	Infuse and drink by cupful.

First Aid Chart

Condition	Herbs to Use	Method of Use
Earache	Yarrow, aloe vera, papaya, roast onion, olive oil, horehound, wormwood	Apply as poultice.
Eye—to remove foreign object	Flax seed, clary sage seed	Gently place in corner of eye, close eyelid; foreign object can be removed with seed.
Fainting	Lavender, borage, fern, valerian, ginseng, gentian, mint, rosemary	Infuse and drink by cupful.
Fever	Peruvian bark, angelica, boneset, willow, meadowsweet, wintergreen, borage, cleavers, dill, goldenseal, horehound, calendula, sage, sorrel, yarrow, elder, wormwood, black currant, catnip, Chinese ephedra	Infuse and drink by cupful.

First Aid Chart

Condition	Herbs to Use	Method of Use
Headache	Feverfew, meadow-sweet, willow, wintergreen, peppermint, yerba mate, yerba santa, basil, camphor or oil of peppermint applied externally (See also Analgesic in Glossary)	Infuse and drink; use only two or three leaves yerba santa; warm poultice
Indigestion	Peppermint, chamomile, gentian, calamus, most culinary herbs	Infuse and drink freely.
Insect Bites	Feverfew, savory, elder, goldenseal, borage, calendula, lemon balm, comfrey, witch hazel, yellow dock	Apply fresh leaves or poultice of softened dry leaves.
Insomnia, Restlessness	Valerian, skullcap, passionflower, peppermint, lemon balm, catnip, savory, chamomile, thyme, watercress, lavender (see also Sedatives in Glossary)	Infuse and drink a cup at bedtime.

First Aid Chart

Condition	Herbs to Use	Method of Use
Menstrual cramps	Chamomile, lemon balm, peppermint, mother of thyme, feverfew, motherwort (see also Analgesic and Antispasmodic in Glossary)	Infuse and drink as needed.
Nausea, vomiting	Ginger, peppermint, spearmint, anise, caraway, clove, ginseng, chamomile, raspberry leaf, goldenseal, lavender	Infuse and drink by half cupful.
Poison ivy/ poison oak	Jewelweed, white oak bark, yellow dock	Use as poultice.
Sore throat	Horehound, lemon balm, marjoram, peppermint, sage, yarrow, goldenseal, myrrh, woundwort (see also Astringents in Glossary)	Infuse and use as gargle.
Sprains	Spirits of juniper (gin), spirits of angelica, spirits of calamus, henbane oil, oregano	Apply cold compresses.

First Aid Chart

Condition	Herbs to Use	Method of Use
Sunburn	Aloe vera, Chinese tea, white oak bark, witch hazel, burnet, cucumber, comfrey	Apply aloe or cucumber directly to skin; make strong infusion of herbs and apply to skin with cotton.
Toothache	Oil of clove, peppermint, anise, marjoram, garlic, calamus root and stem, garden sage or lemon balm steeped in wine, angelica juice, tulip tree bark, prickly ash	Apply to cavity of tooth.
Wounds	Comfrey, aloe vera*, echnacea,* chamomile, Saint-John's-wort, calendula, crocus, witch hazel, garlic*, hops,* sphagnum moss (for bandage), goldenseal,* myrrh,* sweet gum resin,* water lily,* wild daisy, lady's mantle, woundswort	Use as infusion to clean wound. Apply aloe directly; use infused herb in compress or mashed herbs in poultice.

*Antiseptic

Part Three

The Herbal Kitchen

Chapter 15

Herbs in the Kitchen

Seasoning a dish with herbs or spices is a custom at least as old as civilization. Indeed, it is one that we equate with civilization. The use of particular spices, either alone or in combination, is a distinct way of expressing both a culture and a cuisine; their absence or neglect is one way of determining just how civilized a particular culture is.

The term *herb*, as I have used it here and as herbalists for centuries have used it, is very elastic, encompassing virtually everything not of animal or mineral origin that can be used for medicine, seasoning, or scent. For most cooks, a spice is any plant used for seasoning, regardless of where it comes from or how it tastes. *Larousse Gastronomique* defines a spice as an aromatic condiment that stimulates gastric juices; it includes pepper, bay leaf, and marjoram in the definition. For some cooks, though, spices are . . . well . . .

spicy, and rather sweet—the ingredients that lend their characteristic flavor to desserts: cinnamon, allspice, ginger, nutmeg, and clove; herbs, although many of them, such as basil and tarragon, are quite aromatic, are the seasonings used for flavoring soups, salads, main dishes, and other courses that come before dessert. Spices, by this definition, would be appealing to children and others with a relatively unsophisticated palate, while a taste for herbs is an acquired one. If none of these definitions clarifies the distinction between herbs and spices for you, perhaps Avonelle Day and Lillie Stuckey's definition, in *The Spice Cookbook,* will suffice: "True spices are parts of plants that usually grow in the tropics; herbs are always leaves of plants that grow in temperate zones."

In consequence, herbs, which can be gathered by the wayside or cultivated in gardens, have always been less costly, while spices, until modern transportation made them accessible to all, were rare in most parts of the world except the tropics where they grew. In former times they were often worth their weight in gold. Peppercorns, for example, were once used in trading as a substitute for money; in medieval France, a serf could buy freedom with a pound of peppercorns. The ancient Egyptians had a variety of uses for spices, including embalming. In biblical times, the Queen of Sheba brought spices as a gift to King Solomon, whom scholars believe may have gained much of his wealth by trad-

The history of the table of a nation is a reflection of the civilization of that nation. To show the changes in the order and serving of meals from century to century, to describe and comment on the progress of the French cuisine, is to paint a picture of the many stages through which a nation has evolved since the distant time when, as a weak tribe, men lived in dark caves, eating wild roots, raw fish and the still pulsating flesh of animals killed with the spear.

August Escoffier

ing in spices. In ancient Greece and Rome, spices were used to perfume the bath and the skin. The source of these precious materials was a secret closely guarded by Arab merchants who grew rich on the spice trade. Later, during the Crusades, the lure of wealth to be gained by opening trade routes with the Orient was perhaps as inspiring to the Crusaders as the prospect of reclaiming the Holy Land from the Moslems.

As every schoolchild learns, it was the search for spices that propelled Columbus from the shores of Italy, and in the New World the spice trade was a lucrative occupation. New England's first millionaire, Day and Stuckey tell us, gained much of his fortune from the pepper trade.

Spices were the stuff of legend, romance, commerce, and religion, while herbs were the mainstay of everyday life both in the infirmary and in the kitchen.

The vegetable garden, as we know it, is relatively modern and did not come into its own until after the Renaissance. Before that time, the herb garden reigned supreme, although here and there one might find a few onions or globe artichokes, which were considered herbs at that time. Indeed, the category of herbs was a broad one and included plants that today are grown in the area set aside for flowers: roses, lilies, "gillyflowers" (a variety of carnation), marigolds, poppies, peonies, and violets. The flowers, as well as the herbs, were used as stuffings or accompaniments to meats, which our ancestors consumed in vast quantities.

Cooks distributed herbal and floral bounty liberally. Salad, for example, was no mere lettuce-cucumber-tomato-avocado affair enlivened by a timid pinch or two of dried herbs and maybe a whiff of garlic; it was often a lusty celebration of young herbs, nuts, and eggs, dressed with herbal vinegars and crowned with flowers. For grand occasions such as banquets, the salad was arranged according to color in tiers surrounding a central figure. This figure, composed of paste colored with green herbs and glazed with egg yolk, might take the form of a tree or even a castle. Flowers added a delicate tint and flavor to sweet puddings, which, along with other desserts, were often served with syrups made from roses, violets, or cowslips.

Herbs and flowers were also the basis for wines, cordials, and certain nonalcoholic drinks. While elderberry or dandelion wine is about as adventurous as most contemporary home vintners get, during the sixteenth to eighteenth centuries one could sample strawberry wine (Sir Walter Raleigh's favorite cordial) or wines made from ginger, raisins, lemons, red or black currants, the sap of birch trees, turnips, quince, cherry, gooseberry, apricots, damson plums, raspberries, marigold, or saffron. Then there was sack, a white wine made from rue, fennel, and honey. Methaglin was a glorious and often potent alcoholic creation composed of honey, water, yeast, herbs, and spices. In the few recipes I have read for this drink (one calls for no less than sixteen different herbs), the choice of green ingredients seems to have been determined by what was available at the time, although rosemary and ginger seem to be constants. Sir Kenelm Digby, who put together the sixteen-herb recipe "out of sundry receipts," explains that "the strong herbs preserve the drink and make it nobler." Some years ago, at a New Year's Eve celebra-tion, I did have occasion to sample a homemade metheglin that had been lovingly aged for six months in an earthenware crock. I can attest to the potency of this remarkable beverage, the taste of which was sweet and strong, not to be taken in large quantities.

Spices, herbs, and flowers were also used to garnish and flavor the wine cup, sometimes for medicinal purposes (herbal prescriptions often stipulated that they be taken in wine), more often for the subtle flavor or scent they im-parted to the beverage, or sometimes "to comforte the heart." The blue petals of borage were most often used for this purpose.

Before the days of refrigeration, herbs and spices were often used as preservatives or to mask the off-flavor of meats that were well past their prime. Then, too, in those days when the average diet was not what we would consider well balanced but consisted largely of meats and pastries, many of

*A*lso borage is hoote and moyste in the fyrste degree, for it hathe the propertye of engendrying gladness, if it be drunk in wine. And it doth most comfort the harte, for it healpeth such wyche bee payned with the sycknes of the harte.

From First Garden Book
(the first published in
the English language)
by Thomas Hyll

the herbs and spices used to season them also aided digestion and helped dispel the flatulence occasioned by such rich fare.

In the seventeenth century, European immigrants who made the passage to America brought their enthusiasm for herb gardening to the New World. Seeds were imported from their homelands or arrived, uninvited, in the fur of animals or the straw in which they had been bedded, or clinging to travelers' clothing.

Some plants that grew wild in America were already familiar to the settlers, who used them as they had at home. The uses of others, which are native to the New World, they learned from the Indians. The most commercially important of these New World herbs was sassafras. The spicy, mucilaginous, mitten-shaped leaves are still used today for thickening gumbo, while the bark and roots were used for flavoring, especially by the root beer industry, until the 1960s when it was discovered to be carcinogenic and banned for commercial use. Sassafras bark, one of America's first export crops, was brought to England by Sir Walter Raleigh, who cornered the market—until other enterprising Englishmen began sending ships over to bring it back. As a consequence, the British market was soon flooded with this once-lucrative import and the price dropped drastically.

The repertoire of culinary herbs used in American cooking expanded with each new wave of arrivals from Northern Europe, the Mediterranean, Africa, and South America. Like her European counterpart, the American housewife copied the new recipes she had learned or discovered through experiment into family "receipt" books, later to evolve into cookbooks as we know them.

The Industrial Revolution and the development of steam transportation, which made it possible for perishable goods to be shipped back and forth across the country, brought radical changes to the ways people lived, worked, and gardened. Spices, once so precious, were widely sold at little cost in grocery stores. A few enterprising farmers grew herbs commercially. The Shakers were the first people to do so, and by the nineteenth century, herb gardening was an important source of income for them. Tomatoes and other vegetables gradually displaced herbs from the garden, and the leisurely days and evenings spent in preparing and using herbs and enjoying elaborate meals were replaced by less homely pleasures and more commercial activities. By World War II, when many housewives left home to work at jobs vacated by men who had gone to war, the kitchen hearth was no longer the center of the home or of daily life, and the "victory gardens" so vital in those days of food shortages and rationing were mostly limited to vegetables.

An appreciation of herbs and the culinary miracles they can bring about has never, of course, disappeared entirely. Those who prepare food as their profession or their pleasure have preserved and enriched the art. The back-to-the-land movement of the 1960s and 1970s and the current American obsession with what we eat and how it affects our bodies have revived an interest as old as the pyramids. So, for those who are embarking on herbal culinary adventures, here are a few notes and a few recipes to help you on your way.

General Hints About Using Herbs

For those on restricted diets, herbs provide an antidote to boredom. For example, lemon juice and/or herbs are a tasty substitute for salt. Herbal salt substitutes are now sold in stores, but you can easily make your own custom blend by reducing a mixture of your favorite herbs to a powder, using a mortar and pestle or the back of a wooden spoon. (A mortar and pestle, by the way, is a splendid tool to have on hand if you plan to get serious about herbs. A garlic press is another handy implement, and perhaps a small coffee grinder, which also grinds seeds, nuts, and spices.)

For those on reducing diets, herbs, which have a negligible number of calories, add substance to a dish, making even a limited portion more satisfying. If you are a smoker trying to cut down or quit, strongly flavored herbs and spices—especially hot ones—may relieve your craving for the taste of tobacco although they don't, of course, satisfy the craving for nicotine.

If it is cholesterol you are trying to avoid and the prospect of life without butter seems dismal, you might console yourself for the deprivation by experimenting with the oils of sesame, walnut, avocado, or olive. The last two are monosaturates and said to lower cholesterol. You can transform ordinary salad oil into a flavorful topping for vegetables, salad, pasta, and rice, or a medium for sautéing or frying, by adding peeled garlic cloves, hot peppers, or fresh herbs to the oil and steeping it on a sunny windowsill for at least a week. When the oil is flavored to your taste, strain and bottle.

The same method can be used for making flavored vinegars. If you grow your own herbs, use the flowers as well as the leaves. The flowers of purple basil, for example, tint the vinegar. At harvest time place your herbal vinegar in a sunny spot—a garden, if you have one, is perfect for this—and leave the herb-and-vinegar mixture to steep for about a month. A homemade herbal vinegar with an herbal bouquet floating inside makes a pretty gift.

The flavor and aroma of fresh herbs are far superior to dried. Fresh herbs are sold in many supermarkets and greengrocers, or you can grow them yourself. Although fresh spices are largely the privilege of those who live near where they grow, freshly grated dried spices are the next best thing. You can buy special spice graters for this purpose, or simply use the finest mesh on a cheese grater.

If you are using dried herbs, remember that they are much more concentrated than the fresh. Because they are dried, they don't yield their full flavor and aroma until they are rehydrated, so use them judiciously. If you are new to herbal cooking, use small amounts at first—a quarter to half a teaspoon to a dish that serves six. The flavor of herbs varies in intensity according to variety, method of drying, and age; too strong a flavor will overpower rather than enhance a dish.

An experienced cook uses herbs with a subtle hand, and this light touch should pervade the entire meal. A dinner composed of only highly seasoned dishes is rather like a costume made up of checked, striped, and patterned garments, each one distracting attention from the others. Instead, choose one—or at most two—foods to season, and heighten your artistry with a background of contrasting textures and flavors.

The Herbal Kitchen

The best way to learn about herbs is gradually, one at a time, the way we usually sample unfamiliar wines or teas. Descriptions of herbal qualities can do no more than suggest their scents and flavors. The flavors of tarragon, fennel, and chervil, for example, are often characterized as being like anise. They are more like anise, I suppose, than clove or marjoram, but they aren't anything like each other, or much like anise, either, for that matter, and you wouldn't use them interchangeably. Some herbs are aggressive, others are mild; some are bitter, or sharp, or biting, or sour. The way they are used is often determined and limited more by ethnic convention than anything else. An American cook, for example, would be unlikely to enrich a meat or poultry sauce with chocolate; Mexican cooks sometimes do. American cooks, as a rule, don't put allspice in salad dressing, but Middle Eastern cooks do.

Like any other art or craft, fine cooking demands not only skill but imagination. Following the rules will surely earn you praise, but following your instincts may win you laurels.

Storing Herbs

If you grow your own herbs, you can enjoy them at their peak of flavor. If you buy fresh herbs, remove them from their plastic bags, wrap them loosely in a damp paper towel, and store in the crisper compartment of your refrigerator. As with any perishable item, buy only small amounts of fresh herbs at a time—no more than you expect to use in the next few days. Dried herbs should also be purchased in small amounts, preferably from an herbal supplier who sells them loose rather than packaged. If there is no herbal supplier in your vicinity, the next best thing is to order by mail. A few suppliers are listed in the "Resources" section.

Your dried herbs and spices will keep better if you store them in a cool, dark place. And don't forget to label them—an omission I regretted one evening when a visitor who was preparing dinner in my kitchen cheerfully sprinkled the remaining contents of a bottle labeled "Basil" into the tomato sauce he was making. Some hours and a few fiery mouthfuls later, we made the unhappy discovery that the "basil" had come from the container where I had stored my black pepper.

In the following pages you will find listed some common and not so common seasonings, ways they can be used, and a few notes about their lore and history.

The Lore and Uses of Herbs and Spices

Allspice is not, as the name suggests, a combination of spices; it is the purplish-black berries of the evergreen pimento tree that grows in the West Indies, particularly Jamaica, and in South and Central America. The dried berries resemble large peppercorns and taste something like a combination of clove, cinnamon, pepper, and juniper. Like most aromatic plants, allspice has been used internally as a stimulant and carminative, added sometimes to laxatives to improve the taste and prevent griping; it has been used externally to relieve rheumatism. Once used for preserving meat, allspice was favored by pirates, who called their allspice-flavored meat "boucan," a name that inspired the seventeenth-century appellation for pirates—buccaneers.

Allspice is a popular baking spice, good in fruit dishes, spiced cakes, cookies, steamed puddings, and coffee cakes. A pinch of allspice adds zest to meats and meat loaf; in Jamaica it is used to season chicken. Allspice is delicious with sweet yellow vegetables such as yams, sweet potatoes, carrots, pumpkin, and winter squash. Try some in salad dressing, too.

Angelica, which grows wild in the Alps and is easily cultivated in gardens, has culinary and medicinal uses dating back at least as far as the Middle Ages, when it was carried as a protection against the plague. According to legend, the protective powers of angelica, also known as the Holy Ghost plant, were revealed to a monk in a dream. Since that time, angelica has been considered a strong defense against witchcraft—one of the few ingredients no witch would ever add to her cauldron. The flowers are greenish-white and grow in umbrels, somewhat like Queen Anne's lace, to which the plant is related. Medicinally, the roots or seeds have been used for stomach and intestinal problems, to promote sweating and stimulate urination and for nervousness and spasms. It is applied externally for rheumatism and skin problems. The oil is used for flavoring Chartreuse and vermouth as well as creams and custards. In former times the leaves and stalks were eaten as vegetables, either raw or boiled; they are said to taste something like parsley, also a botanical relative. The candied stalks are a popular confection in Europe and a specialty in French regions.

Anise is a member of the same large family that includes angelica, dill, and fennel. Anise seeds have a taste similar to licorice, but more concentrated and less sweet. Native to Greece, Asia Minor, and Egypt, anise was known to the ancient Egyptians and early Greek physicians and is mentioned in the Bible. The seeds are still used in folk medicine for cramps, gas, indigestion, and insomnia, to promote the flow of milk in nursing mothers, and to improve the tastes of other medicines. In former times, anise was appreciated as a sachet as well as a medicinal and seasoning. In Virginia, early settlers were required by law to plant six seeds. Oil from the seeds is used to flavor liqueurs, most notably anisette and the infamous absinthe. Anise seeds are most often used to flavor sweet rolls, cakes, cookies, and fruit, but they also add interest to cole slaw, mild cheeses, meats, eggs, beets, and cucumbers.

Asafetida is a gum-resin extracted from the root of *Ferula foetida,* a plant native to Afghanistan. Asafetida was the "in" drug of the time of Shakespeare, who mentions it in his plays, and was still official in America at the turn of this century. The nickname "devil's dung" may give you an idea of the taste and odor. According to the sharp-tongued Dr. Bush, who was not one of its admirers, "Asafetida formerly had the reputation of being a powerful anti-spasmodic, a nerve and cerebral stimulant, a stimulating expectorant; as well as tonic, laxative, diuretic, diaphoretic, emmenagogue, aphrodisiac and anthelmintic. It is much more probable, however, that the benefits assumed to have accrued from the administration were due to the mental impression pro-duced by the odor and taste than to any actual medicinal virtue. To avoid taking a sec-ond dose most patients would have a rapid amelioration of symptoms." Nonetheless, the ancient Romans were very fond of asafetida's culinary properties and used it for sea-soning. Indisputedly an ac-quired taste, asafetida is still used in Indian and other cui-sines. The Persians, who used the juice as a condiment and enjoyed the leaves as a boiled green and the root roasted like a potato, called asafetida "food of the gods." I must confess

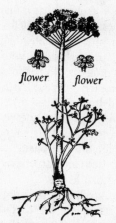

flower   *flower*

Asafetida-Ferula asafoetida

that I have no firsthand experience with this interesting plant, but if you care to experiment, Aphrodisia (see "Resources") lists it in their catalog.

Basil. I grow basil on my windowsill if for no other reason than the warm, clove-like fragrance that arises every time I water the soil or brush against the leaves. The medicinal efficacy of basil was a matter of controversy among the ancients, but they all did agree that the sowing of the seed should be accompanied by curses to ensure proper growth. In Italy, however, the plant was associated with love, a notion immortalized by both Keats and Boccaccio, who each wrote of a grieving maiden who kept her lover's severed head buried in a pot of basil. Basil is sacred to the Hindus, who grow it near their temples. In Indian mythology, basil was once the nymph Tulasi, beloved of Krishna, who turned her into a basil plant. Basil was also beloved by Vishnu, whose followers wear rosaries made of basil stalks and roots. In ancient Greece, basil was regarded as a royal plant fit only for sovereigns, who cut it with a golden sickle. One thing all cultures seem agreed upon is that basil is a marvelous seasoning, good with just about any vegetable, fish, or meat, indispensable with tomato or lamb. No Italian sauce is complete without basil, and it is delicious in potato salad. Possibly the best-known use of basil, though, is in pesto, the uncooked pasta sauce composed almost entirely of fresh basil leaves.

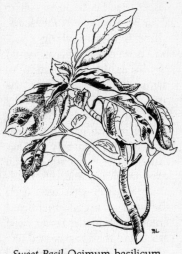

Sweet Basil-Ocimum basilicum

Bay Leaf, or laurel, an evergreen tree native to the Mediterranean, has been extolled in cookery, employed in medicine, and enshrined in mythology for centuries. The tree was sacred to the Greek god Apollo, who had fallen in love with the nymph Daphne, whose father obligingly transformed her into a laurel tree so she could escape the god's unwelcome advances. Apollo, undaunted by the maiden's unusual rejection, ordained that the laurel evermore would be his tree, its leaves used to crown the victorious poet, athlete, soldier, and emperor. The custom has continued through the centuries, inspiring the expression "to win one's laurels." As one might expect of a tree with such an extraordinary past, branches of the laurel were also thought to protect against lightning, sickness, death, and evil spirits. Greek physicians, who wore crowns of the berries of the salubrious laurel that were called *bacca lauri,* were known as baccalaureates, a term that was later applied to all those who completed undergraduate studies. In medicine, besides their use as a carminative and digestive, bay leaves have been used externally for colds, congestion, rheumatism, and skin problems. In distilling, the berries are used to flavor fioravanti, a spirit made from aromatic herbs, and in cookery the bay leaf is a savory addition to spaghetti sauce, meats, fish, soups, and stews of all kinds. This herb is very pungent—one leaf is enough to use in a dish intended to serve six.

Borage is seldom used medicinally now, but it once was given to reduce fever, soothe nervous conditions, stimulate production of milk in nursing mothers, and relieve sore throat and inflammation. The blue, star-shaped flowers of this lovely perennial, which grows wild as well as cultivated, were often copied in embroidery during the sixteenth century. They were also candied and served as a sweet. Fresh petals were floated on wines and cordials in the belief they would instill courage and gladden the heart. Borage is still used in claret cup to lend a hint of cucumber flavor. In some parts of France, the blossoms are cooked as fritters, and the cucumber flavor of the young leaves seasons salads, vegetables, and iced drinks. The young leaves can also be eaten as a leafy green vegetable.

EDIBLE BLOSSOMS AND FLOWERS

Flowers are no longer commonly used for garnish and flavor in American cooking, but the art of culinary flower use is one you can revive in your own kitchen if you have access to flowers that are not contaminated with pesticides and automobile fumes.

Dried marigolds are still used by Dutch cooks to flavor meat stews; the Elizabethan English used it as a substitute for saffron to give a golden tint to rice.

You can make your own custom-blended floral teas by adding the dried blossoms of orange, lime, or jasmine to Chinese tea.

Squash blossom fritters are still a summer treat in certain areas of the country; elder blossoms also make good fritters. Flowers also add a touch of elegance to salads.

Violets, rose petals (the white base is bitter, so snip it off before using), nasturtiums, red clover blossoms, daylilies, rose geraniums, carnations, and marigolds are all edible and make lovely garnishes for aspics or gelatin desserts. Arrange the blossoms at the bottom of a gelatin mold, then add the cooled gelatin mixture and place in the refrigerator to harden.

Plain vanilla custard is one of those comforting foods many of us remember from childhood. You can elevate such simple fare into an extraordinary adult dessert by using, instead of vanilla, the petals of marigold, rose geranium, cowslips, or roses for flavor and color. Flower petals can also be used to flavor cakes by sprinkling a few petals on the bottom of your baking pan before you add the batter.

Candied flowers are a lavish treat at the end of a meal, and provide an elegant pastry decoration. They are easily made by dipping the flowers in sugar syrup that has been boiled and cooled. When candied flowers were in fashion, rosewater, instead of plain water, was often used to make the syrup.

In the days before artificial dyes were used for food coloring, the deep hues of certain petals were used. Colored sugars were made by gently simmering dried powdered petals with sugar that had been slightly moistened. When the moisture evaporated, more dried petals were stirred into the hot sugar.

The distilled "waters" of certain flowers were also used as flavoring, much as we use vanilla and other extracts. Rosewater is still used in pastry making in many parts of the world and can be found in some supermarkets and other stores that sell imported specialties. If you like the tint as well as the taste of roses in your confections, you can add deeply colored rose petals (without the white heel) to rosewater and let the mixture steep in the sun until the water turns rosy.

Caraway. Like most kitchen spices, caraway is both digestive and carminative. In addition, it has been used to "bring down the courses" and promote milk in nursing mothers. A wild and cultivated perennial thought to have originated in Asia Minor, the caraway plant looks a bit like carrot, to which it is botanically related. The taste and scent are sharp and somewhat resinous.

Although the leaves and shoots of the first-year plant can be eaten, it is the seeds that are used for seasoning; they are most often associated with rye and pumpernickel breads. Caraway is also used in flavoring the liqueur kümmel and eaten in sugar-covered "comfits," but this by no means exhausts its culinary possibilities. The seeds add delicious flavor to sausage, pork, and boiled cabbage, stews, both dried and fresh beans, cheeses and omelettes as well as meatballs, apple desserts, and all sorts of breads.

Cardamom, a native of India, has limited medicinal uses as a digestive and carminative and for flavoring other medicines; it is best known as a spice in Indian cooking and Danish pastry. The tiny, spicy black seeds, which are encased in a papery beige pod, taste a bit like ginger and are a nice addition to sweet breads and desserts, cantaloupe and honeydew melon, sweet yellow vegetables, cooked greens, fish, chicken, veal, cream sauces, and salad dressings. In the Middle East, cardamom is used to flavor coffee. For extra zip, try adding a few seeds when you brew coffee. Two or three seeds per six-ounce cup of water.

Cayenne is a small, hot red pepper native to tropical America, used in medicine as an appetite stimulant, tonic, and circulatory stimulant, and externally for rheumatism and muscular stiffness. Cayenne appears frequently in cuisines of the tropics because it stimulates perspiration. This pepper is extremely hot—a pinch goes a long way. It adds warmth and zest to just about everything except dessert, and is preferable to black pepper in avocado and cream dips, eggs, cheese, and milk sauces, where black pepper specks would detract from the appearance. When you use paprika, add a pinch of cayenne to bring out the spicy flavor.

Celery Seed. My mother and many other women of her generation used celery seed in beef stews and homemade pickles and tomato juice. Medicinally, the seeds have been used as a carminative and sedative and for bronchitis and rheumatism. The seed has a concentrated celery taste, and, if my father is any example, is tolerated even by those who have no appetite for herbal seasonings. Use sparingly in seafood and poultry and in seasoning cheese casseroles, zucchini, and summer squash.

Chervil, writes Gerard, "groweth in my garden, and in the gardens of other men who have been diligent in these matters." The boiled roots, he asserted, are "very good for old people that are dull and without courage; it rejoiceth and comforteth the heart, and increaseth their lust and strength." Juice pressed from the fresh flowering herb is used for skin problems, gout, dropsy, "female complaints," and high blood pressure. Originating in Russia and Central Asia, chervil is for the most part neglected in American cooking, probably because the dried leaves are as tasteless as dried parsley. The fresh leaves are quite another matter, having the savor of fresh Italian parsley with a hint of anise. The French use chervil as a component of *fines herbes,* their most popular seasoning, which also includes finely chopped parsley, tarragon, and chive. Cultivated since antiquity, chervil was eaten as a leafy green vegetable and was often used to flavor breads. The Elizabethans used it as a major salad ingredient, and as far as I'm concerned, that is the best use to make of it. Chervil blends well with any nondessert, but the subtle flavor is best appreciated in delicately flavored foods such as fish, poultry, cream sauce, eggs, zucchini, summer squash, and cottage cheese.

Chive, which may have originated in the Alps, grows wild in temperate and northern climates all over the world. An appetizer and digestive, chive contains iron and arsenic (the latter in harmless amounts); both are good for anemia. The slender, onion-flavored spears of chive are a familiar ingredient in cream and cottage cheese, salads, and on sour cream served with baked potato.

When I live outside the city, I never take the trouble to grow or buy chive, because this "onion grass" grows profusely on lawns, in meadows, beside streams, in the woods—just about everywhere. To find it, you have only to follow your nose to where the air is scented with a mild onion savor in early spring. Like chervil, chive is best fresh on foods with a bland or subtle flavor.

Sweet Cicely. A perennial with fern-like leaves native to Europe, sweet cicely has a faintly anise-like flavor and can be used for flavoring cream soups and to add sweetness to some desserts. The herb is seldom used in American cooking.

Cinnamon. Is there anyone who doesn't love cinnamon? Centuries ago, the ancient Phoenicians cornered the trade in cinnamon, protecting its whereabouts with tall tales of fearsome bats, birds, and inaccessible cliffs that made gathering it a perilous undertaking. In biblical times, cinnamon was used for annointing during religious ceremonies and for perfuming.

Like most aromatic spices, cinnamon has been used to aid digestion, correct flatulence, and render obnoxious medicines more palatable.

Unlike other spices, the part of the cinnamon tree that we use for flavoring is not the fruit or the seed but the bark, which is harvested during the rainy season when it can be peeled from the tree and wound in slender scrolls.

The culinary uses of cinnamon are limitless, from the simple cinnamon toast we enjoyed as children to flavoring Indian curry, Greek beef stew, and Mexican coffee and hot chocolate. It is used in all kinds of sweet desserts and is indispensable with apple. Spiced wines, once very popular, were laced with cinnamon. Hot cider stirred with a cinnamon stick is ambrosial; I like to add a jigger of vodka to hot cider and cinnamon and serve it to guests at Christmas and New Year. Cinnamon is also good in cranberry juice and cranberry sauce, and with sweet yellow vegetables.

Clove. The evergreen clove tree probably originated in China, then was cultivated in the Moluccas by the Dutch. Medicinally, clove is used to prevent vomiting, and, being both antiseptic and anesthetic, is a common household remedy for toothache. It was also once thought to be aphrodisiac. The unopened buds of the clove tree are almost synonymous with baked ham and are indispensable to home picklers and bakers. Cloves are very pungent; one or two make a lively addition to soups and stews and also add zest to sweet yellow vegetables.

Coriander, long neglected in American gardens, has become quite fashionable in the past few years. Its medicinal uses date back to ancient Egypt, where it was used for headache. It is also antispasmodic as well as digestive and carminative and can be used to relieve rheumatic complaints when applied externally.

Coriander, which grows wild in Europe, is thought to be native to Asia. The seeds were used in early India to flavor curry. The ancient Greeks used the seeds to flavor bread and preserve meats. In biblical times coriander was a treasured seasoning and was among the bitter herbs eaten at Passover. The seeds have also been used to flavor liqueurs and comfits. Today the leaves, which to me taste like soap, are added to salads. The taste of the seeds has been variously described as similar to anise, fennel, and orange; they are used to flavor baked confections, meats, cheeses, pickles, salads, soups, and puddings. Ground coriander seeds will ennoble a simple roast chicken. Try sprinkling ground coriander, crushed sage, and dill over the oiled skin of chicken before you roast it—the aroma alone suggests a feast.

Cumin, an ingredient of curry powder, is thought to have originated in Asia, and has been cultivated in Egypt, China, and Palestine since antiquity. Medicinally, it has been used as a tonic since the days of ancient Egypt. It has also been used for stomach upsets, eye irritations, and sores on the hide of cattle. The tiny yellowish seeds, which were used in early Greece and Rome as a substitute for the more costly peppercorn, were a symbol of greed and stinginess; in biblical times they were used for paying tithes. During the Middle Ages, and for some time after, coriander seeds were thought to keep husbands and sweethearts from straying. In ancient Egypt the acrid, spicy seeds, botanically related to caraway, were used to flavor meats, fish, and stews. The ancient Hebrews and early Romans used ground cumin as a spread on bread, much as tahini is used today. The spice is popular in Spanish cooking and is used to flavor meat, sausage, soups, stews, pickles, cheeses, and certain liqueurs. Add a pinch of cumin when you make hamburger patties or meat loaf.

Dill. I suppose that every cook has a favorite herb, and mine is dill. The tart, feathery leaves, which look a bit like carrot tops, are wonderful for seasoning just about anything, but are particularly good in mayonnaise, sour cream, and cheese toppings, as a seasoning for potato salad, cole slaw, green or cucumber salad, zucchini and summer squash, fish, and poultry. Dill pickles would not, of course, deserve their name unless they were made with dill, which is also wonderful in other pickles, such as those made with string bean, purslane, and cauliflower. A friend of mine is so fond of dill that he eats sandwiches composed only of dill between buttered slices of bread. Dill leaves taste best when fresh or frozen but are acceptable when dried. The seeds, which are often described as having an anise flavor, are used along with the leaves in pickling and in seasoning fish, poultry, vegetables, and meats.

Decoctions of the seeds are used medicinally for colic, insomnia, and nervous conditions, and to promote the flow of milk in nursing mothers. Native to the Mediterranean, southern Russia, and Egypt, dill was used by the Pharisees in biblical times to pay their tithes, as a garland in early Greece and Rome, and, through the ages, as powerful protection against witches and the evil eye.

Fennel, which looks like dill and belongs to the same botanical family, has similar uses in medicine. In addition, it is one of the best herbs to use for relieving eyestrain, and has a centuries-old reputation for helping dieters shed unwanted pounds. Like dill, fennel was used as a garland in ancient Greece, crowning victorious warriors as well as youths and maidens who attended festivals. In the Greek legend of Prometheus, the rebel who stole fire from the gods, the Olympic flame was carried to earth concealed in the hollow stalk of a giant fennel. Fennel was also used during the Middle Ages to ward off witches.

All parts of this plant have a licorice flavor, particularly the seeds, which are used to flavor breads and baked apple dishes. Both seeds and leaves add a pleasant resonance to fish and poultry; Italians eat the entire plant as a boiled vegetable.

Fenugreek grows in Europe, the Middle East, and the Orient. Both the seeds, which have a maple flavor, and the leaves are used lavishly in Middle Eastern cooking for flavoring and as a salad ingredient and cooked green vegetable. Medicinal and culinary uses date back to ancient India, Egypt, and China, where fenugreek was used as a restorative and aphrodisiac, among other purposes. Try a pinch in stews, soups, rice dishes, and desserts. The flavor is rich and interesting.

Garlic. As you may be aware, garlic is the best weapon to have on hand if you expect to meet a vampire. On the other hand, garlic has a sinister reputation in biblical history, being the plant that sprang up in the left footprint of Satan as he fled from the Garden of Eden. Egyptian laborers ate garlic for endurance, and the Israelites took it with them on their exodus from Egypt. Greek and Roman soldiers and sailors ate garlic to give them strength in battle; during the Middle Ages it was considered proof against witches and the plague as well as vampires.

The medicinal uses of this miraculous bulb are listed elsewhere in this book. In America garlic became popular when soldiers returning from World War II brought with them a new familiarity with the cuisines of Italy and other countries where garlic was popular. Rare is the cook who needs to be instructed in the use of garlic, which enhances most foods, especially meats, fish, poultry, tomato, and green vegetables. Bits of garlic browned in olive oil have a crunchy texture and nutty taste and make a delicious topping for asparagus, broccoli, string beans, zucchini, summer squash, and cauliflower. Many cooks would not consider proceeding with a vegetable salad until they have first rubbed a cut garlic clove over the surface of the salad bowl. If the flavor is too pungent for your taste, try elephant garlic, which has a milder flavor than ordinary garlic. Elephant garlic has cloves equal in size to three or four ordinary cloves, and a flavor that is especially pleasing in salads and other dishes that call for raw garlic. You should be able to find it at greengrocers who stock specialty items. I keep the unused portion of elephant garlic cloves in a tightly sealed jar in my refrigerator. If you prefer the convenience of having your garlic ready peeled, soak the cloves in vinegar for twenty-four hours. The acid retards spoilage and prevents browning, and you can use the vinegar in salad dressings. After marinating, the garlic should be covered in oil and stored in the refrigerator, where it will keep for several weeks.

Ginger, native to tropical Asia, is one of the warming herbs used in

Chinese medicine to ward off colds, among other things. Tea made with ginger stimulates perspiration and is stimulant, stomachic, and carminative, good for preventing motion sickness. As a seasoning, ginger is best known as the spice in gingerbread, a confection that originated in ancient Greece and may have been enjoyed in early Egypt as well. A sweet with universal appeal, gingerbread was among the gifts sent to celebrate the birth of Peter the Great of Russia and was a favorite of Queen Elizabeth I and her court. During the sixteenth century, ginger was used in spiced wines and beer as well as confections. The American Indians used a variety of wild ginger to season cornmeal and fish. Sliced ginger lends a clean, pungent savor to Chinese cooking and is good with fish, poultry, and sweet yellow vegetables. To keep ginger fresh, bury the root in clean sand.

Horseradish. The above method will also keep the root of horseradish fresh. Native to southeastern Europe and western Asia, horseradish grows wild as well as cultivated and has medicinal uses in treating gout, rheumatism, and bladder infections. Applied externally, horseradish stimulates circulation and relieves congestion in those conditions where mustard plasters are used.

Horseradish is best known as a condiment for boiled beef and ham; it is also good with oily or fatty foods because it aids digestion. Horseradish root, which has a penetrating odor and a hot, peppery taste, can be used as a marinade or cooked with tough meats as a tenderizing agent. The fresh, grated root adds zest to canapes, boiled eggs, and cold meats.

Marjoram. (Sweet marjoram) is a member of the mint family and related to oregano, which has a similar but stronger taste. The botanical name for marjoram means "joy of the mountain," a reference to the sweet perfume that arises from the Mediterranean hills where the herb grows wild. The crushed leaves, which have a fragrance reminiscent of pine needles, were a favorite strewing herb in former times, serving as cushions for lounging, air fresheners in crowded halls, and a perfume and moth repellent for stored garments. A symbol of honor and happiness, marjoram was formerly woven into crowns worn by bridal couples; bouquets were carried to repel witches. Medicinally, the uses of marjoram are similar to those of mint: it can be used to treat headache, nervous conditions, indigestion, flatulence, and respiratory problems. Oil distilled from the leaves is used for muscular stiffness, rheumatic complaints, and toothache, and to "bring out" scarlet fever and measles.

Marjoram has a strong, distinct flavor that can overpower other ingredients if you use too much. It is used best in foods with robust flavor such as tomato sauce, meat loaf, paté, dried beans and snap beans, leafy green vegetables, stuffings, herb breads, and roasted and braised poultry.

Mint. In Greek mythology, this fragrant herb was once the nymph Mentha. Like most male deities, Pluto, ruler of the Underworld, had a roving eye, and carried Mentha off to the Underworld to be his lover. Pluto's wife, Persephone, who herself had been abducted by Pluto, did not enjoy the competition and began stomping Mentha into the ground. Pluto, in order to protect the maiden, transformed her into the herb we know as mint. Later in Greek mythology, the leaves were used to scour the table of Philemon and Baucis in Ovid's tale of an elderly married couple who, though very poor, offered hospitality to two strangers who appeared at their door begging a meal. The visitors later revealed themselves as Zeus and Hermes and rewarded the couple by ordaining that their wine pitcher be miraculously filled each time it was emptied. The couple, along with the mint they had used to freshen the dining table, became ever after a symbol of hospitality.

Mint was a favorite strewing herb in ancient Greece and Rome, where it was also used to perfume the bath. It was one of the herbs used to pay the tithe in biblical times. In colonial America peppermint was used for medicine, as it had been since antiquity. Spearmint was used for flavoring, and other mints were used as a substitute for the Chinese tea so heavily taxed by the British Parliament.

There are several varieties of mint besides peppermint and spearmint, including field mint and horse mint, often found growing in

the wild, and orange, lemon, chocolate, apple, and pineapple mints. The uses of peppermint as a flavoring in candy and syrup are well known. In the Middle East, fresh peppermint leaves are added to salads as a green and also used liberally as a vegetable in cooked dishes. Peppermint and the flavored mints are lovely in fruit salads and as a garnish for iced drinks. On hot summer days I like to start a meal with cold fruit soup made with equal parts of plain yogurt and strawberries, raspberries, mulberries, or blueberries pureed in a blender, crowned with mint leaves (any of the flavors are good) and served on a bed of crushed ice. Mint julep, of course, wouldn't deserve its name unless iced bourbon was crowned with a fresh mint leaf. Spearmint is the traditional accompaniment to lamb, either in mint jelly or used as a seasoning. Mint can also be used to flavor cream cheese, carrots, and peas. For a savory summer dish with a French touch, steam fresh garden peas with a leaf of fresh lettuce and a few fresh mint leaves.

Mustard is another plant a country gardener scarcely needs to grow because it is free for the picking just about everywhere. Mustard is native to Asia and has been used since ancient times for both medicine and seasoning. Even if you have no firsthand knowledge of mustard's medicinal use, you have probably seen references in literature and films, because it was a popular home remedy until fairly recently. Recently, on two mustard containers that were at least twenty years old, I found recipes for mustard plaster (equal parts of mustard, flour, and tepid water); poultice (three quarters of a cup linseed meal made from ground seeds of the flax plant, one cup boiling water, one third of a cup mustard); footbath (two or three tablespoons mustard to two or three gallons water); and an emetic (one teaspoon mustard to a glass of warm water). If mustard has been deposed from its reign in the family medicine chest it is because our fast-paced lifestyles leave no time for the mess and bother of preparing mustard plasters and footbaths, not because its medicinal value is any less than that of drugstore preparations. The paste made from crushed mustard seeds is a familiar accompaniment to meats of all sorts, especially beef and ham. The young leaves lend piquant flavor to boiled greens and salads. A pinch of powdered mustard seed is good in mayonnaise, salad dressings, cheese sauces, and casseroles. For a homemade mustard guaranteed to clear your sinuses, not to mention your palate, make your own fresh mustard paste by mixing the powdered seeds with equal parts of vinegar, wine, or water. A pinch each of salt and sugar and a dash of cream brings out the full flavor. In Elizabethan times, rosewater was sometimes used to moisten the mustard.

Nutmeg/Mace. The nutmeg tree, an evergreen native to the tropics, produces a sweet fruit that is eaten as we in temperate zones eat peaches and pears. The seed of this fruit is a pale brown stone—the nutmeg—encased in a reddish membrane—mace.

Like most spices, nutmeg is digestive and carminative. Back in the 1960s and '70s, when any number of botanicals were smoked, sniffed, ingested, or injected in the search for a high, nutmeg was eaten for its euphoriant effects. The seed does have psychedelic properties, but the visions could be fatal—a dose sufficient to get you high is also poisonous.

Although in contemporary American cooking nutmeg is mostly confined to eggnog and desserts, in former times it was used as freely as we use salt and pepper today. In seventeenth-century recipe books, nutmeg appears in every sort of main dish. Today it adds the characteristic flavor to Swedish meatballs. A pinch of nutmeg adds distinction to cheese and cream sauces, cooked green and sweet yellow vegetables, and poultry, beef, and veal. Next time you bake winter squash, add a pat of butter and a little brown sugar, then grate nutmeg over the surface. The flavor and scent of mace is similar to nutmeg, but more potent, so use sparingly.

Oregano, well known to Americans as the seasoning in pizza and spaghetti sauce, is a relatively new name for an herb that was formerly known as wild marjoram, or, in some areas, Mexican sage. In appearance, the herb we know as oregano more closely resembles marjoram than sage, but the exact botanical classification is still a bit fuzzy.

Medicinally, the uses of oregano for digestive and respiratory problems are similar to those of other members of the mint family. In cookery, oregano is most often used for the Italian specialties already mentioned, but it is also good with any tomato, egg, or meat dish, or with dried beans, broccoli, or cabbage; it is very good sprinkled on pork chops or roast and it combines well with thyme and basil, making it a natural for tomato sauce.

Parsley. The history and folklore of parsley are, to my mind, more interesting than its flavor, which has little to recommend it other than its inoffensiveness. In ancient Greece, parsley was considered an omen of death and was used for funeral wreaths and adorning tombs and, later, to crown victorious athletes. During the Middle Ages, two legends sprang up around parsley: one was that it belonged to the Devil, the other was that babies were gotten from parsley beds.

Parsley has important medicinal uses, described elsewhere in this book. Chewing a sprig of parsley is said to remove garlic from the breath, and that may be its main importance for the dining table other than as a garnish. In cookery it is used to flavor everything except dessert—it certainly won't harm any dish, and it combines well with other seasonings. The most refreshing use I have seen made for parsley is in the salad bowl, where a quantity of the leaves were used as a salad green—more flavorful than lettuce, and, due to its high vitamin A content, certainly more nutritious. Fresh parsley is also used in Middle Eastern cooking as a salad green or vegetable.

Poppy Seeds are rich in nutrients, and add a delicate nutty flavor to a variety of foods. They are most often used in breads and pastries, but also make delicious toppings for casseroles, noodles, vegetables, and poached fish or poultry. The seeds are packed with protein and other nutrients.

Sesame seeds are equally nutritious and have similar culinary uses. Tahini, a paste made from ground sesame seeds, is used in

Middle Eastern cooking and is popular in this country as a sauce or a spread.

Rosemary is one of the most resonant seasonings. The quill-shaped leaves of this evergreen look and taste a bit like pine needles and in ancient times were used in medicine, cosmetics, and cookery.

The Latin name for rosemary means "dew of the sea," a reference to its birthplace on the Mediterranean seashore, and also to the Virgin Mary, who, according to legend, threw her blue cloak over a rosemary bush, changing the color of its blossoms from white to blue. Used as a garland to crown youths and maidens in early Greece and Rome, rosemary was carried as a protection against the plague during medieval times. It was also used in embalming as a disinfectant and was buried with corpses. Arabian physicians of the thirteenth century praised it for its ability to "comfort the brain" and restore memory.

Shakespeare's contemporary, Gerard, recommends rosemary for sweetening the breath and lifting the spirits. Culpeper prescribed it for nervous headache, trembling, and female complaints, and as a tonic. Externally, rosemary has been used for rheumatic complaints.

Rosemary is a potent seasoning, so use sparingly in stuffings, chicken, lamb, game, beef, and green vegetables; it adds a mysterious savor to stir-fried dishes. Crushed rosemary leaves are also wonderful in biscuits and breads. Use about a quarter-teaspoon to every cup flour.

Saffron, the tips of the orange pistils of the autumn crocus (*Crocus sativa*), is and always has been the most costly spice in the world because several thousands of flowers must be harvested to produce one pound of the pistils. Native to Europe and Asia, saffron was used in ancient Greece, Rome, and Egypt in cookery, perfumery, and fabric dyeing. Homer and the Greek playwrights refer to the saffron hues of the sunset, or garments dyed with golden saffron. During the Middle Ages, saffron, along with other cosmopolitan luxuries, all but disappeared from European culture, but it was later brought to Spain by the conquering Moors and to England by a pilgrim who carried a bulb concealed in the knob of his pilgrim staff. Saffron was beloved by the English, who used it to impart golden color to puddings, sauces, and tea breads. You need only a few threads to give flavor and color to rice, poultry and seafoods, cream cheese, or eggs.

Sage. "He who would live for aye must eat sage in May" is an old expression that more or less sums up the high esteem in which sage was held for centuries. In early Egypt, sage tea was prescribed to restore women's fertility. Somewhat later, Europeans believed that sage flourished in the gardens of families where the wife was dominant, or in gardens of the wealthy, withering when the wealth declined. In medicine, sage was used as a snuff for nasal congestion, as a tea for coughs and spitting of blood, palsy, the "bitings of serpents," and to preserve the wit and memory. *Sage* in English and French is a synonymn for wisdom, presumably bestowed by partaking of the herb.

Gerard writes, "No man needs to doubt of the wholesomenesse of sage Ale, being brewed as it should be, with Sage, Scabious, Betony, Spikenard, Squinath, and Fennel seeds." The leaves were frequently used in brewing beer before hops were employed as a bitter, and as a staple of English cookery from Anglo-Saxon times. Parkinson, in *Paradisi in Sol,* writes that sage was boiled with calves' heads, and the juice of the herb was used to season roasted pigs' brains, which were served with currant sauce and also used with other herbs in a sauce for pieces of veal. The crushed leaves have been used for centuries to flavor cheese, breads, stuffings, and strongly flavored meats, particularly pork. The flavor of sage is assertive, and may well overpower a dish unless used with discretion.

Savory—Summer and Winter. In Germany savory is known as "the bean herb" and used to flavor that vegetable not only for its delicious flavor but because, being stomachic and carminative, it is believed to render the beans more digestible and less gas-producing.

Native to the Mediterranean, summer savory is an annual with a sweet, slightly resinous flavor; winter savory is a perennial, more woody than summer savory, with foliage that can last all win-

The Herbal Kitchen

ter, even in Northern regions. The flavor is similar to summer savory, but stronger. Both savories have been used for stomach upsets, diarrhea, and sore throat, and also as aphrodisiacs. In cookery, savory is used to flavor cucumbers, tomato, carrots, fish, poultry, meats, and stuffing as well as beans.

Tarragon is an artemisia, one of a botanical genus that includes some of our most aromatic plants. The species name for tarragon, which is native to Siberia, is "little dragon," a reference to the serpentine shape of the roots. Tarragon was cultivated in ancient Greece and Egypt for its distinct sweet flavor, somewhat like chervil, sweet basil, or anise, and was used in early Arabian medicine. Like most culinary herbs, tarragon has been used as a digestive. The tea is said to bring on menstruation, promote urine, and induce sleep. In sixteenth-century England, tarragon was a popular ingredient in salad and salad vinegar, but it was most appreciated by the French, who used it to create sauce béarnaise, a hollandaise seasoned with tarragon, and tarragon cream, a puree of tarragon leaves boiled in white wine, then mixed with cream sauce or mashed potatoes and used for stuffing vegetables or making canapes. Tarragon is also an essential ingredient in *fines herbes*. A pinch of tarragon is wonderful in salad dressing, scrambled eggs, sautéed or braised veal, and sprinkled over poultry before roasting or fish before poaching; it adds character to summer squash and zucchini, creamed onions, tomato juice, and sauces.

Thyme, native to the Mediterranean, is a favorite plant of bees and, probably by association with these industrious insects, a symbol of activity and courage. An old folk song of the British Isles begins, "Come all ye fair and tender girls, who flourish in your prime, beware, beware, keep your garden fair, let no man steal your thyme. For when your time is past and gone, he'll care no more for you," suggesting that thyme was also a symbol of virginity. Thyme was frequently included in tussie mussies, tiny bouquets of fragrant herbs and flowers that ladies carried about with them— a much-appreciated custom, no doubt, in those days when bathing was infrequent.

Thyme is a popular culinary herb, particularly when used to

season fish, seafood chowders and bisques, stuffings, and tomato sauce. It is one of those herbs that enhances just about everything except dessert, good with all meats, zucchini and summer squash, beets, carrots, onions, potatoes, mushrooms, and tomatoes.

Turmeric, a native of Asia, is more widely used in India than America, where it is best known as an ingredient in pickles, prepared mustard, and curry powder. The root is the useful part of this plant, which is related to ginger and somewhat gingery in taste. In former times, turmeric was used in place of the more expensive saffron as a yellow dye for fabric and to give a golden tint to rice and other foods. Next time you marinate a beef steak or roast, add turmeric to your marinade. It is also good with chicken, fish, pork, chick peas, and cabbage.

Finding a good herbal recipe will probably be as easy as leafing through the pages of your favorite cookbook, for the best dishes are seasoned with herbs. Each herb has a different character, and you may find that you like some better than others and perhaps a few not at all. Using some of the seasoning ideas in the descriptions of herbs above can turn an ordinary recipe into an interesting one. Don't be afraid to experiment. In the following pages I have included a few recipes to get you started. Some are my own inventions, some contributed by friends, others are from sixteenth-century "receipt" books. The historic recipes are set forth here exactly as they appeared in the early recipe books; therefore you may have to guess at the ingredients or methods, since they were chosen mainly for their charm and the inspiration they may offer to the modern cook.

Recipes

Beverages

Hot Tea

1 part hibiscus
1 part orange blossoms
4 parts black Chinese tea
4 parts gotu kola

In a scalded teapot place 1 teaspoon tea mixture for each serving and one for the pot. Steep for ten minutes and serve.

Iced Tea

5 teaspoons Oolong tea
5 teaspoons crushed rosehips
½ cinnamon stick
1 quart cold water

Place all ingredients in a glass jar and let the mixture steep on a sunny windowsill for at least 4 hours. Strain, refrigerate, and serve over ice. Garnish with borage, burnet, mint, or a slice of orange or lemon.

A Queen's Delight

From The Queen's Closet Opened, *one of the most popular "receipt" books, published in 1655*

Take a Gallon of good Rhenish Wine, put into it as much raspberries very ripe as will make it strong, put it in an earthen pot, and let it stand two days; then pour your Wine from the Raspberries, and put into every bottle two ounces of Sugar. Stop it and keep it by you.

A Cordial Water of Sir Walter Raleigh
From The Queen's Closet Opened

Take a gallon of strawberries, and put them into a pint of Aqua vitae, let them stand for four or five days, strain them gently out, and sweeten the water as you please, with fine sugar, or else with perfume.

To Make Metheglin
From The Compleat Cook, 1655

Take all sorts of Herbs that are good and wholesome, as Balm, Mint, Fennell, Rosemary, Angelica, wild time, Hop, Burnet, Egrimony, and such other as you think fit, some field Herbs, but you must not put in too many, but especially Rosemary or any strong Herb, less than half a handful will serve of every sort, you must boyle your herbs and strain them, and let the liquor stand till to morrow and settle them, take of the clearest liquor two Gallons and a half to one Gallon of Honey, and that proportion as much as you will make, and let it boyle an houre, and in the boyling skim it very clean, then set it cooling as you do Beer, when it is cold, take some very good Ale Barme, and put into the bottom of the Tub a little and a little as they do Beer keeping back the thick settling, that lyeth in the Bottom of the Vessell that is cooled in, and when it is all put together, cover it with a Cloth, and let it work very neer three days, and when you mean to put it up, shine of all the Barme clean, put it up into the Vessell very close in three or four days, but let it have all the vent for it will work, and when it is close stopped, you must look very often to it, and have a Pegge in the top to give it vent, when you heare it make a noise as it will do, or else it will break the Vessell. Sometime I make a bag and put in good store of ginger sliced, some cloves and Synamon, and boyle it in, and other times I put it into the Barrel and never boyle it, it is both good, but Nutmeg and Mace do not well to my tast.

Vegetables

Wild Spring Greens

Both nettles and dandelion greens are wonderfully health-giving, as you have read in earlier chapters. In the following recipe you can use any combination of greens that is appealing. Wintercress and mustard greens, which also can be gathered fairly early in spring, are tasty additions to this dish.

1   pound young spring greens (if you are using nettles, harvest only the tender tops, wearing gloves to do so)
1/2   cup feta cheese
    olive oil to taste
    freshly grated nutmeg

Steam the greens or boil them in a little water for about 10 minutes, or until tender. Break up the cheese with a fork or your fingers and mix it into the greens. Drizzle on as much olive oil as you like, then sprinkle on freshly grated nutmeg. Served with fresh whole-wheat bread this makes a hearty vegetarian meal for one or a side dish for two or three.

Stuffed Artichokes with Pignolias

Recipe by Claudia Jessup
Artichokes, which also have been discussed in the medicinal section, are good for your liver, gallbladder, and cholesterol level. They are an elegant vegetable, whether topped with hollandaise or added to other dishes.

4   large artichokes
1   cup cooked brown rice

1   tablespoon chopped fresh parsley
3   scallions, sliced
1/2   cup grated parmesan
1/4   cup pignolias, roasted
1   tablespoon chopped fresh basil
1   tablespoon salt
2   tablespoons olive oil and
      wine vinegar

Cut off artichoke stems, bottom row of leaves, and top third of leaves. Force center leaves apart and remove inner choke. Fill with stuffing made of the rest of the ingredients, mixed. Arrange artichokes in a pan. Add two cups water. Drizzle the two tablespoons oil and wine vinegar to taste. Cover and simmer 30 minutes.

Soybean Chili

Recipe by Claudia Jessup. Note: Herbs and spices, except for garlic, are dried and ground.

1   cup soybeans
1/2   cup chick peas
1/2   cup wheat berries
6   cups water
2   tablespoons oil
1   tablespoon chili powder
1/4   teaspoon cayenne
1   teaspoon oregano
1–3   cloves garlic, finely chopped
1   medium onion, chopped
2   canned hot jalapeño chili peppers, or 1 fresh
4   tomatoes, chopped
2   bay leaves
1/2   teaspoon nutmeg
1/2   teaspoon cinnamon

$^1/_4$ teaspoon ginger
$^1/_4$ teaspoon anise
     soy sauce to taste
     chopped scallions
     chopped parsley

Place soybeans, wheat berries, and chick peas in a bowl. Cover with water and soak overnight. Transfer to a heavy saucepan. Bring to a boil; cover and simmer 3 to 4 hours or until beans are nearly tender. Heat oil in skillet, add chili powder, cayenne, oregano. Cook, stirring for a minute or so. Add garlic and onion and cook for another 5 minutes. Add chili peppers and tomatoes and bring to a boil. Add all this to the soybean mixture along with the other spices. Cook until beans are tender. Season to taste with soy sauce and garnish with scallions and parsley.

Brazilian Chick Pea Salad

Recipe by Antonio Coelho

1   15-ounce can or 2 cups chick peas
1   medium plum tomato, finely chopped
$^1/_2$ onion, finely chopped
1   clove garlic, finely chopped
4   sprigs parsley, finely chopped
1   teaspoon dried or 2 teaspoons fresh basil
1   teaspoon dried oregano
2   teaspoons olive oil
1   teaspoon crushed tarragon
     juice of $^1/_2$ lime
     salt and freshly ground pepper to taste

Drain chick peas and rinse in hot water. Mix in a bowl with other ingredients. Serve in soup bowls.

Potato Salad

The secret of good potato salad is to make it while the potatoes are still warm and the other ingredients are at room temperature.

2 cups peeled cubed russet potatoes (boiled in their jackets)
1/4 cup mayonnaise
1/4 cup sour cream or plain yogurt
1/4 cup onion, finely chopped
1 tablespoon fresh basil, finely chopped
1 tablespoon fresh dill, finely chopped
1 tablespoon fresh Italian parsley, finely chopped
3/4 teaspoon salt
1/4 teaspoon paprika
pinch cayenne

Combine yogurt, mayonnaise, and seasoning and toss onto potatoes. Serve immediately at room temperature or chill for a few hours.

Side Dishes

To Fricat Champignons

A fresh mushroom dish from *The Compleat Cook*, 1655, this can either be served as a side dish or as a topping for meat.

Make ready your Champignons as you do for stewing and when you have poured away the black liquor that comes from them, put your Champignons into a Frying pan, with a piece of sweet Butter, a little Parsley, Time, Sweet Margirum, a piece of Onyon shred very small, a little Salt and fine beaten Pepper, to fry them till they be' enough, to have ready to leave abovelaid, and put it into the Champignons, whilst they are in the Pan, toss them two or three times put them forth and serve them.

Cumin Rice

1	cup uncooked brown rice
4–5	cloves garlic, sliced
1	onion, chopped
3–4	tablespoons salad oil
2²/₃	cups boiling water
1	teaspoon dried summer savory
1/2	teaspoon dried cumin
1/4	teaspoon coriander seeds
1/2	teaspoon dried chervil
	pinch cayenne pepper
	pinch salt

Sauté rice, garlic, and onion in salad oil. When the mixture is golden brown and the rice smells a bit like popcorn, add boiling water, summer savory, cumin, coriander seeds, chervil, cayenne pepper and salt. Simmer until rice is tender and water is absorbed—about 45–50 minutes. Serve as a side dish with meat or poultry. Accompanied by black beans, a garnish of fresh orange slices, and a green salad, makes a hearty vegetarian dinner.

Main Dishes

Lamb and Eggplant Istabul

For the best flavor, make this the day before you serve it to allow the flavors to marry in the refrigerator overnight.

1	medium eggplant
	salt
1	medium onion, sliced
2	pounds stewing lamb, cubed
1	four-ounce can tomato paste
1	pint fresh tomatoes, scalded and peeled (or canned tomatoes)

4   cloves garlic, crushed
1   bay leaf
1   tablespoon fresh basil
¼   teaspoon dried thyme
    pinch rosemary
    pinch seasalt
6   artichoke hearts, canned, fresh, cooked, or frozen

Peel and cube eggplant, place in bowl, and sprinkle salt over the pieces; set aside for 20 minutes. Sauté the onion until transparent, set aside, then brown the lamb in the oil used for cooking onion. Drain the water from the eggplant and pat dry with a paper towel. Sauté until transparent, and set aside. Combine lamb and onion with tomato paste, tomatoes, and seasonings. Cover and simmer 2 hours. Add eggplant, cover, and simmer another hour, or until lamb and eggplant are tender. Ten minutes before serving, add the artichoke hearts. Serve over rice or pasta and garnish with lemon slices.

Roast Lamb in Mustard Sauce

This recipe was handed down to my neighbor, Loretta Nieminski, from her Polish mother. Loretta claims that the mustard sauce tones down the "wild" taste of the lamb and made it acceptable to her daughters when they were young. If your lamb roast is large, you might want to increase the quantities of the other ingredients accordingly.

1   tablespoon dry mustard
1   tablespoon brown sugar
2–3   tablespoons vinegar
1   leg or other roast of lamb, about 3 pounds

Combine mustard, sugar, and vinegar and spread the paste over the lamb. Marinate in the refrigerator overnight, then roast at 350°—about 1½ hours for a three-pound roast.

The Herbal Kitchen

Ghormeh Sebzi

Yelena Melikian created this low-calorie version of a dish traditional in her native Iran. You should be able to find the fenugreek and dried limes in stores that sell foods used in Middle Eastern cooking.

1 cup blackeyed peas or kidney beans
3 pounds chicken, cubed, with all skin and fat removed
2 leeks, finely chopped
1 cup scallions, finely chopped
1 large onion, finely chopped
4 bunches parsley, finely chopped
1 pound spinach, finely chopped
1 tablespoon dried tarragon
   pinch to 1 teaspoon dried fenugreek, to taste
4 crushed dried limes or 1/4 cup fresh lemon juice and the grated rinds of 2 lemons
   chicken stock (2 or 3 cups)

Soak beans overnight or parboil them for about an hour. Sauté leeks, scallions, onions and chicken in 1/4 cup oil until brown, add water or chicken stock to cover. Sauté spinach and herbs in oil until spinach is wilted, add to onions and stock. Add beans and limes or lemon juice/rind, boil for 5 minutes, then simmer for about 1 1/2 hours, or until tender. This stew is best if it is made the day before it is served. In Iran, this meal often ends with a plate of fresh basil, mint, radish, and feta cheese.

Potée

A French recipe from Auvergne, this version is from Joanna and Ted Krauss.

1/2 head cabbage
4 cups beef stock
1 large onion studded with cloves
2 turnips, 3 carrots, 3 potatoes, peeled, cut into small chunks

½   cup parsley
1   bay leaf
½   teaspoon dried sage
½   teaspoon dried thyme
3   tablespoons olive oil
    salt and pepper to taste
1   garlic clove, minced (optional)

Break cabbage into pieces and put in large pot. Cover with beef stock. Add other ingredients. Bring to boil, cover, and simmer slowly for 1½ hours.

To Make The Best Sausages That Ever Was Eat
From The Compleat Cook

Take the lean of a Legge of Porke, and four pound of Beef suet, shred them together very small, then season it with three quarters of an ounce of Pepper, and halfe an ounce of Cloves and Mace mixed together, as the pepper is, a handful of Sage when it is chopped small and as much salt as you think will make them taste well of it, Mingle all these with the meat, then break in ten Eggs, all but two or three of the whites, then temper it all well with your hand and fill it into Hoggs gutts, which you must have ready for them, you must tye the ends of them like puddings, and when you eat them you must boil them on a soft fire; a hot fire will crack the skins and the Goodness boyle out of them.

To Make a Chicken Pye
From The Compleat Cook

Take four or five Chickens, cut them in pieces, take two or three Sweet Breads parboyld and cut in pieces as big a Walenuts, take the udda of Veale cut in thin slices or little slices of Bacon, the bottoms of Hartichokes boyld, then make your coffin proportionable to your meat, season your meat with Nutmeg, Mace and salt, then some butter on the top of the Pye, put a little water into it as you put it into the Oven and let it bake an houre then put it in a leere of butter, Gravy of Mutton, eight Lemonds sliced. So serve it.

Chicken in Sour Cream

1   tablespoon salad oil (approximately)
1   tablespoon butter (approximately)
1/2   medium onion, sliced
1/2   cup sliced mushrooms
2   cloves garlic, sliced
1   frying chicken, skinned, disjointed, and cut into large chunks
1   teaspoon dried thyme
1/2   teaspoon dried tarragon
1   teaspoon dried dill
1/2   cup white wine
1/2   cup sour cream or plain yogurt at room temperature
1   tablespoon flour
    pinch cayenne

In a Dutch oven or heavy skillet melt butter and combine with equal amount of oil so you have enough fat to cover bottom of skillet. Sauté onion, mushrooms, and garlic until brown; remove and set aside. Brown chicken, adding more oil and butter if necessary. When chicken is browned, sprinkle one side with half the herbs. Cover and cook for 5 minutes over medium heat, then turn the chicken over, sprinkle remainder of herbs on the uncooked side, turn the chicken again, and cover and cook for 5 minutes. Add wine, mushrooms, garlic, and onion; cover and simmer for 20 minutes, or until tender. Remove ingredients to a warmed serving platter, leaving the broth. Mix flour and cayenne thoroughly into the sour cream or yogurt and stir into the broth. Cook over low heat until thickened, then pour over the chicken. Serve over rice. *Note:* If you use fresh herbs, double the quantity and do not add until you make the sauce.

To Dress Flounder or Place With Garlick and Mustard

From The Compleat Cook

Take flounders very new, and cut all the finns and tails, then take out the Gutts and wipe them very clean, they must not be at all washt, then with your knife scotch them on both sides very grosly, then take the tops of tyme and cut them very small, and take a little salt, Mace and Nutmeg and mingle the Tyme and them together, and season the flounders; then lay them on the gridiron and bast them with Oyle or Butter, let not the fire be too hot, when that side next the fire is brown, turne it, and when you turne it, bast it on both sides til you have broyld them Brown, when they are enough make your sauce with Mustard two or three Spoonful according to discretion, fix Anchovies dissolved very well, about halfe a pound of butter drawn up with Garlicke, Vinegar, or bruised Garlick in other Vinegar, rub the bottom of your Dish with Garlick. So put your sauce to them, and serve them, you may fry them if you please.

Sauces, Dressings, and Pickles

Pesto

Pesto freezes well, so make some extra. One January night when the winds are howling, you will be immeasurably uplifted by this summery treat. The following recipe makes two or three generous servings, and in most kitchen blenders that's about as much as you can make at one time, so if you are having a dinner party, plan on making more than one batch. It is one of the most quickly prepared and elegant repasts.

2 cups fresh, washed basil leaves
1/2 cup olive oil
2 cloves garlic
1/4 cup pignolia nuts

In a blender, pack basil leaves, olive oil, garlic, and pignolia nuts. Blend at medium speed until reduced to a fragrant puree. Serve at room temperature over hot pasta. A fresh tomato salad and garlic bread are all you need to complete the feast.

Note: Lorel Nazzarro, a basil grower and cookbook writer who lives in Maine, also uses pesto in other dishes such as biscuits and tomato sauce for squid. If you care to experiment, add a tablespoon or two of pesto to your favorite Italian or bread recipes or use as a topping for homemade potato salad.

Mint Vinegar

Recipe by Bonnie Warner. This recipe can be used for other herbal vinegars.

2–3 cups fresh mint, or 1/2–1 cup dried mint
1 quart vinegar, warmed

Combine mint and vinegar and pack into jars. Cover and set in a warm place for two weeks. Strain into bottles.

Bread and Butter Pickles

An old family recipe handed down to my mother, Helen Wilcox, years and years ago. The results are so delicious that I have had dinner guests sit down with a plate and a knife and fork and gobble up the pickles as a first course. Don't omit the ice—it makes the pickles crisp.

4 quarts cucumbers, sliced

8   small onions
2   green peppers, sliced thin, mixed with ½ cup salt

Cover with ice and let stand 3 hours, drain, and cook in the following mixture:

5   cups sugar
1½   teaspoon dried, ground turmeric
½   teaspoon ground clove
2   teaspoons mustard seed
1   teaspoon celery seed
5   cups vinegar

Heat slowly to the boiling point in a stainless steel or fireproof glass saucepan, then take off the fire immediately, pack in warm, sterilized canning jars, either pint or quart size, and seal.

To Pickle Pursleine
From The Compleat Cook

Take pursleine, stalks and all, boyle them tender in faire water, then lay them drying upon linnen Cloathes, then being dryed, put them into the Gallypots, and cover them with wine vinegar mixt with Salt, and not make the pickle so strong as for cucumber.
Note: Fresh dill would be a good addition to this recipe.

Breads

To make Bisket Bread, otherwise called French Bisket
From The Compleat Cook

Take halfe a pecke of fine flower, two ounces of Coriander Seedes, one ounce of anise seedes, the white of foure eggs, half a pint of ale yeast, and as much water as will make it up into a stiff paste, your water must be but blood warme, then bake it in a long roll as big as your thigh, let it stay in the oven but one houre, and when it is a day olde, pare it and slice it overthwart, then sugar it over with fine powdered sugar, and so drie it in an oven againe, and being drie, bake it out and sugar it againe, then bake it, and you may keepe it all the year.

Herb and Olive Bread

1	yeast cake (or 1 package dry yeast)
1/4	cup warm water
1	cup scalded milk
1	cup boiling water
2	tablespoons butter
2½	teaspoons salt
1	tablespoon honey
2	tablespoons powdered dried rosemary
1	teaspoon dried thyme
1	teaspoon dried oregano
1/4	cup fresh basil, finely chopped
2	tablespoons fresh marjoram, finely chopped
1/2	cup black olives, drained, seeded, and coarsely chopped
2	cups whole-wheat flour
3	cups unbleached all-purpose flour

Dissolve yeast in water. Meanwhile, combine scalded milk, boiling water, honey, and butter in a large, heavy mixing bowl. Stir until butter has melted, then add salt, herbs, and olives. When this mixture has cooled to lukewarm, add yeast mixture and stir in three cups of flour gradually. At this point, your mixture should be thick, and you will find it easier to mix in the remaining flour with your hands. Add a little more flour if need be to make a stiff dough. Knead the dough in the bowl until it feels light and elastic, bubbles can be seen under the surface, and the dough squeaks when you work it. Form the dough into a ball and cover the bowl with a towel that has been drenched in hot water and squeezed out. Place the covered dough in your oven with a pan of hot water on the floor of the oven. Let rise until double in bulk. This will take about 1½ hours. The oven should be warm and steamy, so keep checking the temperature of your water, and when it cools, add more hot water. When the dough has risen, punch it down, knead briefly, form into loaves, and place in two or three greased baking pans. Let the dough rise again until it doubles in bulk, about 45 minutes. Meanwhile, preheat your oven to 350°. Set a pan of water in the bottom of the oven (to give the bread a moist interior and a crunchy crust) and bake about 1 hour,* or until the bread sounds hollow when you tap it. Cool on wire racks. Hot bread tastes wonderful, but do not slice it when it is hot; instead tear off portions to eat.

Onion Rosemary Rolls

3	cups unbleached white or whole wheat flour
½	yeast cake (or ½ package dry yeast)
¼	cup warm water
1	cup boiling water
1	tablespoon butter
1	tablespoon sugar
1	teaspoon salt
1	teaspoon dry rosemary, crushed fine
¼	cup onion, finely chopped
1	raw egg
1	tablespoon cream

Dissolve yeast in water. Mix, knead, and let rise as for Herb and Olive Bread. When you have punched and kneaded the dough

*Note: Three smaller loaves take about 45 minutes.

again, shape into balls and drop into greased muffin tins or onto a greased baking sheet. Beat egg and cream together. Brush the top of the rolls with mixture. Bake at 375° for 10 or 15 minutes, or until brown.

Desserts

Apple Ginger

I found this recipe scribbled in the flyleaf of a very old edition of *The Boston Cooking School Cookbook.*

8   parts apples
8   parts sugar
1   part green ginger root

Slice apples and cover with half the sugar and leave stand overnight. Scald and scrape ginger root, run through food chopper, and add to apples and remainder of sugar and cook until clear.

To Make Sugar Cake
From The Queen's Closet Opened, *1655*

Take three pound of the finest Wheat Flower, one pound of fine Sugar, Cloves, and Mace, of each one ounce finely searsed, two pound of Butter, a little Rosewater, knead and mould this very well together, melt your Butter as you put it in, then mold it with your hands forth upon a board, cut them round with a glasse, then lay them on papers, and set them in an Oven, be sure your oven be not too hot, so let them stand til they be colored enough.

A Trifle

From Archimagirus Anglo Gallicus or Excellent and approved Receipts and Experiments in Cookery. *Copied from a choice Manuscript of Sir Theodore Mayerne Knight, Physician to the late K. Charles, 1658.*

Take three pints of pure thick Cream, and boil it with cinnamon, and nutmeg, and sugar; when it is boiled, keep it stirring till it be but blood-warm, then put in some rennet, and when you think good serve it.

To Make Snow

From Archimagirus

Take a quart of cream not too thick, beat it with a birchen rod with whites of Eggs in it, take off the snow as it rises til you have enough of it for a dish, boil some cream for the bottom, set a penny loaf in the bottom of it with a rosemary sprig set in the midst, throw your snow on top of it.

To Make Almond Butter

From Archimagirus

Take a pottle of the best Sweet Cream, a pound and a half of Almonds beaten with rose water to a soft paste; then take three pints of water or more, with half a spoonful of Coriander seeds well boiled together, when it is cold strain out your almonds with this water, getting the substance of the Almonds as much as you can, then mingle your cream with it, set it altogether upon a clean fire, when it is ready to boyl put in a little salt, and when it boyls up, seruch in some juice of Lemons all over it, not too much, but a little to curdle it. Then take it off the fire, let the whay run through a thick cloth or napkin very softly, when it sticks something dry, tye it up round like a pudding, hang it upon a tack all night, then beat it with fine sugar and a little rose water; afterwards make dishes of it.

A Way to make sugar plate both of color and taste of any flower

From Delights for Ladies *by Sir Hugh Plat, 1609*

Take violets and beat them in a mortar with a little hard sugar, then put into it a sufficient quantitie of Rosewater, then lay your gum in steepe in the water, and so worke it into a paste, and so will your paste be both of the color of the violet, and of the smell of the violet. In like sort may you work with Marigolds, Cowslips, Primrose, Buglose or any other flower.

To Make Paste of Flowers of the Color of Marble Tasting of Natural Flowers

From The Queen's Closet Opened, *1655*

Take every sort of pleasing flowers, as Violets, Cowslips, Gilly flowers, Roses or Marigolds, and beat them in a mortor, each flower by itself with Sugar, til the Sugar become the color of the flower, then put a little Gum dragon steeped in water into it, and beat it into a perfect paste, and when you have half a dozen colors, every flower will take of his nature, then rowl the paste therein, and lay one peece upon another, in mingling sort, so rowl your paste in small bowls as big and as long as your finger, then cut it off the bigness of a small nut, over thwart, and so rowl them thin, that you may see a knife through them, so dry them before the fire, till they be dry.

Candied Angelica
From Larousse Gastronomique

Cut angelica stalks into pieces of six to eight inches; soak in cold water, then boil until the pulp yields slightly when pressed with the fingers. Cool under a cold tap, drain and peel, removing all stringy parts. Put into a syrup made with one cup sugar to one cup water for 24 hours. Drain, cook the syrup to 225° and pour over the pieces of angelica. Repeat this operation for three days; on the fourth, cook the syrup to a small pearl (245°). Put angelica into this syrup and bring it to the boil several times. Remove the pan from the fire and let it stand. Drain the pieces of angelica on a sieve. When they become dry, lay them out on a marble slab, sprinkle with fine sugar and put them to dry in a very slow oven. Store in tins.

I will end this recipe section with one of the most beguiling uses of thyme. Dorothy Jacobs, in *The Witch's Guide to Gardening*, records the following "recipe," whose original is preserved in a museum in Oxford, England:

To Enable One to See Fairies

A pint of salad oyle and put in a vial glasse; and first wash it with rose-water; the flowers to be gathered towards the east. Wash it til the oyle becomes white, then put into the glasse, and then put thereto the budds of hollyhocke, the flowers of may-golde, the flowers or tops of wild thyme, the budds of young hazel, and the thyme must be gathered near the side of a hill where fairies are use to be; and take the grasse of a fairy throne; then all these put into the glasse and set it to dissolve three days in the sun and keep it for thy use.

Seasoning Chart

Herb or spice	Culinary use
Angelica	Leaf and stalk as vegetable, stem for candy, liqueur flavoring
Anise	Fruit, especially apple; sweet breads, custards, cookies, cakes; cottage, cream, and other mild cheeses; cucumber, summer squash, zucchini; shellfish; liqueur flavoring
Basil	Pesto; all vegetables, especially tomato; salad dressing; potato salad; lamb, beef, veal, poultry; fish and shellfish; pizza; Italian tomato sauce; yeast breads and baking powder biscuits; vinegar
Bay Leaf	Meat stews; meat or vegetable soups; meat, vegetable, or fish broth; pot roast; Italian tomato sauce; poached fish or poultry
Borage, Rose, Geranium, Violet, Marigold, and Other Flowers	Fresh as garnish for iced drinks, chilled fruit soups, salads, and aspics; candied as confections or pastry decoration; fresh petals flavor cakes and custard; crushed petals color and flavor sugar; whole fresh blossoms as fritters; dried petals flavor tea; marigold in stews
Caraway	Yeast breads, especially rye; roasted and stewed meat, especially pork; sausage; cole slaw, boiled cabbage, string beans; cheese; scrambled eggs, omelettes; baked and stewed fruit, especially apples; young leaves and shoots as vegetables

Cardamom	Danish pastry, sweet breads, cakes, cookies; cantaloupe, honeydew melon; carrots, winter squash, leafy green vegetables; fish, chicken, veal; sour cream sauce, salad dressing; coffee
Cayenne	Avocado or cream dips; eggs; cheese, cream, and milk sauces; cheeses; canapes; salad dressing; soups, stews; dried beans; chili; all meats, fish, game, poultry
Celery Seed	Pickles; beef stew; meat or vegetable stews and soups; seafood, poultry; cheese casserole; zucchini, summer squash; deviled eggs
Chives	Cream, cottage, or other bland cheeses; scrambled eggs; baked potato, potato salad; vegetable salad; fish, poultry
Cinnamon	Stewed and baked fruit, especially apple; cakes, cookies, puddings, whipped cream; curry; beef stew; veal; rice; tea, cocoa, coffee, hot cider, spiced wine, cranberry juice; cranberry sauce; carrots, winter squash
Clove	Cakes, cookies; stewed or roast meat, especially ham; pickles; soup; carrots, parsnip, winter squash
Coriander	Fresh leaves in salad, Mexican dishes; ground seeds with meat or poultry, cheese, pickles, salad dressing, soups, stews, rice, puddings, cakes, cookies
Cumin	Curry, sausage, pickles, cheese, hamburger or meat loaf, rice, meat stew, dried beans, lentils

Dill	Cucumber, string bean, cauliflower, or purslane pickles; mayonnaise, sour cream, or cheese sauces and dips; fish, poultry; potato salad, cole slaw, cucumber salad, string beans, zucchini, summer squash; yeast breads; vinegar
Fennel	Entire plant as boiled vegetable; leaves with fish, poultry; seeds in baked apple desserts, breads
Garlic	Meat, fish, poultry; tomato, green vegetables; salad; soups; meat stews; sautéed with string beans, broccoli, asparagus, cauliflower, zucchini, summer squash; Italian tomato sauce; vinegar
Ginger	Dried, ground in gingerbread, cakes, cookies, candy, pudding, stewed or baked fruit, especially apples, spiced wine; fresh with fish, poultry, carrots, parsnip, winter squash, stir-fried dishes, soup, as candy
Horseradish	Boiled beef, ham; pork, cold meats, canapes, boiled eggs
Marjoram	Italian tomato sauce, meat loaf, paté, dried beans, lentils, string beans, poultry, meat or poultry stuffing, leafy green vegetables, yeast bread
Mint	Candy, syrup, ice cream; fruit or vegetable salad; garnish for iced drinks, cold fruit soup; lamb; cream cheese; carrots, peas; vinegar
Mustard	Young leaves in boiled greens or salads; ground seeds in mayonnaise, salad dressings, cheese sauces, casseroles; paste with beef, ham, pork, lamb, and all cold meats

Nutmeg/Mace	Cake, cookies, pudding; spiced wine, hot cider; stewed or baked fruits, especially apple; Swedish meatballs, meat loaf, veal, beef, poultry, fish; cheese or cream sauce; leafy green vegetables, carrots, parsnips, turnip, winter squash
Oregano	Pizza, spaghetti sauce, and other Italian specialties; meat, especially pork; eggs; tomato dishes; dried beans, lentils, broccoli, cabbage; chili; bean, tomato or minestrone soup
Parsley	As leafy green vegetable in soups and salads; all meats, fish, shellfish, poultry, vegetables; scrambled eggs, omelettes; cream, cottage, and other bland cheeses
Poppy or Sesame Seed	Breads, cookies; topping for casseroles, noodles, all vegetables, poached fish, poultry
Rosemary	Beef, lamb, game, poultry; stuffing; green vegetables; stir-fry; biscuits, yeast bread
Saffron	Pudding, sweet breads, cream cheese, eggs, rice, poultry, seafood
Savory	Beans, cucumber, potato, tomato, carrots, zucchini, summer squash; salad; stuffing; poultry, fish, all meats
Tarragon	Salad dressings; scrambled eggs; sauce béarnaise, canapes, stuffed vegetables; poultry, poached fish, sautéed or braised veal; zucchini or summer squash, creamed onion, tomato juice, tomato sauce, vinegar
Thyme	Fish, seafood chowder or bisque; stuffing; tomato sauce; all meats, poultry; zucchini or summer squash, beets, carrots, onions, potatoes, mushrooms, tomatoes
Turmeric	Pickles, mustard paste; beef steaks and roasts, chicken, fish, pork; chick peas, cabbage

Part Four

The Herbal House

Chapter 16

Herbal Cosmetics

And what about the bark of the wild black cherry, do you scorn it? I actually find its aroma pleasing. But how many bottled perfumes have disappointed me!

Colette

It was not until fairly recently that beauty has been sustained by the blessings of chemistry. Your great-grandmother and generations of her ancestors probably relied on the contents of their pantries or the herbs that grew in their gardens or surrounding neighborhoods to keep their skin soft, their hair shining, and their fragrance sweet. Such time-tested beauty aids have none of the unpleasant side effects of some of our contemporary skin-softeners, hair dyes, and deodorants. Alcohol and the chemicals used to perfume, color, and preserve cosmetics can dry out skin and hair and irritate allergic or sensitive skin. Some of the chemicals in dyes used to color the skin and hair are not only toxic, but the result is not as subtle or pleasing as natural preparations. The cosmetics sold in health food stores are, for the most part, free of harsh chemicals and alcohol. Even they are several steps away from nature, however, having been highly refined to remove irritants and increase shelf life. Many are also quite expensive. So why not experiment with some of the ingredients used by great beauties through the ages?

Making your own cosmetics is a sensual experience, far more satisfying than trying to pronounce the names of the chemicals on the labels of cosmetics sold in department stores. All the ingredients I have listed in this chapter can be purchased from a well-stocked herbal supplier. If you do not have such an outlet in your community, you can order the ingredients by mail from one of the sources listed in the "Resources" section.

Homemade cosmetics will not stay fresh indefinitely because they are not highly refined, as those available in health food stores are, nor do they contain the chemical preservatives that keep proprietary cosmetics fresh. A pinch of gum benzoin, a natural resin, helps retard spoilage; so does storing the cosmetics in your refrigerator as you would any perishable. To avoid bacterial contamination, which can cause skin rashes, be sure that your skin and utensils are clean when preparing, handling, or applying homemade preparations. And before you use any product on your face, it's a good idea to try it out initially on a small area of your skin, such as the inside of your wrist, to make sure it agrees with your skin and body chemistry.

Herbal Cleansing

Some skin care experts believe that you should not use soap on your face. Ever. Especially if your skin is dry. This is because most soaps are alkaline and upset the natural pH balance of the skin, which is slightly acidic. As a result, soap-washed skin is less supple and tends to dryness. Those beguiling bars of glycerin soaps aren't the answer, either, unless you have oily skin, because glycerin, although it is a skin softener, draws water from body tissues. Continental beauties creamed their faces clean. This can be done very simply by using olive, sesame, or any good vegetable oil. Or you can try my adaptation of the ancient Greek physician Galen's recipe for cold cream, recorded by Helen M. Fox in *Gardening With Herbs for Flavor and Fragrance*:

Almond oil	1 part
Rosewater	1 part
White wax or beeswax	1 part
boric acid	1 part
Attar of roses	$1/16$ part

Manipulation: place wax and boric acid in top of double boiler made of enamel or fireproof glass and large enough to contain twice the quantity of cream to be made. Place over boiling water until the wax and boric acid are melted, then add the oil and again heat until the specks of wax and boric acid are liquified. Add rosewater slowly, stirring constantly. If your kitchen is cold, heat the rosewater first so as not to cool the wax. Keep stirring until all of the rosewater has been incorporated. Cool and add the attar of roses.

Attar of roses is very expensive, so you may want to omit that ingredient. If you have trouble finding white wax in your local pharmacy, look for it in a craft shop that sells candlemaking supplies, or use beeswax instead. Beating your mixture until cool is important for a creamy consistency. This should be done with a flat spoon or a paddle. The mixture will thicken faster if you set the bowl in cold water.

Cold creaming is not appealing to everyone. For some, myself included, steaming is a better way to dislodge dirt and thoroughly cleanse the pores, to stimulate the circulation, and to help moisturize. To steam, simply fill a washbasin with boiling water to which you have added a handful of peppermint, rosemary, chamomile, thyme, rose leaves, rose hips, or orange blossoms. Drape a large towel to cover both your head and the basin and remain in your steamy tent for about ten minutes. You can eliminate the towel by leaning over a simmering pot of this herbal mixture, or use a facial sauna. Rinse with cold water if you have oily skin, then use an astringent (see below). If you have dry skin, rinse with a quart of warm water to which a tablespoon of cider vinegar has been added to restore your skin's acid balance. Moisturizers are better absorbed when your skin is warm.

Facial scrubs wash away dead skin cells, cleanse the pores, and discourage the development of whiteheads and blackheads, leaving the skin healthy and glowing. Using finely ground almonds, apricot seeds, oatmeal, bran, fine cornmeal, wheat germ, brewer's yeast, or a combination of these ingredients, make a paste by adding water or rosewater, smooth gently over your face and neck, then rinse and towel dry. Use no more than once a week if your skin is dry, twice a week for oily skin.

Milk, buttermilk, and yogurt, being alkaline, are all very good for cleaning oily skin. Mix any of these dairy products with equal parts of a strong herbal infusion made with one tablespoon peppermint and one tablespoon borage, yarrow, or geranium leaves to one cup water.

Skin Fresheners

After cleansing, treat your face to a freshener to tone, firm, and refine the skin, stimulate circulation, and remove any traces of cleanser or debris. Fresh aloe vera gel did wonders for Cleopatra's beauty and will do the same for you. The gel tones, firms, and softens the skin, helps smooth out wrinkles, kills bacteria, and provides a sunscreen. To use, simply cut off a section of the leaf, split it open, and rub over the face and neck. Unused portions can be wrapped and stored in the refrigerator. A solution of equal parts aloe vera gel and water also makes a very soothing and healing after-shave lotion.

Other skin fresheners can be made by infusing a tablespoon or two of the herbs listed below.

Common Fresheners

Smooths and heals irritated skin	Marigold petals; chamomile; elder blossoms; comfrey; witch hazel bark, twigs, or leaves; aloe vera
Smooths wrinkles	Cowslip petals, orange blossoms, comfrey, elder blossoms, fennel, lemon balm, rose petals, linden or lime blossoms, aloe vera
Moisturizes	Orange blossoms, chamomile
Stimulates cell replacement	Orange blossoms, comfrey
Stimulates circulation	Rosemary, peppermint
Whitens skin	Cowslip petals, elder blossoms
Soothes sunburn	Aloe vera, elder blossoms, comfrey, witch hazel
Astringent, corrects oily skin, shrinks large pores	Rose petals, comfrey, bay leaf, witch hazel, yarrow, sage, nettles, strawberry leaves, raspberry leaves, horsetail
After-shave lotion	Aloe vera, comfrey, witch hazel
Softens skin	Orange blossoms, comfrey, elder blossoms, rose petals
Improves skin tone	Bay leaf (also for bruises), aloe vera, rose petals

Moisturizers

Overexposure to sun, wind, or steam-heated rooms, or simply the passage of time can rob our skin of essential moisture. Women of the British Isles are noted for their fine complexions, which are constantly moistened by ever-present fog, mist, and rain. You can simulate these conditions by spraying your face with water from an atomizer or mister several times a day. Using a strained infusion of moisturizing herbs will not only replenish your skin but also surround you with a refreshing aura of scent. Try orange, chamomile, or rose blossoms (with the astringent white heel removed).

Moisturizing creams can be easily made by adding a tablespoon strong infusion of moisturizing herbs to a quarter-cup cocoa butter, lanolin, petroleum jelly, or plain, unscented moisturizing cream and whipping the heated mixture until cool and creamy. Or you can start from scratch, using the following recipe, which produces a rich cream:

- 1/3 cup orange blossom infusion (1 tablespoon to 1/2 cup boiling water)
- 1/3 cup olive oil
- 1/3 cup fresh aloe vera gel
- 1 tablespoon beeswax or carnauba wax
- 1/8 teaspoon borax
  pinch of gum benzoin

Melt oil, borax, benzoin, and wax in top of double boiler. Blend warm infusion and aloe vera in electric blender. With blender running at medium speed, slowly pour in oil mixture. Blend 30 seconds, remove to a bowl at least twice the size of the ingredients and whip briskly until mixture is cool and creamy. Good for dry hands as well as your face.

Skin Problems

Here are two recipes from *The Queen's Closet Opened* for problem skin:

An Excellent remedy for Heat and Pimples in the Face

Take of Plantain leaves four little handfuls, and of Mallows or Tansy one little, of Cinquefoil half a little handful, and as much of strawberry leaves, there must be this quantity of every sort, when they are pict clean, then take a pottle of new Milk hot from the Cow, and put it in a still with the same herbs, until it hath dropped a quart, then let it drop no more; you may keep it a whole year in a glass; when you use it, wet a cloth in some of it, and wash your face at night to bed, and often in the day; the best time to still it is in May.

For Heat or Scurf in the Face

Take a pint of cream as thick as can be scummed then take of chamomile one handful, pick, wash and shred it very small, then put it into the cream, and let it boil very softly, til it come to an Oil, never stirring it after the putting in the herbs at first, but scum it clean, when you see the oil come to the top, then boil a little faster, and strain it out through a thin linin cloth, and then anoint the Face therewith.

Face Packs

Facial packs are a luxurious beauty treatment for cleansing and moisturizing. Depending on your skin type, make a warm poultice of either moisturizing or astringent herbs (lady's mantle and burnet nourish the skin) and spread on your face, keeping well away from the eyes. Lie down for fifteen minutes and let the herbs do their magic. For dry skin, add honey to the mixture. Whey, as dairymaids of yore knew well, is a wonderful skin softener. Whey is the watery residue that remains after cheesemaking, the liquid that separates from the curds that form in sour milk. You can produce your own curds and whey by filling a cup with warm milk, adding a slice of lemon, and allowing the mixture to stand for several hours in a warm room. Strain off the curds and use the whey to moisten your facial pack or add a strong infusion of your favorite beauty herb—one part infusion to three parts whey—and apply to your face with a piece of cotton, leaving it on for a few minutes. Good for skin on all parts of your body.

Hair

Hair is mostly composed of protein and is slightly acidic in composition. The simplest way to nourish your hair with protein and keep it strong and glossy is to add a raw egg to your shampoo mixture or shampoo with only the raw egg. Contrary to what you might expect, the egg doesn't leave your hair sticky, but clean and tangle-free. A hot oil treatment before you wash your hair adds gloss and strength and is particularly good for hair that is shampooed often. Rosemary, nettle, burdock root, bittersweet, and plants of the nightshade family are reputed to be particularly good for the hair, encouraging growth. To make hot oil for hair treatment use two tablespoons herbs to one cup oil and steep on a sunny windowsill for two to three weeks. Castor oil is best if you don't mind the odor (try it on your eyelashes and see how luxuriantly they grow); lanolin, olive oil, and corn oil are also very good. Massage this oil into your scalp. Cover your head with a hot, wet towel for fifteen minutes or cover the oiled strands with a shower cap and leave on overnight. Shampoo and rinse in tepid water, which rinses away the oil more thoroughly than hot water does.

A simple but very effective shampoo can be made by grating a quarter of a bar of nonalkaline soap (about a quarter-cup) and mixing it with a quarter-cup aloe vera gel and a half-cup hot strong herbal infusion (two tablespoons herbs to one cup water). If your hair is light, use chamomile to bring out the blonde highlights; use sage, rosemary, or nettles for dark hair. If you prefer not to use soap, try yucca root or soapwort. In the West, where it grows, yucca was used by American Indians for food and as a soaping agent. Used as a shampoo it imparts a healthy sheen. The root of soapwort, also called bouncing Bet, makes a lather and has been used for cleaning delicate fabric.

Follow your shampoo with a rinse containing either vinegar (for dry and normal hair) or lemon juice (for oily hair) to restore the acid balance. Use about one teaspoon to one quart water.

Thinning hair is a common problem. A vigorous daily massage with a strong infusion of one or a combination of the herbs listed for hot oil treatments may help. Father Kneipp, a physician-priest who practiced in the latter part of the ninteenth century, recommended two hundred grams of nettle veins (try a homeopathic pharmacy for this ingredient) with one liter water and half a liter of cider vinegar. Boil half an hour, then strain and rub into the scalp before bedtime.

Some people consider gray hair quite striking, and indeed it is if you and your hair are healthy and glowing. But if your original shade is more appealing to you, you can try some herbal strategies that have worked for centuries. Sage or stinging nettle will darken your hair gradually if you rinse with a strong solution after every shampoo. Simmer one ounce sage in one quart water for twenty minutes, steep for another ten minutes, and when the solution has cooled to a comfortable temperature, pour over your hair. If your hair is very dark, gradually increase the proportions of herbs to water. If your hair is light, brew chamomile, marigold petals, or mullein flowers—about one half to one cup to a pint of water—for use instead.

If you have ever compared wool or other fabrics dyed with plants to those dyed with chemicals, you have some idea of what nature can do for your hair. The colors are never harsh; rather, they are natural-looking and soft. Henna, a tropical shrub, yields a lovely hair coloring that penetrates the hair shaft and conditions the hair. When the color fades, the tones become muted, and there is no telltale darkening or graying at the roots. Henna comes in a wide range of shades including neutral and can either enhance or alter your natural hair color. To use, mix the powdered henna with hot water to make a paste the approximate consistency of porridge. For best results, apply the henna treatment before you shampoo. Apply the henna paste with a toothbrush if your hair is very short, a hairbrush if your hair is longer. When you have coated all the strands, work the remaining paste into your hair. Cover with a plastic bag and leave on for fifty minutes—no more. Careful timing is very important when you use henna because the red flowers are used in varying proportions in all hair shades, and these red tones, which usually don't show up in the blondes and browns, can make a startling appearance if you leave the paste on for too long. (I learned this the hard way.) As with any hair coloring, do not use henna for a month before you have a permanent and do not use more frequently than every eight weeks or so.

Hands and Body

While not everyone needs a face cream, we all use hand lotions from time to time for moisturizing and softening. Rosewater-and-glycerin is an old-fashioned hand lotion still sold today. You can easily make it for yourself by combining equal parts of the two ingredients. However, while both ingredients do soothe and soften, glycerin, as I pointed out at the beginning of this chapter, is also drying and may not answer your needs.

The following recipe makes a good hand or body lotion: Prepare an herbal oil by steeping two tablespoons of one of the herbs listed below in half a cup of safflower, sunflower, or almond oil in a sunny window for two or three weeks. Strain out the herbs and heat the oil, one teaspoon beeswax, one quarter-teaspoon honey, and a pinch of gum benzoin in a double boiler until melted. Whip until cool and creamy. Herbs to use include marigold or comfrey for skin that is irritated, cut, or sore; elder, linden, or lime blossoms to soften and whiten; mint or chamomile, antiseptic and healing; marshmallow root or Irish moss to soften; lady's mantle for problem skin. Lavender or rose petals can be added for fragrance.

Nails

Horsetail, which herbalists consider effective in treating connective tissue and use for joint disease and rheumatic problems, is also very good for your fingernails. Its high silica content strengthens the nails if you soak them for a few minutes in a strong infusion. You might want to alternate the horsetail treatment with soaking your nails in an infusion of myrrh or warmed wheat germ or olive oil.

Herbs for the Bath

For centuries folk healers have recognized the therapeutic value of herbal baths. The skin is stimulated by the hot water, and tests have shown that it actually absorbs medicinal properties of certain herbs, while the aroma of the herbs is transmitted by the olfactory nerves to the centers of emotion and memory in the brain, influencing, some therapists believe, the functioning of the body through the nervous system. So when we add our favorite herbs to the bath, the benefits may extend beyond beauty and fragrance.

Lavender, for example, has been used in the bath since the days of ancient Rome—hence the herb's name, meaning "to wash." Since then, lavender has been used for scenting toilet soaps, clothing, and household linens, as well as for treating headache, dizziness, fainting, and hysteria. A whiff of the oil applied to a handkerchief was used in bygone days to revive ladies who were having attacks of "the vapors." Rose petals, chamomile, and mint have similar medicinal applications. Violet has been used for both headaches and skin diseases. As you read in Chapter 15, many of the herbs and spices we use for seasoning have medicinal uses as well, and most have also been used in making soaps, perfumes, colognes, and toilet water. The list of such herbs includes cinnamon, clove, saffron, marjoram, calamus, angelica, anise, dill, tarragon, sweet woodruff, caraway, coriander, cumin, wintergreen, hyssop, bay leaf, lemon balm, geranium, and thyme. Other herbs you might use are lovage, which is a deodorant, and pine or spruce needles, which are invigorating. The herbs I have already listed for skin preparations are wonderful, of course, in the bath. To use them, tie the herbs into a bag made from a porous fabric, such as net or cheesecloth, and suspend from the water faucet so the hot water will run through them. When the bath is drawn, place your herbal sachet directly into the water.

Bath oils can be made by the same method as skin and hair oils. If you use blossoms or gracefully shaped herbs, leave them in the oil. A pretty jar or bottle with herbs or flowers swimming in it adds a decorative touch to the bathroom.

Flowers can be used for scenting oils with a lasting, subtle fragrance to perfume your hair or skin. Lavender, roses, violets, and other fragrant flowers are lovely to use, but you can also make scented oils from the blossoms of culinary herbs; basil and sweet marjoram are particular favorites of mine. Saturate a piece of cotton with bland salad oil and place in a glass jar. Cover the cotton with a layer of petals, screw the lid on the jar, and place in the sun for a few weeks. Squeeze the oil from the cotton, add new flowers, and repeat the process until you have as much oil as you wish.

You can make your own talcum powder by mixing dried powdered Irish moss with pulverized leaves or blossoms. One of the most fragrant is orris root, which you will read about in the next chapter.

Robert Frost once wrote that the advantage of cutting your own wood is that it warms you twice. So, too, the gathering of your own herbs and flowers for cosmetics: first, when their sweetness in wood or field seems to contain all the warmth of the sun, and again, rising from the waters of the bath or releasing their fragrance in rainbowed oils, silken as the ghost of a summer day.

Chapter 17

Herbal Fragrance

For fragrance is indeed what the past well knew it to be, a refreshment and a strength, a sweet and human pleasure, an exorciser of demons from the body and the beseiged and troubled spirit. Subtlest of influences, touching the emotions directly, asking nothing from the mind, it not only works in us an emotion of place, but summons up as well a poignant emotion of ourselves as we were in time and place remembered.

From Herbs and the Earth by Henry Beston

Researching an herbal is a delight not only to the mind but to the senses, and of the many experiences I had tracking down information, perhaps the greatest feast for nose and eye was a vist to the Caprilands herb farm in Connecticut one autumn afternoon.

Since she bought the land in 1929, owner Adelma Grenier Simmons has planted thirty-one small herb gardens where visitors can stroll and read about the lore of individual herbs from signs posted throughout the gardens. Wearing a flowing cape and looking every inch the high priestess of gardening that she is, Simmons gives daily lectures in the spacious barn where herbs are dried.

On a table just inside the entrance to this barn stands an enormous wooden bowl filled with potpourri—a heady rush of fragrance that seems to contain all the sweetness of summer. A few minutes later, when I took my place among the audience assembled for her lecture, I was enveloped in a fragrance that seemed to take me back through time and space to the mountains of New Mexico, where I had lived at one point. Sagebrush, which perfumes the air of the Rockies in spring and summer, was not a scent I would ever expect to encounter in the Northeast. When I inquired about the origins of this nostalgic fragrance, someone pointed out the great bunches of silver king, an artemisia used in herbal wreaths, drying in the rafters above us. Sagebrush, not related to our garden sage even remotely, is an artemisia, a botanical relative of the silver king, mugwort, and other artemisias grown for their lasting fragrance and cool, silver-green beauty.

When I left New Mexico, I brought a few branches of sagebrush with me as a reminder of my stay in the West, and every so often a friend would send me a sprig or two from there. A branch of eucalyptus affects me similarly, the warm, penetrating aroma reminding me of the year I lived in the California mountains near a forest of eucalyptus trees.

As Marcel Proust wrote so eloquently in *Remembrance of Things Past*, our sense of smell can re-create past moments more powerfully than any other sense. This is not surprising when you consider that other species attract or communicate with each other through scent. The art of perfumery certainly takes such psychological factors into account, creating scents chosen to express the personality of the one who wears it and evoke an emotional response in those nearby. You will be most successful when you take these emotional factors into account when you create your potpourri.

Potpourri is a French word meaning "rotten pot," an accurate description of the process used to make moist potpourri by partially decomposing the ingredients with salt. Such potpourris are said to last longer than dry potpourri, although they are not as appealing to the eye, and hence not so popular.

The ingredients that make up a potpourri, and their proportions, are largely a matter of individual taste, the ingredients available at the time you make it, and the ambience you wish to create. For example, at Christmastime I send a mixture containing pine cones and bay leaf to my parents in Florida to remind them of our Maine woods. I use a lavender mixture as a bathroom air freshener, spicy stovetop mixtures in the kitchen, and so on. A potpourri can be as personal as the scent you wear, a subtle evocation of a range of moods and memories.

The basic ingredients of potpourri are flowers, roses being the oldest and most widely used because of their color and lasting fragrance. The cabbage rose and tuberose have traditionally been chosen for their deep color and scent; most other flowers—with the exception of lavender, cassia, lemon verbena, and rose geranium—lose their fragrance after drying. Dried ingredients can be purchased from specialty dealers (see "Resources"), or you can gather them yourself. Blossoms that have not fully opened contain the most essential oil. Gather them early in the day, after the dew has dried, and lay them out on old window screens (paper or cloth will absorb the essential oils) in a dark room (colors fade in sunlight) with good air circulation. Other materials you can dry and add to the mixture are the leafy parts of herbs and other fragrant plants, grasses, pine cones, cedar, or other fragrant bark, berries, and brightly colored blossoms chosen for their visual interest rather than scent. When your ingredients are completely dry, place them in a large bowl and add a fixative to keep the essential oils from evaporating. Use about one tablespoon of fixative to four or five cups flowers. Orris root, which has a fragrance like violets, is most often used as a fixative. Others are gum benzoin (balsam fragrance), tonka bean (like vanilla), angelica root, calamus (sweet, like grass), myrrh, oakmoss, patchouli (woodsy), sandalwood (woodsy), and frankincense. Add about one tablespoon ground spice (cinnamon, clove, nutmeg, allspice, anise, vanilla bean, coriander) and perhaps a tablespoon of dried orange or lemon peel. Finally, add a drop or two of essential oil to reinforce the fragrance. Bergamot enriches the fragrance of the other essential oils in your herbs or flowers. Seal in a large container for about six weeks, shaking or stirring the mixture every day or two. Dry potpourri is pretty to look at, so display it in a clear glass jar with a tight lid. When you want to release the scent, remove the lid and give the mixture a stir. Here are three basic recipes to get you started; see "Resources" for places where you can order supplies.

Lavender Potpourri

3	cups lavender flowers
1½	cups rosebuds
¼	cup oakmoss
¼	cup deer tongue leaves
1	tablespoon powdered orris root
1 or 2	drops essential lavender oil

Christmas Mix

½ cup each:
   small pine cones
   sweet marjoram leaves
   bay leaf
   red eucalyptus leaves
   rose buds
   calendula flowers
   balsam fir tips
   balm of Gilead buds
1 tablespoon powdered benzoin
1 or 2 drops essential pine oil

Stovetop Simmering Spices

1 orange, dried, chopped peel
1 lemon, dried, chopped peel

½	cup allspice berries
2	tablespoons star anise
¼	cup German or Egyptian chamomile
½	cup whole cinnamon, broken
3	tablespoons whole clove
½	cup whole nutmeg, broken
1	tablespoon vanilla bean, crushed

To use, simmer 2 tablespoons of this mixture in 1 pint water.

Moist potpourri, which does not have the visual appeal of the dry mixture, should be stored in opaque containers. To make a moist potpourri, place a layer of rose petals or other fragrant flowers in a container and cover with a layer of sea salt, alternating the layers of petals and salt until the container is filled. Cover and leave undisturbed for two weeks, then break up the caked mixture with a wooden spoon, add fixative, essential oil, and ground spices in proportions similar to dry potpourri.

Potpourris have many uses. Spicy mixtures can be simmered on the top of the stove for a country kitchen aroma. If you keep a container of water on your radiator to humidify the air in winter, add a handful of floral mixture or one containing mint or eucalyptus.

Sachets have been used for centuries to scent clothing and linen and can be easily made by sewing your potpourri (or a single herb such as lavender, anise, or roses) into a cloth bag or small pillow. Some plants also repel insects, and a sachet of one of these is far pleasanter than mothballs for storing with woolens. Herbs that repel insects include mint; marjoram; wormwood, mugwort, and other artemisias; eucalyptus; pine needles; and red cedar chips. Pomanders are another old-fashioned way to scent closets. To make one, simply insert whole cloves into an orange or lemon, and dry.

Another way of scenting the air with spices and resins is to burn them, a practice dating back to ancient times when the smoke of incense replaced human sacrifices as a way of propitiating the gods and goddesses. Freshening the air with burnt spice is a trick I learned at my mother's knee when she poured a little ground clove into a

The Herbal House

dish and lit it after she had cooked fish, liver, or other odorous foods. Most ground spices, as well as frankincense and myrrh, have a spicy fragrance when they are burned. Put a teaspoon or so into a metal dish or ashtray, then light a wooden kitchen match and lay it gently over the spice. By the time the match was burned out your spice will be smoldering. If you have a woodburning fireplace or stove, toss a little spice into the fire—the perfect ending to an herbal feast.

Chapter 18

Grow Your Own

One cold and gloomy winter morning, I woke feeling stuffed-up and groggy, with an ominous rasp in my throat. Disinclined to reach into the medicine chest, which doesn't offer much in the way of cold preparations anyway, I went instead to the indoor garden growing on my kitchen windowsill. Here I found the makings of an aromatic, healing broth that helped me avoid debilitating flu bouts all last winter. (See page 95 for recipe.)

The basil I had planted the previous spring had succumbed to soil line fungus during a wretchedly hot and humid summer. Now it was putting out new leaves on the desiccated and blackened stems. Beside the basil, a pot of sweet marjoram, planted in mid-autumn, offered young leaves on sprawling stems, and a tiny rosemary bush, purchased in autumn, stood ready for its bimonthly pruning.

A few leaves of each herb, all of them cold remedies, went into a soup pot along with fresh garlic and a teaspoonful of dried wild

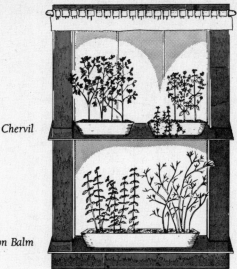

Chervil

Thyme and
Sweet Marjoram

Lemon Balm

Dill

mountain thyme I had gathered a few months before in the Catskills. This was my daily lunch for the next few days.

Although I can't claim an instant cure—most herbs don't work that instantly or dramatically—I did feel somewhat better, and what ordinarily would have been weeks or even months of debilitating flu symptoms never became more than a mild and temporary cold. Moreover, I was spared the drowsy, mind-clouding side effects that invariably accompany commercial cold preparations.

The following spring and summer, my indoor herb garden was much more extensive, and since the windows that frame it all face south, I enjoyed fresh herbs throughout the winter, not only for home remedies, but for the freshest possible seasoning.

No matter how carefully an herb is harvested and preserved, there is always something lost in the freezing or drying: aromatic oils and other chemicals, perhaps unknown as yet, that contribute nutrients, healing properties, and flavor. Some herbs, such as chervil and parsley, can only be enjoyed when fresh; when dried, they don't taste like much of anything.

Reaching over to snip a handful of chive or a few sprigs of dill or tarragon adds a crowning touch to a sauce or salad and is much more impressive to dinner guests than shaking out a pinch or two of dried seasoning. But best of all is the joy of watching seeds I have sprinkled over the soil of a plant pot burst into tiny points of green and develop and bloom almost before my eyes. Watching the cycle of growth, decay, and rebirth taking place on my windowsill keeps me sane during those months I spend in the concrete jungle and puts me in close touch with nature.

If you have a suburban backyard or country property, you can, of course, practice gardening on a more extensive scale than I do when I am in the city. There are many fine books on the subject that offer more advice than I possibly could in the limited space of a chapter. Gertrude B. Foster's *Herbs for Every Garden* is one of the best; Helen M. Fox's *Gardening With Herbs for Flavor and Fragrance* is also excellent. However, since both are New England gardeners, you may find other books more suited to your climate.

With some exceptions, the three essentials for an herb garden are good drainage, plenty of sunlight and poor soil that is slightly alkaline. If your soil is rich, Pat Repert of Shady Hill Farms in Saugerties, New York, advises mixing equal parts of soil, peat moss, and gravel, sand, or perlite with a handful of lime added to provide the proper medium for herb growing. Sweet woodruff, she says, is an exception, preferring the acid soil, shade, and moisture of woodland areas. Thyme is also more tolerant of acid soil, while lavender requires more alkalinity than you would use for most herb plantings. To provide this, Repert uses wood ashes for a winter mulch.

Other herbs that can do without one or more of the essentials are sweet basil, which can be planted in your vegetable garden, especially around tomatoes because it helps protect them against insect predators; peppermint, which tolerates wet conditions; watercress, which, as the name implies, will grow in water; and rosemary, which does well in the shade.

Generally speaking, if you find yourself with a patch of land that appears to be unsuited for growing other crops, herbs will be your answer. The exceptions, Foster points out, are the subsoil left over after digging a house foundation and areas under large trees where nothing grows.

The size and design of your garden will depend on the available space and your personal inclinations. The plan can be as simple as a tiny clump of your favorite culinary herbs or as ambitious as a knot garden, a labyrinth, or similarly elaborate design. Many of the seed suppliers listed in the "Resources" section produce catalogs with detailed information about cultivation and descriptions of the mature plant. Most also suggest the best herbs for a novice's garden.

If you fancy a lawn and the soil is inadequate for growing grass, which is actually a fairly modern lawn material, try growing chamomile instead. Roman chamomile is a perennial, and preferable to German chamomile, which is an annual. When the flowers are kept clipped, the Roman chamomile spreads over the ground to form a fragrant green mat. Chamomile lawns were popular for centuries in Europe. In monastery gardens, chamomile was planted over earth that was heaped up to form benches on which the monks could rest and contemplate nature. Chamomile is known as the plant's physician, and if planted near ailing vegetation the chemicals in the roots supposedly spread to the sick plant to make it well.

Most herbs—again, with exceptions—will grow easily from seed; most germinate in five to seven days. French tarragon, more flavorful than the Russian variety and preferable for culinary use, cannot be grown from seed, so you must obtain the plant and propagate by root division. Lavender can take as long as a month to germinate. When I planted the seeds indoors in late May, only three frail, spindly seedlings came up, and they eventually died. When I sowed again in August, however, four or five seedlings did appear in about a week and a half. One explanation for this may be that in the May planting the seeds were still dormant. Pat Repert claims that the seeds must be subjected to frost to break their winter dormancy. She stores her lavender seeds in the freezer for a couple of weeks to accomplish this.

The difficulty of growing parsley has been publicized for centuries in many old sayings such as "It must be planted at Easter, then go nine times to the Devil and back again so the Devil can have his share," "Only the wicked can grow parsley," "Only the pregnant can," "It must be grown apart from other herbs because it doesn't like company."

Repert's theory is that the seed won't germinate until the tough outer covering is cracked, so she pours hot water on the seeds. Or, she adds, you can try Gertrude Foster's method: Place the seeds between layers of wet paper towels for seven days.

Personally, I think this is a lot of fuss for such an insignificant-tasting herb, and after one failed attempt many years ago, I haven't tried again, preferring the more accommodating and flavorful Italian parsley. Even this variety, though, can germinate slowly, sometimes taking over a month. By July, I could harvest the fat sprigs, and the plant remained hardy throughout the winter.

Other herbs that are difficult to grow from seed include: rosemary, best propagated by cuttings; winter savory, best propagated by division; and costmary, which propagates by division or being grown from plants.

In contrast to these reluctant growers, mint is one of the most prolific in the garden, reproducing not by seed but by spreading runners that in time will take over a garden if they are not contained. Repert deals with this problem by sowing in large, saucer-shaped terra-cotta planters set into the soil, or by pruning twice a year so the leaves will not root when the plant flattens against the ground.

Compost is your best fertilizer because it will not burn the tender roots. Weeds, which are high in vitamins and minerals, will greatly enrich your compost pile. Nettles, for example, are rich in iron; so are dandelions, which draw nutrients from deep in the soil with their long roots. It is best to use young plants, before they go to seed, or their progeny may establish themselves in your garden.

A layer of mulch conserves moisture and supresses weeds in summer. Avoid evergreens, however, because they will add unwanted acidity to the soil; and do not use mulching material that will seed the soil with weeds. A winter mulch will protect your perennials from alternate freezing and thawing, sun, and winds.

The most frequent insect guests in your herb garden will be bees, who are especially fond of thyme and bee balm. However, you may be troubled from time to time by predatory insects, although the aromatic oils in herbs usually act as a repellent. Marigolds are often planted as a border in both vegetable and herb gardens to discourage insects. If this doesn't do the trick, try soaking the heads of feverfew in water and use as a spray, or dust on the dried powdered flowers. In addition to its medicinal value, feverfew yields pyrethrum, which is used in certain commercial insecticides because it is nontoxic to warm-blooded animals and thus the safest of the insecticides. You can also rub the leaves or flowers on your skin to repel bugs while you are gardening. If you live in the country where rabbits, deer, and other wildlife like to browse in your garden, use dried blood as a repellent. You can buy this product where gardening supplies are sold.

While outdoor gardens are a joy to behold and work in—merely breathing the mingled fragrances of herbs seems to be health-giving—city dwellers must usually be content with more modest space. If you have south-facing windows, you should have adequate light for even your sun-loving herbs. If your windows face in other directions, you should be able to grow rosemary, sweet woodruff, or bay laurel in natural light. Other herbs require more sun, so the natural light will have to be supplemented by special lighting. The blue end of the spectrum in flourescent lighting nourishes the leaves but not the flowers; the red end of the spectrum in incandescent lighting nourishes flowers but not the leaves. If your herbs are to thrive, your lighting must include the entire spectrum. Some gardening suppliers sell full-spectrum lighting; you also may be able to buy directly from the manufacturer.

For a growing medium, I have found that the nearest thing to poor soil is the pebble-strewn mixture of sand, soil, and humus sold as potting soil for cactus. You should be able to find this at your local supermarket. To three parts of this mixture I add about one part peat moss and a handful of bone meal. Shallow pans are the recommended vessel for the initial seedbed, but since I didn't have any on hand the first time I sowed, I improvised with ice cube trays and found the compartments ideal for separating the few seedlings I needed. Eggshells are also good for starting seeds because they can be transplanted to a larger pot, adding calcium to the soil when they decompose.

To plant, I first moisten the soil with a fertilizing solution made with 5-10-5 fertilizer, then scatter three or four seeds in each compartment and cover the whole with a plastic bag. The plastic provides a humid greenhouse atmosphere that eliminates the need for frequent watering. When I wanted a somewhat larger planting of an herb—in this instance, it was marigold—I experimented with the clear plastic container in which I buy hydroponic lettuce. This, in fact, proved to be an ideal miniature greenhouse. Much to my astonishment, the morning after I had planted the marigold seeds, I lifted the lid and found a thick sprinkling of green tips sprouting through the soil. Some gardening suppliers sell miniature greenhouses for starting seeds—see the "Resources" section for details. The greenhouse idea is especially good for parsley, lavender, or any other seeds whose germination time is so long that you may forget to water them. Whatever you use as a seedbed, keep it out of direct sunlight until the seedlings appear.

When your seedlings have four true leaves, it is time to transplant them. Cardboard milk cartons or drinking cups are good for the plant's first home after the seedbed and they can be recycled to use as initial planters for a later season. After transplanting, keep the seedlings out of direct sunlight until the next day to allow them to recover.

Damp or muggy weather or abrupt changes in temperature can make seedlings vulnerable to damping off fungus, which attacks plants at the soil line and causes the stems to shrivel and turn black. Sprinkling a layer of peat moss on top of the soil helps avoid this; so does watering from below by placing the container of seedlings in a pan of tepid water so the soil will soak up by capillary action the moisture that seeps in through holes in the container. Watering from below is also good for African violets and other plants that have parts that shouldn't come in direct contact with water.

In the springtime, before I have my windows open all day, my seedlings develop better if I set them on top of the lower window sash where they get more sunlight. Suspending the plants so they hang in the upper half of the window is also good. Be sure you turn the plants every day or so for even development, and fertilize every two weeks with a 5-10-5 solution or a fish or seaweed emulsion.

In summertime, the best place for your plants is in an open window where they get fresh air and sunlight. They will do even better outdoors, in direct sunshine. You're in luck if you have access to a fire escape, rooftop, or outside window ledge wide enough to hold a potted plant. You can also suspend the plants outside your window with hooks, or plant them in a window box. The last is an attractive way to present herbs, but you can only set about three plants in a window box, and if you want to bring them in for winter you will have to dig them up and repot them.

Last summer I had windowsill gardens both inside and outdoors on window ledges. The difference in size and hardiness between plants grown in these two locations was quite dramatic. My outdoor basil, for example, grew to be about four times the size of those I have indoors. My indoor peppermint grew close to the soil and had tender leaves with a barely detectable taste or scent of mint, while the leaves of my outdoor mint were much larger and tougher, sharply toothed along the edges, with a pronounced scent and taste of peppermint. The dill I grew inside was downright peaked, producing no flowers, while my outdoor dill was strong, tall, and hardy, with a vigorous flower.

Delightful, too, in my outdoor garden were the wind-borne seeds that sprouted where I least expected them. Sumac, Japanese knotweed, and wood sorrel all made an appearance. The sorrel, which adds a pleasant tartness to dips and salads, was the most enthusiastic volunteer, turning up in several of my plant pots, even indoors, and putting out tiny yellow flowers in summertime.

It is best to start your plants by the middle of May so they will be hardy enough to be set outdoors in pots or planted in a garden when summer comes. Wait until all danger of frost is past before doing this. If I am setting houseplants outdoors, I wait for mild days with temperature close to 60°, so the plants won't be shocked by an abrupt change in temperature, and take them in at night until the weather is fairly mild.

Although spring is the usual time for propagation, I have made autumn indoor plantings of sweet marjoram and spicy globe basil for the pleasure of seeing new life in a season when everything else is dying down. The seedlings developed very slowly all winter, and by mid-May the basil was budding and the marjoram had flowered. My autumn plantings thrived on an outdoor window ledge all summer and remained hardy indoors throughout the winter.

In order to flourish, herbs need good drainage and large pots to accommodate their root systems, so you will need to transplant to larger planters when your herbs begin to outgrow their original containers. This is particularly true for rosemary, which has strong, fibrous roots and needs a large container. Terra-cotta, which is porous, is an excellent material for repotting plants. To make sure I have adequate drainage, I line the bottom of the pot with drainage material. Pebbles or broken terra-cotta plant pots are recommended. In the city, however, pebbles are hard to come by, and most apartment dwellers lack the storage space for keeping old planters on hand. One solution is to save bottle caps, which don't take up much space, and put a layer or two at the bottom of the planter. On top of this goes a layer of sand or perlite, then some more of the potting mixture used for the seedlings. To repot, fill the new planter about halfway up with soil, then turn the old planter with the plant in it upside down, keeping your fingers spread to hold the plant in place. Tap the bottom of the cup so the plant, along with the soil, slides out smoothly. Then position the plant, with the old soil still attached, in the new planter so the old soil comes almost to the rim of the new planter. Fill in the planter with new soil, water with a fertilizing solution, then wait a day before you place your transplant in direct sunlight.

Your indoor plants need to be shaded from the midday sun on hot summer days. Ironically, aloe vera, so useful in treating burns, can actually get sunburned. If the leaves turn rosy, indicating sunburn, you only have to move the plant out of direct light for it to recover.

During the heat of summer, you will probably need to water every day. This should be done early in the morning or at evening, although Gerard says basil and marjoram should be watered at midday. I'm not sure why, but he seems to be right; basil seems to need more watering than other plants. According to tradition, the watering of basil should be accompanied by oaths. I'm not into plant abuse, though, and they seem to thrive in spite of that.

As soon as the leaves grow large and abundant, you can begin snipping them off for use. Your herbs will benefit from this casual pruning, which makes the plant bushier and more compact. The tops of rosemary should be trimmed every two months.

The time for bringing your plants in for winter will depend on the weather in your vicinity. During the transitional months, you can leave them out when the days are warm and take them in at night to the coolest place you have available.

As a rule, the flavor and medicinal properties of an herb are the most po-

The quiet of winter is wearing through upon the land. Human voices which seemed lost in the vast snow have again the open earth beneath them, and over the unfrozen soil, across field and pasture and darker wood comes the bold and distant cry of chanticleer. What a fine sound it is, that triple and unearthly cry, heard here in the garden through the pale and quiet of the northern spring. All the animal defiance of circumstance and fate, all the acceptance and challenge of the animal blood come with it into our human world seeking an echo there, before melting away into the light. Pressing on with the sun the furrow shall follow north the sun retreating, and the earth shall be sown again and shall part, giving life to the seed and to the herbs of man's remembrance, the ancient leaves dear at once to ploughman and woman of the distaff, to priest and golden-circleted king.

From Herbs and the Earth
by Henry Beston

tent just before flowering. After that, the essence is concentrated in the flower and seed, and the plant, if it is an annual, having completed its natural function, will die. The way to keep herbs over the winter is to interrupt the cycle of reproduction and decay by snipping off the buds so the plant won't flower.

The best time to harvest an herb is just before it flowers. This should be done in the morning, before the heat of the day has dissipated the essential oils. The leaves should be as dry as possible, however, so wait until the morning dew has dried and harvest on a fair day. If you want to collect the seeds, let at least one plant flower and set seed if yours is a windowsill garden, more if your garden is outdoors.

Most herbs will dry quite successfully if you hang them upside down in a dark, dry place. Wash the herb first, then pat it dry with a towel and cover with a paper bag to protect it from dust and insects. The bag should be large enough so it will not absorb essential oils by coming into contact with the leaves. If the weather is damp or you want to accelerate the drying process, you can dry the herbs in a warm oven set at the lowest temperature. If it is basil you are drying, the oven method is preferable because basil easily molders and turns black. Leaves are dry when they feel brittle, which should take about an hour in the oven. Strip the dry leaves from the stems and seal them tightly in tins or dark glass bottles to keep out light and moisture. Used vitamin bottles are ideal for this purpose.

A few herbs are better frozen. Dill loses much of its flavor when dried; chervil and parsley lose just about all of their character; and basil, as noted, molders easily. Herbs do not require blanching before freezing, but merely have to be washed and sealed in plastic bags or cartons. When you need them for teas or seasoning, cut off only as much as you will use immediately and add them to your teapot or casserole while they are still frozen.

Although dried or frozen herbs you have grown yourself can enliven a January meal with memories of summer, fresh herbs are the most uplifting, and their flavor cannot be surpassed. You can extend this pleasure into the winter months by potting up your garden herbs and bringing them indoors, or keep your indoor garden growing by setting the plants in the upper portion of a south window or under gardening lights. Rosemary, bay laurel, and sweet woodruff require less sunlight, so you may get by with placing them in a less sunny window. The flavor and fragrance of herbs grown indoors is less intense, but still superior to dried herbs.

Before bringing your herbs indoors, spray them with a solution of Ivory dishwashing soap—one teaspoon to one quart water—to eliminate any insects that might be clinging to them. This is also a good way to deal with the white flies and soil gnats that often plague indoor gardens.

Herbs should be watered as soon as the soil feels dry. Rosemary, especially, should be well watered and never allowed to dry out. You may need to water every day. Your herbs, especially rosemary, will also appreciate a daily misting.

Herbs should be grown as far as possible from radiators and other heating appliances, in a room that is cool, moist, and well ventilated. On very cold winter days they should be placed at some distance from windowpanes, which will be much colder than the rest of the room.

When spring returns, it is time for trimming, pruning, repotting, and refreshing the soil as you do with your houseplants. This is also the time for seeding new varieties and increasing the number of established plants by cuttings or root division.

Herbs are wonderful for gift-giving, as you may have discovered already if you have been making herbal cosmetics or condiments. There are few homemade gifts more welcome than a bottle of dandelion or elderberry wine at Christmas, unless it's a young plant, with its promise of delights for nose and palate, presented on an early summer day.

Chapter 19

Boiled Christmas Tree
and Other Rejuvenations

How does one recycle a Christmas tree? I pondered that interesting question last New Year's morning as I undressed the branches, still fragrant with pine, and put away the lights, the circular mirrors, and the miniature wooden toys I use for ornaments for another year.

In the country there wouldn't be a problem. Dry pine trees make good kindling, if nothing else, or possibly a mulch for acid-loving plants. In some states you can even buy a Christmas trees with the roots still attached so you can later return it to the dealer for re-planting, or replant it yourself in your own back yard. But last winter I lived in Brooklyn, where there are no tree farms and little demand for mulch or kindling. In Brooklyn, as in most cities, once Christmas is over, you wrap the tree in twine, making a compact bundle to avoid littering the floors and hallways with dry needles that will cling to rugs and lurk in corners and cracks. Then you set the tree out on the street for the sanitation crews to cart away, along with similar vegetable corpses—a whole forest of them—to decay in some landfill or waterway.

There must, I thought, be a better way. I don't much like artificial trees, possibly because the one I remember most vividly adorned my mother's parlor in Florida one Christmas when I visited her. In an attempt to evoke the Yuletide pungency of a spruce forest in Maine, she had sprayed on some artificial tree scent, which, if it resembled any aroma at all to be found in nature, suggested the glandular eruptions of a startled skunk.

While I am not one of your urban enthusiasts willing to spend a week's salary on a temporary decoration, I had paid something for this tree, and it didn't seem economical, ecology-wise or money-wise, not to get more for my investment. So I decided to boil it.

Years ago, as a treat, I bought myself a bath gel that had a wonderful alpine fragrance and produced an invigorating sense of rejuvenation as I emerged from the bath. Maybe, I thought to myself, I could recapture that wonderful feeling by extracting the oils from my Christmas pine. My guide for this operation was John Lust's *The Herb Book*, which described the process of making such a potion from the young twigs and cones of spruce trees. My tree, of course, was not a spruce, and the twigs weren't exactly young, but I was hopeful. Lust's recipe called for two or three pounds of tree parts to four gallons of cold water, to be steeped for a night and day, then boiled for two hours. Not having a scale handy, I guessed at the amounts, filling a kettle about three quarters full of branch tips, then adding water to the rim of the pot. After twenty-four hours, when the broth didn't smell exactly alpine, I let the mixture sit for an extra day or two, then set the kettle on my gas burner to simmer. The aroma, I must tell you, was penetrating. Temples pulsing and eyes smarting, I chided myself for my frailty, overlooking the rather important fact that pine trees are the source of turpentine.

The finished product, I am happy to report, did not smell like turpentine, although its russet hue would disqualify it from being a hot seller at the cosmetics counter. Nevertheless, I bottled the stuff and went ahead and used it as I had originally intended. Adding about a cupful to a bath when I felt a cold coming on did bring relief for sniffles and congestion and the aches and stiffness that come with a cold. Next year, though, for my recycling project, I think I'll try a spruce.

Some of my other recycling experiments have been less arduous, and often accidental. For example, a cold compress consisting of the teabag left over from a cup of fennel tea I had sipped as a carminative proved wonderfully soothing to my sore and tired eyes. It was only later that I discovered that infusions of fennel are used for just this purpose, along with many other ones, which include smoothing out wrinkles and toning the skin. On another evening, after I had sipped a cup of peppermint tea for a nightcap and also for a mild headache, I tried applying the warm teabag as a compress to my forehead and found its penetrating warmth immensely soothing. Peppermint is also, paradoxically, very cooling as well as antiseptic, and good for stimulating and toning the skin. You can either rub the teabag on your face, as I did, being very careful not to get it near your eyes, or add to a facial steam or a bath.

There are many herbs that you may first savor as tea before you go on to enjoy their cosmetic benefits, and they can be used in all the ways I have just mentioned. If it is loose tea you are steeping rather than a teabag, you can simply tie the leaves in a porous cloth—cheesecloth is good. Some of the herbs you may take first for medicine or relaxation include chamomile

Eucalyptus-Eucalyptus globulus

flowers, which tone and soften the skin and soothe eye irritations, and elder flowers, which are soothing and mildly astringent and can be used to whiten and soften the skin and smooth out wrinkles. Elder has long been a favorite for facials and skin salves because of these qualities. A weak infusion also soothes irritated eyes. Linden and lime blossoms stimulate circulation, smooth wrinkles, and whiten the skin. Orange blossoms and rose petals both soften and moisturize; yarrow is astringent and good for skin toning.

Herbs you may have used as air fresheners can also have a second career after their original one is exhausted. At the end of winter, when your eucalyptus bouquet is tired and dusty, use branches to protect your woolens from moths and fleas when you put them away for summer storage. The lingering fragrance when I first wear a scarf or sweater again in the fall is one of the nicest I know. Eucalyptus in your bath water is also a wonderful decongestant as well as antiseptic and soothing to sore or tired muscles.

A bouquet of wilted flowers, instead of going into the trash can, could go into a potpourri, you will find instructions for making one in Chapter 17. I have also found that the buds I snip from the herbs growing on my windowsill, especially basil and sweet marjoram, add a refreshing scent to potpourri. The potpourri, when past its prime, will serve for a floral bath a time or two if you wrap the ingredients in a piece of cloth or muslin and attach the sachet to the faucet so the hot water will run through it.

Herb blossoms can also be used for flavoring oils and vinegars (see Chapter 15) or as a base for scented oils (see Chapter 16).

Finally, if you live in a dry climate, you can also use your leftover herbal tea leaves as a mulch for potted herbs. In the heat of summer, when daily watering is essential and you have more interesting things to do, your leaf mulch will keep the soil moist. A caution, though: This does not work well with very young plants, which are vulnerable to soil line fungus, nor is it good in humid climates, which may cause damp leaves to molder.

If you make your own compost, herb tea leaves are an excellent addition, contributing vital nutrients to your soil. Nettles and dandelions are particularly good for composting because of their rich mineral content.

There are some of the ways you can recycle your plants, both great and small. You will surely think of other ways yourself. Sniff their aroma, experience their feel and texture, and your plants and herbs will reveal their secrets to you as they have for centuries to shamans and witches, sages and peasants, monks, poets, and all the gardeners and gatherers who have loved them well.

Resources

Seeds

Abundant Life Seed Foundation
P.O. 772
Port Townsend, WA 98368
Nonprofit company devoted to
preserving wild plants and
distributing seeds. Herb,
wildflower, vegetable, grain seeds;
good selection herb, ecology,
gardening books.

W. Atlee Burpee & Co.
Warminster, PA 18974
Thick catalog of all kinds of seeds,
including herbs. Reliable.

Caprilands Herb Farm
534 Silver St.
Coventry, CT 06238
Seeds, live plants, dried herbs,
books by owner, Adelma Grenier
Simmons, herbal craft items, dried
flower and herb wreaths a
specialty. Extensive gardens, nice
to visit, serves superb herbal
luncheons.

Fox Hollow Herbs
Box 148
McGrann, PA 16236
Small packets of seed available for
only 25¢.

Horticultural Enterprises
P.O. Box 810082
Dallas, TX 75381-0082
Chili seeds—over thirty different
varieties.

Johnny's Selected Seeds
203 Foss Hill Rd.
Albion, ME 04910
Grow their own seeds or contract
from ecological small farmers,
exchange seeds with customers.
Organic gardening supplies,
informative catalog.

Orol Ledden & Sons
Center and Atlantic Ave.
P.O. Box 7D
Sewell, NJ 08080
Seeds, live plants, gardening
supplies. Oriented to commercial
grower.

Lily of the Valley Herb Farm
3969 Fox Ave.
Minerva, OH 44657
Extensive list live plants and seeds, herbs, and scented geraniums; also dried herbs, potpourri ingredients. Informative catalog includes gardening hints.

Sandy Mush Herb Nursery
Rt 2 Surret Cove Rd.
Leicester, NC 28748
Extensive list live plants and seeds, nice handbook.

Nichols Garden Nursery
1190 North Pacific Hwy.
Albany, OR 97321
They introduced elephant garlic. Exotic herb and vegetable seeds from all over the world, also live plants, dried culinary and medicinal herbs including fo-ti-tieng, supplies for home vintners, brewers, and gardeners, books, potpourri.

Park Seed
Cokesbury Rd.
P.O. Box 46
Greenwood, SC 29648-0046
Specializes in flower seeds, but good selection herb seeds.

Plants of the Southwest
930 Baca St.
Santa Fe, NM 87501
Seeds and live plants native to Southwest. Herbs, including devil's claw, wildflowers, some medicinal, grasses and vegetables. Interesting booklist, beautiful catalog.

The Redwood City Seed Company
P.O. Box 361
Redwood City, CA 94064
Interesting herb selection, also wild plant seeds, old-fashioned vegetables, several varieties basil and chili, books. Catalog $1.00.

Richter's
Good Wood, Ontario
Canada LOC IAO
Seeds, live plants, tools, fertilizers, books. Live plants resonably priced, seeds rather expensive but has very comprehensive list including skullcap, ginseng, fuller's teasel, tormentil; $2.50 for catalog.

Clyde Robin Seed Co., Inc.
P.O. Box 2855
Castro Valley, CA 94546

Wildflower Seeds, Some Medicinals, Also Wildflower Mixtures

Shale Hill Farm and Herb Gardens
6856 Hommelville Rd.
Saugerties, NY 12477
Seeds I planted produced hardy specimens that lasted two winters so far. Newsletter packed with recipes and gardening tips. Concerts, lectures, festivals, and other events.

Territorial Seed Co.
P.O. Box 27
80030 Territorial Rd.
Lorane, OR 97451
Herb, vegetable, and flower seeds guaranteed to grow in Northwest. Also beneficial insects and insecticides, tools, supplies. Catalog has detailed gardening information.

Le Jardin du Gourmet
Box 7
St. Johnsbury, VT 05863
Live plants and seeds from France or their own Vermont garden. They also sell sample selections for 25¢ a packet.

Gardeners' Supplies

Gardener's Supply
128 Intervale Rd.
Burlington, VT 05401
Develop many of their own products. Committed to organic gardening and local farming. Exclusive North American distributor for Accelerated Propagation System, a miniature greenhouse for starting seeds. Tools, cold frames, seeds, fertilizer.

Also see Johnny's Selected Seeds, Territorial Seed Co., Richter's.

Dried Herbs

Aphrodisia
282 Bleecker St.
New York, NY 10014
Wide variety of medicinal and culinary herbs, some organic, including Chinese and Aryurvedic botanicals, ginseng, homeopathic remedies, essential oils, potpourri ingredients, books, cosmetics. Catalog $2.00.

Indiana Botanic Gardens Inc.
Box 5
Hammond, IN 46325
One of the best. Quality products, wide assortment single herbs and mixtures based on early American and European spa recipes. Excellent book list.

Meadowbrook Herb Garden
Route 138D
Wyoming, RI 02898
Dried herbs, seeds, tea mixtures,
elixirs, cosmetics, potpourri herbs.
Grown by Bio-Dynamic gardening
method. Catalog $1.00.

Stewart Laboratories
122 South Wabasha St.
St. Paul, MN 55107
Comfrey leaves grown by special
process to reduce pyrrolizidine
alkaloids to almost nil. Leaves sold
by the pound extremely
reasonably. Also skin-care products
for moisturizing and infections.

Weleda Inc.
30 S. Main St.
Spring Valley, NY 10977
Started in Switzerland over sixty
years ago. Bio-Dynamic dried
herbs, home remedies, cosmetics,
baby products, books.

Potpourri Ingredients

Tom Thumb
Route 13
P.O. Box 357-HC
Mappsville, VA 23407
Extensive list potpourri ingredients,
also their own mixtures, potpourri
containers, craft accessories, books.

Also see Aphrodisia.

Organizations

American Botanical Council
P.O. Box 201660
Austin, TX 78720
Nonprofit; disseminates
information on herbs and
medicinal plants. Publishes
Herbalgram in conjunction with
Herb Research Foundation.

Garlic Seed Foundation of New
York State
Rose Valley Farm
Rose, NY 14542-0149
Has tested over seventy-five garlic
strains for New York state farmers,
distributes growing stock,
information, newsletter.

Herb Research Foundation
P.O. Box 2602
Longmont, CO 80501
Membership gets you *Herbalgram*,
an excellent quarterly publication
detailing current research on
medicinal herbs.

Scientific Names for Herbs and Spices

Common name(s)	Botanical name
Allspice	*Pimenta dioica*
Aloe vera	*Aloe barbadensis*
Amaranth	*Amaranthus hypochondriacus*
Angelica	*Angelica archangelica*
Anise	*Pimpinella anisum*
Apple	*Pyrus malus*
Arnica	*Arnica montana*
Artichoke	*Cynara scolymus*
Asafetida	*Asafoetida ferula*
Asparagus	*Asparagus officinalis*
Basil, sweet	*Ocimum basilicum*
Bay leaf, laurel	*Laurus nobilis*
Bearberry, kinnikinnick	*Arctostaphylos uva-ursi*
Belladonna, deadly nightshade	*Atropa belladonna*
Birch, white or paper	*Betula alba*
Blackberry	*Rubus fruticosus*
Black cohosh	*Cimicifuga racemosa*
Blueberry, bilberry, huckleberry	*Vaccinium myrtillus*
Blue cohosh	*Caulophyllum thalictroides*
Boneset	*Eupatorium perfoliatum*
Borage, bugloss	*Borago officinalis*
Buchu	*Agathosma spp.*
Burdock	*Arctium lappa*

Burnet, great burnet	*Sanguisorba officinalis*
Calamus, sweet flag	*Acorus calamus*
Calendula, marigold	*Calendula officinalis*
Caraway	*Carum carvi*
Cardamom	*Elettaria cardamomum*
Cascara	*Rhamnus purshiana*
Catnip	*Nepeta cataria*
Cayenne pepper	*Capsicum annuum*
Celery	*Apium graveolens*
Chamomile, Roman or garden	*Anthemis nobilis*
Chamomile, German or wild	*Matricaria chamomilla*
Chervil	*Anthriscus cerefolium*
Chicory	*Cichorium intybus*
Chinese ephedra, ma-huang	*Ephedra cineca*
Chive	*Allium schoenoprasum*
Cinnamon	*Cinnamomum verum*
Cinquefoil, silverweed	*Pontentilla veptans*
Cleavers, bedstraw	*Galium aparine*
Clove	*Syzgium aromaticum*
Clover, red	*Trifolium pratense*
Comfrey	*Symphytum officinale*
Coriander	*Coriandrum sativum*
Corn	*Zea mays*
Cotton	*Gossypium spp.*
Cowslip	*Caltha palustris*
Cucumber	*Cucumis sativus*
Currant, black	*Ribes nigrum*
Currant, red	*Ribes rubrum*
Daisy, wild or European	*Bellis perennis*
Dandelion	*Taraxacum officinale*
Desert or Mormon tea	*Ephedra viridis*
Dill	*Anethum graveolens*
Dogwood	*Cornus florida*
Echinacea, Black Sampson coneflower	*Echinacea purpurea*
Elder, American or sweet	*Sambucus canadensis*

Elder, black	*Sambucus nigra*
Elder, red	*Sambucus racemosa*
Ergot	*Claviceps purpurea*
Eucalyptus, blue gum	*Eucalyptus globulus*
Eyebright	*Euphrasia officinalis*
Fennel	*Foeniculum vulgare*
Fenugreek	*Trigonella foenum-graecum*
Feverfew	*Chrysanthemum parthenium*
Flax	*Linum usitatissimum*
Fo-ti-tieng	*Hydrocotyle asiatica minor*
Foxglove	*Digitalis purpurea*
Garlic	*Allium sativum*
Garlic, elephant	*Allium ampeloprasum*
Gentian, yellow	*Gentiana lutea*
Ginger	*Zingiber officinale*
Ginseng, Chinese	*Panax schinseng*
Ginseng, American	*Panax quinquefolius*
Goldenrod, sweet, or common	*Solidago odora*
Goldenrod, European	*Solidago virgaurea*
Goldenseal	*Hydrastus canadensis*
Goldthread, canker root	*Coptis groenlandica*
Gotu kola	*Hydrocotyle asiatica*
Hawthorn, English	*Crataegus oxyacantha*
Hayflower, yellow melilot, or sweet clover	*Melilotus officinalis*
Henbane	*Hyoscyamus niger*
Henna	*Lawsonia inermis*
Hibiscus, flower-of-the-hour	*Hibiscus trionum*
Hops	*Humulus lupulus*
Horehound	*Marrubium vulgare*
Horseradish	*Armoracia rusticana*
Horsetail, shave grass, scouring rush	*Equisetum arvense*
Hyssop	*Hyssopus officinalis*
Imperial masterwort	*Imperatoria ostruthium*
Iris, blue flag	*Iris versicolor*

Irish moss, carageenan	*Chondrus crispus*
Jasmine	*Jasminum officinale*
Jewelweed	*Impatiens biflora*
Jimsonweed	*Datura stramonium*
Jojoba	*Simmondsia chinensis*
Juniper	*Juniperus communis*
Lady's mantle	*Alchemilla vulgaris*
Lady's slipper, nerve root	*Cypripedium pubescens*
Lavender	*Lavandula angustifolia*
Lemon balm	*Melissa officinalis*
Licorice	*Glycyrrhiza glabra*
Licorice, Chinese	*Glycyrrhizae uralensis*
Lily of the valley	*Convallaria majalis*
Linden, European lime	*Tilia europaea*
Lobelia	*Lobelia inflata*
Loosestrife, purple, or New England heather	*Lythrum salicaria*
Lovage	*Levisticum officinale*
Madder	*Rubia tinctorum*
Mallow, common	*Malva sylvestris*
Mandrake, European	*Mandragora officinarum*
Marigold (see calendula)	
Marijuana	*Cannabis sativa*
Marjoram, sweet	*Origanum majorana*
Marshmallow, Althea	*Althaea officinalis*
Meadowsweet	*Filipendula ulmaria*
Milk thistle	*Silybum marianum*
Mistletoe, European	*Viscum album*
Monkshood, wolfsbane	*Aconitum napellus*
Motherwort	*Leonurus cardiaca*
Mugwort	*Artemisia vulgaris*
Mullein	*Verbascum thapsus*
Mustard, black	*Brassica nigra*
Mustard, white	*Brassica hirta*
Myrrh	*Commiphora abyssinica*
Nettle, stinging	*Urtica dioica*

Nutmeg	*Myristica fragrans*
Oak, white	*Quercus alba*
Oat	*Avena sativa*
Oregano	*Origanum vulgare*
Oregon grape	*Mahonia aquifolium*
Orris root	*Iris germanica*
Papaya	*Carica payaya*
Parsley, curled	*Petroselinum crispum*
Parsley, Italian	*Petroselinum crispum neapolitanium*
Passion flower	*Passiflora incarnata*
Pennyroyal, American	*Hedeoma pulegioides*
Peruvian bark	*Cinchona*—various species
Pipsissewa	*Chimaphila umbellata*
Plantain, broad-leaved	*Plantago major*
Poison ivy	*Rhus toxicondendron*
Pomegranate	*Punica granatum*
Prickly ash, toothache bush	*Zanthoxylum americanum*
Primrose	*Primula vulgaris*
Purslane	*Portulaca oleracea*
Radish	*Raphanus sativus*
Raspberry, wild	*Rubus strigosus*
Raspberry, garden or European	*Rubus idaeus*
Rose, cabbage	*Rosa centifolia*
Rose, damask	*Rosa damascena*
Rose, sweetbrier, or eglantine	*Rosa eglanteria*
Rosemary	*Rosmarinus officinalis*
Saffron, Spanish (culinary)	*Crocus sativus*
Saffron, meadow	*Colchicum autumnale*
Sage	*Salvia officinalis*
Sage, clary	*Salvia sclarea*
Saint-John's-wort	*Hypericum perforatum*
Sarsaparilla, Spanish	*Smilax officinalis*
Sassafras	*Sassafras albidum*
Savory, summer	*Satureja hortensis*

Savory, winter	*Satureja montana*
Saw palmetto	*Serenoa vepens*
Senna	*Cassia genna*
Shepherd's purse	*Capsella bursa-pastoris*
Silver king	*Artemisia ludoviciana*
Skullcap	*Scutellaria lateriflora*
Soapwort, bouncing Bet	*Saponaria officinalis*
Solomon's seal	*Polygonatum multiflorum*
Sorrel, common or garden	*Rumex acetosa*
Sorrel, wood	*Oxalis acetosella*
Squaw vine	*Mitchella repens*
Star anise	*Illicium verum*
Sweet cicely	*Myrrhis odorata*
Sweet gum	*Liquidambar styraciflua*
Tarragon, French	*Artemisia dracunculus*
Thyme, garden	*Thymus vulgaris*
Thyme, wild, or mother-of-thyme	*Thymus serpyllum*
Tormentil	*Potentilla erecta*
Trillium, wakerobin, birthroot	*Trillium grandiflorum*
Valerian, European	*Valeriana officinalis*
Vervain	*Verbena officinalis*
Violet, sweet	*Viola odorata*
White pine	*Pinus strobus*
White pond lily, water lily	*Nymphaea odorata*
Willow, white	*Salix alba*
Wintergreen, checkerberry	*Gaultheria procumbens*
Witch hazel	*Hamamelis virginiana*
Woodruff, sweet woodruff	*Galium odoratum*
Wormwood	*Artemisia absinthium*
Woundwort	*Prunella vulgaris*
Yarrow, milfoil	*Achillea millefolium*
Yellow dock	*Rumex crispus*
Yerba santa	*Eriodictyon californicum*

Bibliography

American Council on Science and Health. *Natural Carcinogens in American Food*. Summit, N.J.: American Council on Science and Health, 1985.

Anderson, Frank. *An Illustrated History of the Herbals*. New York: Columbia Univ. Press, 1977.

Appalachian Mountain Club. *Mountain Flowers of New England*. Boston: Appalachian Mountain Club, 1964.

Arber, Agnes. *Herbals, Their Origin and Evolution*. Cambridge: Cambridge University Press, 1953.

Baroja, Julio Caro. *The World of the Witches*. Chicago: Univ. of Chicago Press, 1965.

Beston, Henry. *Herbs and the Earth*. New York: Doubleday, Doran, 1935.

Bethel, May. *The Healing Power of Herbs*. London: Thorsons, 1968.

Boxer, Arabella, and Phillipa Bach. *The Herb Book*. London: Peerage Books, 1985.

Bremness, Leslie. *The Complete Book of Herbs*. New York: Viking, 1988.

British Herbal Medical Association. *British Herbal Pharmacopoeia*. Cowling, West Yorks, Eng.: British Herbal Medical Association, 1981.

Britt, Jennifer, and Lesley Keen. *Feverfew*. London: Century Hutchinson, 1987.

Brooks, Karl L. *A Catskill Flora and Economic Botany*. Albany: New York State Museum, 1983.

Bush, A.D. *Potter's Compend. of Materia Medica Therapeutics and Prescription Writing*. Philadelphia: P. Blakiston's Son, 1917.

Campbell, Joseph. *Oriental Mythology*. New York: Viking Press, 1962.

Clarkson, Rosetta E. *The Golden Age of Herbs and Herbalists*. New York: Dover, 1972.

Colette: Flowers and Fruit. New York: Farrar, Straus and Giroux, 1986.

The Compleat Cook. Cornhill: Nathaniel Brook, 1655. New York Public Library Rare Books Collection.

Coon, Nelson. *Using Wayside Plants.* New York: Hearthside Press, 1957.

Craighead, John, and Frank Craighead. *A Field Guide to Rocky Mountain Wildflowers.* Boston: Houghton Mifflin, 1963.

Culpeper, Nicholas. *Culpeper's Complete Herbal.* London, 1847.

Dioscorides. *The Greek Herbal.* London: Oxford Univ. Press, 1934.

Dodge, Natt N. *Flowers of the Southwest Deserts.* Globe, Ariz.: Southwestern Monuments Association, 1951.

Duke, James A. *Handbook of Medicinal Herbs.* Boca Raton, Fla.: CRC Press, 1985.

Esplan, Ceres. *Herbs for First-Aid and Minor Ailments.* Boulder, Colo.: Shambala, 1972.

Everyday Health Tips. Emmaus, Pa.: Rodale Press, 1989.

Ferris, Roxanna S. *Death Valley Wildflowers.* Death Valley, Cal.: Death Valley Natural History Association, 1962.

Foster, Gertrude B. *Herbs for Every Garden.* New York: Dutton, 1973.

Fox, Helen Morgenthau. *Gardening with Herbs for Flavor and Fragrance.* New York: Dover, 1970. Reprint from 1940 Macmillan edition.

Frazer, James. *The Golden Bough.* New York: Macmillan, 1922.

Freeman, Sally, with Stone Soup. *The Green World.* New York: Berkley, 1975.

Freeman, Sally. *Drugs and Civilization.* New York: Chelsea House, 1988.

Fuchs, Leonhart. *De Historia Stirpum.* 1542. Original manuscript in New York Botanical Garden collection.

Gerard, John. *Leaves from Gerard's Herbal.* New York: Dover, 1969.

——*The Herball, or General Historie of Plants.* 1975.

Gibbons, Euell. *Stalking the Wild Asparagus.* New York: David McKay, 1962.

Griffith, H. Winter. *Complete Guide to Vitamins, Minerals and Supplements.* Tucson, Ariz.: Fisher Books, 1988.

Hatfield, Audrey Wynne. *An Herb for Every Ill.* New York: St. Martin's Press, 1974.

Hirono, Iwao, ed. *Naturally Occurring Carcinogens of Plant Origin— Toxicology, Pathology and Biochemistry.* Tokyo: Kodansha/Elsevier, 1987.

Hoching, George M. *A Dictionary of Terms in Pharmacognosy and Other Divisions of Economic Botany.* Springfield, Ill.: Charles C. Thomas, 1955.

Hyatt, Richard. *Chinese Herbal Medicine.* New York: Schocken Books, 1978.

Hyll [Hill], Thomas. *First Garden Book.* London, 1563.

Jacob, Dorothy. *A Witch's Guide to Gardening.* New York: Taplinger, 1965.

Justice, William S., and Ritchie Bell. *Wild Flowers of North Carolina.* Chapel Hill: Univ. of North Carolina Press, 1968.

Kamm, Minnie Watson. *Old-Time Herbs for Northern Gardens.* New York: Dover, 1972.

Kemp, P. *Healing Rituals.* London: Faber and Faber, 1935.

Kent, Carol Miller. *Aloa Vera.* Arlington, Va.: Carol Miller Kent, 1979.

K'Eogh, John. *An Irish Herbal.* Northamptonshire, Eng.: The Aquarian Press, 1986. Reprint of the 1735 edition edited by Michael Scott.

Keys, John. *Chinese Herbs.* Rutland, Ver.: Charles E. Tuttle, 1976.

Kirk, Donald R. *Wild Edible Plants of the Western United States.* Healdsburg, Cal.: Naturegraph Publishers, 1970.

Kloss, Jethro. *Back to Eden.* New York; Beneficial Books, 1971.

Knight, Sir Theodore Mayerne. *Archimagirus Anglo-Gallicus.* Bedell and T. Collins, 1658. New York Public Library Rare Books Collection.

Kong, Yun Cheung, with Jing-xi Xie and Paul Pui-Hay But. "Fertility Regulating Agents." *Journal of Ethnopharmacology* 15 (1986): 1–44.

Lewis, Walter H., and Memory P.F. Elvin Lewis. *Medical Botany.* New York: John Wiley and Sons, 1977.

Lucas, Richard. *Nature's Medicines.* New York: Award Books, 1969.

Lust, Benedict. *Kneipp Herbs.* New York: Benedict Lust Publications, 1968.

Lust John. *The Herb Book.* New York: Benedict Lust Publications, 1974.

McIntyre, Michael. *Herbal Medicine for Everyone*. London: Penguin, 1988.

Medsger, Oliver Perry. *Edible Wild Plants*. New York: Macmillan, 1966.

Meyer, David. *Herbal Recipes*. Glenwood, Ill.: Meyerbooks, 1978.

Parkinson, John. *Paradisi in Sol, Paradisis Terrestris [A Garden of Pleasant Flowers]*. New York: Dover, 1976.

Patraw, Pauline M. *Flowers of the Southwest Mesas*. Globe, Ariz.: Southwest Parks and Monuments Association. 1951.

Queen Henrietta Maria. *The Queen's Closet Opened*. Cornhill: Nathaniel Brook, 1655. New York Public Library Rare Books Collection.

Rodale Illustrated Encyclopedia of Herbs. Emmaus, Pa.: Rodale Press, 1987.

Rohde, Eleanor Sinclair. *A Garden of Herbs*. New York: Dover, 1969.

Scully, Virginia. *A Treasury of American Indian Herbs*. New York: Crown, 1970.

Shastri, Vijay. *Journal of Scientific Research in Plants and Medicines*. Hardwar, India: Yogi Pharmacy.

Sherman, Ingrid. *Natural Remedies for Better Health*. Healdsburg, Cal.: Naturegraph, 1970.

Simmonite, W.J., and Nicholas Culpeper. *The Simmonite-Culpeper Herbal Remedies*. New York: Award Books, 1957.

Stupka, Arthur. *Wildflowers in Color*. New York: Harper and Row, 1965.

Sturtevant, Edward Lewis. *Sturtevant's Edible Plants of the World*. New York: Dover, 1972.

Teeguarden, Ron. *Chinese Tonic Herbs*. Tokyo: Japan Publications, 1984.

Thompson, A.R. *Herbs That Heal*. New York: Charles Scribner's Sons, 1976.

Tyler, Varro. *The New Honest Herbal*. Philadelphia: George F.S. Stickley, 1987.

Weiss, Rudolph Fritz. *Herbal Medicine*. Gothenburg, Germ.: Arcanum, 1988.

Index

Insect repellent, 147, 240, 246, 250
Insomnia, *see* Sedatives
Insulin, 75, 77
Iodine, 70, 71
Ipecac, 53
Irish moss, 99, 226, 228
Irritable bowel syndrome, 107, 108
Iscador, 142

Jaborandi, 54
Jacobs, Dorothy, 30, 209
Jarvis, D. C., 96, 98
Jasmine, 110, 173
Jerusalem artichoke, 76
Jewelweed, 151–53, 157
Jimsonweed, 33
Joe-pye weed, 92
John, Saint, 26
Juicing, 46
Juniper, 115–16, 124, 126, 157
  berry, 53, 55, 74, 116

Kava kava, 92
Keen, Lesley, 123
Kemp, P., 24
Kidneys (organ), 104, 114–19, 147
Kloss, Jethro, 81
Knotweed, 54

Lady's mantle, 51, 54, 131, 158, 223, 226
Laetrile, 143
Lamb:
  and Eggplant Istanbul, 196–97

in Mustard Sauce, Roast, 197–98
Larousse Gastromique, 161
Laurel, *see* Bay leaf
Lavender, 51, 52, 55, 60, 112, 125, 154, 155, 156, 157, 226, 227, 228, 231, 237–38, 239, 241
  Potpourri, 232
Laxatives, 51, 52, 54, 109–11, 119, 169, 171
  defined, 54
Leeks, 115
Lemon, 55, 95, 98, 139, 225, 231, 232, 233
Lemon balm, 53, 61, 85, 107, 139, 156, 157, 158, 221, 227
Lemon juice, 53, 74
Lemon verbena, 231
Lettuce, 55
Licorice, 52, 53, 72, 75, 81, 82, 89, 98, 110, 111, 147
Lily of the valley, 52, 76
Linden, 52, 53, 97, 221, 226, 249
Linseed, 100
Liver (organ), 54, 103, 104, 105–106, 147
Lobelia, 53, 82
Loosestrife, 54, 55
  purple, 155
Lovage, 154, 227
Lucas, Richard, 67, 90, 99, 129, 140–41
Lumbago, 122
Lungs, 147
Lust, John, 74, 104, 112, 249
Lydia Pinkham, 82, 84

Vulnerary, 128–132
  defined, 55

Wahoo, 52
Wake robin, *see* Birthroot
Walnut bark, 54
Warts, 132
Watercress, 53, 74–75, 115, 156, 237
Water lily, 158
Watermelon, 115
Weiss, Dr. Rudolph Fritz, 104–05, 111, 118, 119, 121, 122, 130
Wheat germ, 86, 220, 226
Whey, 223
White oak, 51, 54, 84, 108, 154, 157
White pine, 148
White pond lily, 84, 100, 153
Wild carrot, 60
Wild cherry bark, 53, 55, 98
Wild mountain thyme, *see* Thyme
Wild Spring Greens, 192
Wild yam, 82
Willow, 52, 53, 55, 63–64, 88, 97, 124, 155, 156
Wintergreen, 51, 53, 64, 88, 92, 97, 98, 124, 125, 145–46, 155, 156, 227
Winter tea, 143
Witches, 28, 29–37, 57, 170

Witch hazel, 31–32, 49, 51, 55, 108, 138, 156, 157, 158, 221
Witch's Guide to Gardening, The (Jacobs), 209
Wolfbane, 34
Woodruff, 52
  sweet, 227, 237, 240, 245
World Health Organization, 4, 23
World Wildlife Federation, 23
Worms, 50, 146, 150
Wormwood, 51, 52, 60, 75, 111–13, 155
Wounds, 55, 131–32, 146, 147, 148–49, 150, 158
Woundwort, 52, 55, 150, 155, 157, 158

Yage vine, 68
Yarrow, 27, 42, 53, 54, 55, 72, 77, 81, 84, 97, 136, 149, 154, 155, 157, 220, 221
Yeast infection, 83–84, 84*n.*, 128
Yellow dock, 51, 52, 72, 95, 156, 157
Yerba mate, 65, 92
Yerba santa, 54, 55, 98, 148, 156
Yogurt, 220
Yohimbe, 92
Yucca, 124, 224

Zhao Zhangguang, 133